A. C. E. FITZSIMMONS

LOOKING FOR ERIK

ADVENTURES IN COLD PLACES

THE CAPER PRESS

Published by The Caper Press, London
www.caperpress.com

Cover art by Anja Sheriden
© Anja Sheriden, 2017

First published 2017

Printed by Clays, www.clays.co.uk

ISBN
978-0-9955384-1-2

In mem.
David and Inge, Lisette and Bill
Words, grammar, journeys

CONTENTS

CONTENTS

PROLOGUE

There's a shriek. I turn towards it and catch a twisting flash of white before I duck - a bird is diving straight for my face. Pulling up my hood, I turn and run. I dodge round tussocks, curse my heavy boots, and stumble. Now I have no more breath. I slow, then stop.

Right here, they threw Erik out of the country.

I sit down on a stone and breathe. Then I look up, and try, as I've tried so many times today, to imagine myself back a thousand years. The same hills, rising in the distance. The same colours – dull greens, mossy browns. The same sound of water lapping at the edge of the fjord.

I'm still nervous about that bird. It's the story of this trip – each time I get close to Erik, something chases me off. I push down my hood and listen.

Just wind, and water, and a sheep, far off.

And now there are longboats in the fjord, ponies grazing, people gathering in judgement. Politicians. Poets. Farmers. Priests. An angry discussion. A judgement. The creation of an outlaw.

And a thousand years later, me – looking for that outlaw, looking, for reasons I still haven't completely understood, for Erik.

ESCAPE

CHAPTER 1

ERIK; SOME KILLINGS; A DUNKING.

I wasn't meant to be there, the day I met him. I was only in the library because our internet had broken and I had to send my CV off for another job I didn't want. I was flicking through the pages of the children's atlases: it seemed less like procrastination than reading a novel.

Erik the Red.

Viking. Explorer. Traveller.

Hmm.

Not someone I'd meet in my day to day life. He was born in Norway, but he and his father left the country 'because of some killings'. The family settled in the wildest corner of Iceland, and for a while, Erik's life looked steady – sensible – like the sort of life I was meant to aspire to, give or take some gender stereotypes and a thousand years' worth of domestic inventions. Erik got married, farmed, had children, moved to more easily cultivated land. And then it all went wrong. A series of fights had half the neighbourhood up in arms, and Erik was outlawed.

If I'd met him in real life rather than in a historic atlas, my family would probably have been concerned about this guy. But outlawry back then wasn't as extreme as it sounds. I'm not arguing that it was a good thing, but his exile was only for three years, and a three-year exile was a relatively common punishment. And it's what he did while he was in exile that started to draw me to him. Although he was banished, Erik could have skulked in central Iceland safely for the whole time. But he didn't. He set sail. He went into barely explored stretches of ocean, looking for land that had been glimpsed just once, during another sailor's voyage. He found it, he explored it, and then he went home, where he named his discovery 'Greenland' – tempting Icelanders (by the boatful) to sail off with him to the new pastures. A happy end for Erik, and the colony he began lasted for centuries. His son, Leif, then used Greenland as a starting point when he set out on his own voyage, reaching Vinland, or North America.

I'd spent the last few days visiting recruitment agencies, or trying to get appointments with them. The only one I'd got anywhere with had asked me questions about office experience. I didn't want any, let alone have any.

There was a picture of Erik, bold and brave and free. There was a map of the world with his route traced on it. There was Greenland, enormous, frozen and, presumably, full of walruses and polar bears. There was Iceland, land of erupting volcanoes, more glaciers, desert.

I tipped my head back and stared up at the ceiling. Would it really be any harder than applying for an as-yet-unspecified, well-remunerated and sensible job? The harder I stared at the ceiling, the more it seemed to make sense. I could put my new archaeology degree to good use figuring Erik out. I could go to where he grew up, and to the lands he discovered, and see whether his 'normal' life was so very different from his life in Greenland. I would make it a proper journey, across land and sea, no shortcuts, no flying, just boats and buses. And all public transport too: not because I had no driving license (not because of that at all) but because it would be better both for the environment and for meeting strange and interesting people.

I would travel and imagine, mentally recreate his journey. I would empathise so hard with this man that some of his boldness rubbed off on me... and when I came back, I would enlighten the world with my new knowledge and become known as a writer and adventurer.

That was the plan, and (as I lowered my eyes back to that picture of Erik in the slightly grimy, but colourful, children's atlas) I could see nothing wrong with it at all.

～～

Eight months later – June. The train is full. Two lunching ladies discuss stag nights, chocolate, and men. I record them for a while, in my new notepad, with my new pencil. Then I decide that even the best writers have to cut the really tedious stuff. I think instead about the various goodbyes I have said over the last few days.

Some of my friends have launched fully into the spirit of the project. A fellow archaeologist even thinks I am not taking it far enough. 'You should hollow out a tree-trunk and use that to travel in,' he keeps telling me. Another friend seems to think it's all about men: she keeps urging me to 'bring back a nice big hairy Viking.' And then there's my schoolfriend who can't understand why I am going, and who is very happy with exactly the life I am fleeing. 'So you're stalking a dead Viking. How – interesting. Er, why?'

I fidget. I check through my tickets for the fifth or sixth time. From London, I am travelling north to Newcastle (yep), then taking the boat further north to Stavanger, in Norway, where Erik's life began (yep, got that one). From there I go on up the coast to Bergen, where a third ship will take me to Iceland – a two-day voyage. Once there, I plan to travel around by bus, departing three weeks later for Greenland with yet more tickets (yep, and yep, and yep). The wedge of documents is about half an inch thick and, because these are only weekly boats and daily buses, if one step goes wrong, all the others follow.

I breathe in, thinking hard about Erik to banish nervousness. But his journey was easier - he didn't have tickets to lose.

The eight months' wait was for a few reasons. I had to plan around the weather – there are parts of Greenland you just can't reach in winter. And I needed to raise some money. Living off economy tinned tomatoes while tutoring fifteen year olds and trying to find a temp job wasn't proving quite lucrative enough to fund a trip to Greenland - and if I got a 'proper' job (assuming that was possible!) I wouldn't have enough holiday time to go. Luckily I found the Winston Churchill Memorial Trust, which funds people travelling abroad to do interesting things. I was both astonished and grateful when they awarded me a grant to cover my travel costs. It meant I could go.

I also needed to do some research. Though my degree in archaeology was recent and very rigorous, I'd focused on the Middle East with occasional forays into parts of Africa. I last studied Vikings in primary school, and I had a lot of catching up to do.

At primary school, as far as I remember, I made a shield with my name on in runes. I also made a papier maché Viking boat which sank. And my friend Sophie and I made a big book about the Vikings out of sugar paper. It had pictures of their wooden boats, which were long and narrow, with stripy sails and dragons on the prows and round shields hanging over the edges. And it had pictures of their gods, Thor and Odin and Frigg, who gave the days of the week their names, Thorsday, Wodinsday, Friggday.

My strongest memory of learning about Vikings was of feeling smug. This was because my teacher – Mrs Cameron – told us that a lot of the books about Vikings were wrong. The books had pictures of enormous blond warriors from Scandinavia, with horns on their helmets and horns to drink gallons of mead from. Mrs Cameron said that they didn't really have horns on their helmets and that probably they were just a bit taller, not giants.

But most of what we learned from the books she gave us is aligned with what my more sophisticated books have told me over the last few months. Viking-style boats have been dug up around Scandinavia, and apart from the dragon on the prow they fit the traditional description. And the dragons may only be missing because they were a removable part of the ship.

The biggest contradiction of my primary school studies was that the Vikings didn't call themselves Vikings. In Old Norse – the language Erik would have spoken – the word Viking means something like fighter or sometimes pirate. It was also used by the much-raided Anglo-Saxon inhabitants of England, and there it seems to mean robber or coastal marauder. It certainly didn't just mean *of Scandinavian origin* as we tend to use it now.

Academics use the word Norse for people like Erik, not Viking. I dithered over it for a while – after all, I needed that intellectual credibility if I was going to be a successful and respected writer. But 'Norse' just didn't seem exciting enough. So I'm calling Erik and his father Vikings. They fit the general meaning of the word: they had no horned helmets and maybe there wasn't a dragon on the prow of their boat, but they were proud, tough men, setting off across the sea from Norway about a thousand years ago. Even if they didn't know it, they were Vikings.

~~

A lack of dragons is about the only thing my first boat has in common with Erik's – that and, unlike my primary school version, being afloat. This vessel will take me from Newcastle to Stavanger. I tug out my notebook and go up on deck.

I write about conversation and laughter, bingo announcements, and behind it all the murmur of Newcastle. Down on the quay, I note carefully that yellow-trousered men are sitting and lying in the sun, near the ropes which still attach us to England. I think about how poetic that sounds. Then the boat gives a shudder. The men, one by one, get to their feet, and at last a rope is cast off. Our hooter blares, and echoes. I can smell seawater, and my hair blows off my face. A motorboat buzzes past us and shoots between two lighthouses into the open sea. I walk round to the back of the boat, to watch the UK disappear, but by the time I arrive it is gone, and there is nothing to see but our wake.

'Nice to be a bird'

It's a stranger - actually talking to me, just like in real travel books! And what's more, he's a red-bearded Norwegian whose hair is puffed out in the wind as he watches the seagulls that are keeping up with us.

'Maybe they'll stay with us the whole way,' I answer, concentrating hard on remembering the conversation but also liking the romance of the idea. After all, maybe they have, many times before. Maybe their ancestors were here in Erik's day, following the longships and many-oared boats.

The Norwegian – whose name is Kyrre – is on his way to North Norway to set up an eco-holiday centre (which I approve of, and note). When I say that I am going to Iceland, Kyrre asks if I'm stopping at the Faroe Islands. He lived there for six months, he says, as a sheep farmer.

Sheep-farming! This is more than a strange fellow-traveller – this is someone who can tell me about Erik's life. Sheep-farming is what I assume, between fights, he spent much of his time doing. I don't know what to ask first:

'Is that hard work? I mean, how much do the sheep need watching, and how much can you leave them to themselves?' Maybe that sounds a bit naïve, I think, too late, but Kyrre laughs.

'No, no, not really hard. They herd themselves mostly. The

Faroes – it's crazy, there are lots of really small islands with steep sides and they put maybe three sheep on one, and leave them there for the summer. They take them by boat and fetch them later.'

'Does someone need to stay with them?' I imagine hundreds of lonely shepherds, each with their three sheep on a private, empty island.

'No, no – they are fine. It's perfect, three sheep and a ram of course so they don't get bored.' He grins. 'Three sheep on an island in the middle of the ocean.' He pauses. 'To get them at the end though, they have to tie their feet together with rope and lower them.' He demonstrates, playing the part of the sheep, leaning backwards until he's looking up at the sky, pulling a confused sort of face and waving his arms in the air. 'Like this!' He rights himself. 'Poor things, they must find it strange.'

'Do they have their lambs on the island?'

'No, no – before. The lambs are put on a bigger island with more of a herd.'

'Are the Faroes very remote?'

Kyrre grins at me again. 'They have cafés, pubs... all you need, really. People are so friendly – they will always help, because that is how it works – everyone needs help sometimes. They still lower people down cliffs to get eggs – not seagulls' eggs, but something close. It's dangerous, people can get killed.

So you see, they are still very close to nature there.'

'What do they use the eggs for? Boil them and eat them?'

'Yes,' nods Kyrre.

~~~

Some of the research I carried out in that eight-month wait has taken me further from, not closer to Erik. For example, I wanted to know what was happening in the world as he set off on his travels. The official date of Erik's arrival in Greenland is AD 985, so taking that literally he possibly left Norway in the 960s or 970s, a thousand years ago and counting. In those centuries, Europe was a shifting battleground. Horsebacked raiders from the Hungarian East, the Magyars, had stampeded across the continent, getting as far west as France and staying there until a Germanic empire appeared and defeated them in AD 955. Further south, there were dangerous Saracen pirates, with bases in Sicily and Sardinia. Vikings were plaguing the coasts and rivers of the north - they had been raiding and settling for two hundred years, and had centres from Ireland through to the Caspian Sea. The Byzantine Empire, which spread from what is now Italy to parts of Turkey, was shrinking, losing control. And it was not only a time of invasion: in corners of Europe, countries like England, Poland, and Norway were starting to form and be formed as kings gained power and tribes cooperated.

What is more, religion was entangled with all this. The old faiths continued in Scandinavia, Thor, Odin and all, and the Norse raiders carried them with them. But at the same time, Christianity and Islam were both expanding. Missionaries were setting out from the Celtic Church and Orthodox Churches. Southern Spain and various Mediterranean islands were Islamic, as was much of North Africa. There were communities of Jewish people throughout Europe, playing an increasingly important role in international trade.

Further away, unimagined by Europeans, the world was changing even more. Europe had at least some connection to (Song dynasty) China, and other lands to the East, through the line of merchants trading with one another along the Silk Road. There, there were printing presses, an invention that would not reach Europe for another four centuries. But many lands were not even imagined. In Peru, the Inca Empire was expanding. New Zealand had been settled for a couple of hundred years, by migrants from Polynesia.

And Erik knew little to none of this. I can look at his past and future, and learn about countries in all directions from Scandinavia, places Europe hadn't even discovered. I can look at them on a historical atlas and see the lines helpfully drawn, showing territory, invasion, naming cultures. But not only could Erik not look into the future, nobody had got around to drawing the map.

The stuff of the texts where Erik's story and others are told is family feuds and loyalties, marriages, local rivalry, the odd royal mention. Even these texts are centuries more recent than Erik, but they are closer to him than the *Times Atlas of World History*.

His land of origin, Norway, had been a kingdom, officially, for less than a hundred years. One Harald Finehair united it at the end of the ninth century, and after his death the kingdom broke up again, and ambitious descendants fought over it. These were changing times. Christianity was not unknown, and there were bishoprics as close as Denmark, but none were established in Norway yet.

I'm about to arrive at the place where Erik's story begins – a southern district of Norway. But in Erik's day the town of Stavanger, my and the ferry's destination, did not exist.

∿

I dodge in and out of the cabin, trading warmth for view for warmth. The fjord is revealing itself, forests and slopes giving way to painted houses on shore, while islands scatter across the water. As we slow down to approach the port, the wind disappears and I keep watch from the top deck, noting down colours and textures of landscape. This is a town built of wood – red, brown and ochre to my left, white to my right. A ship is almost filling the harbour, so big the houses seem doll-sized. I get engrossed in watching and writing notes and then realise with a shock that I need to disembark. Not pausing to think, I race down the gold-railed staircase, pick up my bags, and step ashore.

~~

As I haul my bags across the town, trying to imagine it away, I bump into a retired Scottish couple. They tell me I have too far to walk. I nod, and ignore them, and about an hour later, still walking, realise they were right.

~~

And as I wander through this town that wasn't there, another piece of modern knowledge is bothering me. It's something I have been in denial about for months. And for good reason – it's a fact that makes my whole trip ridiculous. Here it is: Erik the Red may not ever have existed.

Here's how it works. The copy of Erik's story I am carrying round with me was translated from ancient manuscripts kept in Reykjavík and Copenhagen. These manuscripts are copies of copies of an unknown number of copies. And before the first versions of these stories were written down, they were passed on by storytellers, in word and song, from generation to generation.

The stories about Erik are two of a set of tales known as the Icelandic Sagas. The more I have read about the Sagas, the more I have appreciated how hard they are to study. They are full of dates, battles, family feuds, genealogy, ghosts, magic and monsters. Plenty is almost certainly true: plenty is not. For example, one of the Sagas containing Erik's story includes an incident with a monopod – a single-footed bloke who bounds around and shoots arrows at a group of explorers. Academics have come up with a range of ways this could be understood – from simple fiction, to a trick of the light, to poetic flourish or metaphor. Academics also point to politics, human error and saga-writing conventions as reasons not to take everything in these texts literally.

Monopods are easy to dismiss – but what about Erik? As heroes go, he is less ambiguous than some. There has never been a doubt that the Norse settled Greenland - five hundred years of colony left plenty of traces. And there is further help – in another text, which is separate from the Sagas.

From what I can gather, Ari 'the learned' Thorgillsson is more my type than Erik. He lived (and he definitely did live) three or four generations later, in a world where there were (some) books. Rather than committing violent crimes and leaving the country, he wrote a history of Iceland - *Íslendingabók*. In his writing he was unusually explicit about where his information came from, asking only men he considered truthful. Ari wrote that his uncle, one Thorkel Gellison, knew someone who travelled with Erik. So the story is only third hand, when he writes it – and just about within living memory. But Ari does not confirm all the details. Nor is he perfectly neutral - he devotes a lot of effort to discussing his own ancestry and connections to Saga heroes.

So someone, whose name was probably Erik, definitely led the colonisation of Greenland. But the precise detail of his story could be, to put it academically, 'a social or literary construction of later times'. Or, to put it more straightforwardly, it could be completely made up.

~~

There's not much of it either, for his early life. I am in Stavanger because of two sentences. They read: There was a man called Thorvald, who was the father of Erik the Red. He and Erik left their home in Jaederen because of some killings, and went to Iceland.[1]

1 This and all other translations of Erik's Saga and Greenland Saga are from *The Vinland Sagas: The Norse Discovery of America*, translated by Magnus Magnusson and Hermann Palsson, 1965. (And for Mastermind fans - yes, that Magnus Magnusson).

When I ask about Erik, the lady at the tourist office gives me a withering glance.

'No,' she says. 'There is nothing.'

But I need her help. Jaederen or, in modern Norwegian, Jaeren, is the whole district of Norway around Stavanger. It covers hundreds of square kilometres.

I try another tactic and ask what there is to do in Jaeren. She pulls out a bright leaflet and points at it. 'All of these places are in Jaeren. Stavanger is in Jaeren.' She circles activities I might take part in while remaining in Jaeren. I bet Erik would have been into white water rafting, if he'd been born in the twenty first and not the tenth century – but that's not enough of a connection to persuade me to try it.

One thing does catch my eye though – there's an archaeological museum. The people there might be more helpful.

~~

The man in the museum is wearing a t-shirt decorated with a large picture of a runic-looking boat. He is talking about the Bronze Age, pointing to some large, twisted horns that have survived from that period in a bog.

'The circles here, and here, and here,' he explains, 'represent the sun. In this time they believed that the sun moved across in a boat, and this is shown in rock paintings – boats like this'. He tugs at his t-shirt, rocking its runic boat. 'So the people blowing the horns were powerful, magicians or priests.'

The Bronze Age was about a thousand years before Erik's time. But I'm intrigued by the existence of pre-Viking gods. I had assumed that the Viking gods were somehow the original gods of the area, conquered by Christianity. Clearly this was far from the truth.

I steer the conversation back towards the late Iron Age, Erik's period. The climate was much as it is today, so at least I don't need to imagine different weather. Men wore short trousers, shirts and belted tunics, and women wore pinafores over long underdresses, held up by a brooch on each shoulder. The museum has several of the brooches, which have survived long past the clothing in graves and been the main clue in working out the outfit.

I have also spotted some elegant drinking horns, a heavy gold necklace, and some axes. There are coins labelled as Arabic and English, all found in these parts, showing some kind of connection with faraway places. But best of all, there is a huge double-edged sword with an ornate handle. 'Swords were not for everyone,' explains my guide. 'You had to have a certain status to have permission to wear a sword. So they were an important status symbol.

So were horses. That's why you have so many pieces of horse-tackle in graves – showing you had a horse.'

I am not sure if Erik or his father would have had swords or horses when they were in Norway. Erik certainly had a horse by the end of his life, but he was also a more important person by then. I am certain that if I had lived in Viking times I would not have had a sword. Not only am I not chieftain class, I'm female.

I want to understand what the area as a whole would have looked like in Erik's time. Very different, I'm told. Just scattered towns and farms, and the big burial mounds left over from the Bronze Age.

I ask, specifically, about Erik.

'Have you heard of Erling Skjalgson of Sola?' asks my guide.

I shake my head.

'You should look him up. If you go to the Stavanger Museum, you will find his memorial. It used to stand at the entrance to the town, but now it is indoors. He was an important chieftain here.'

~~

Bother Erling. I am in the place, however little locals may care, where Erik's life began, and I need to find out about him. I only have one day left in Jaeren – tomorrow I'm catching a boat. I can't delay it, either – if I miss the boat, I'll miss every connection all the way to Iceland.

Probably, I decide, the best thing to do is to get out of town.

~~

The flaw in this plan is the extent of Stavanger's suburbs. At first, these are sweet and interesting: painted wooden houses and pretty gardens. I discover a Leiv Erikssons Gate – street – and next to it an Erling Skjalgsons Gate. There is no Erik Thorvaldssons Gate, though – I begrudge Leif the publicity in what's Erik's homeland.

After half an hour's walk, the houses get repetitive and, with their conifer- and lobelia-filled gardens, a bit like suburbs everywhere. There is even a craze for monkey-puzzle trees. There are no birch or pine forests at all.

But then, between the rooftops and behind a particularly twisted monkey-puzzle, I spot open hills. A wide fjord is surrounded by low, pine-covered slopes. Through chance, I have come out by the hilts of three swords, each rising ten metres above the ground, their blades thrust into the stone. This is not only countryside as Erik might have seen it – it is also the site of the ninth century battle that resulted in Norway's unity.

Why on earth didn't the tourist office lady think I'd be interested in that?

A row of stepping-stones leads out into the fjord. I step onto the first, noticing that the dark rock is surrounded by heaps of blue mussel-shells. The water is clear – apart from some drifting seaweed, I can see all the way to the bottom. I turn around for a better view and decide to pause, write some notes. At the far end of the row of stones, there is one that looks perfect. I wonder about tides: some of these rocks are a little damp, so perhaps they go under at high water. Certainly the dampness can't be down to waves: the fjord is still, the water only lapping very gently at the edge. How well I will be able to imagine Erik's departure from Jaederen from such a perch.

I step out, and even as my foot slides off the stone I don't realise my mistake. I pull back to regain my balance, but instead I stumble and slip further. Then my other foot is out of control and I wriggle and slither but it is too late: I am up to my chest in water, clinging to the rocks that only a minute before I was walking on. My feet, weighted by my boots, kick against the side of the fjord, searching for anything to rest or grip on. They find nothing: the fjord is surprisingly deep.

CHAPTER 2

STAVANGER FOREVER?

"You are a great example to our children. I tell them repeatedly not to walk on slippery stepping stones, and you have shown them how real the danger is!"

I am trying to feel grateful to my rescuers. But as they haul me out, I'm thinking that at last I am close to a Viking Age experience of this place. I am relishing the cold and the damp, the soggy clothing and, as my feet step on land again, the squelching of my boots. Perhaps Erik did not ever fall into this fjord, but I'd be willing to bet that, if he existed, he swam in it.

They drive me back, going out of their way to transport a soaking wet stranger. I am grateful, honestly. But I am not sure that my B&B is the right sort of accommodation for someone who falls into fjords. I try not to drip too much in the hall, hang my wet clothes in the subtlest corner of the garden I can find, and go out again.

Erik did not mind about wet boots, so why should I?

We – my boots and I – sit on a stile in a field. My passport is dry. So is my notebook. But my phone won't turn on. I pull out the SIM card, rub it, put it back. It works. Triumphant, I eat my damp and salty lunch and try it again. It switches off and won't come back.

Back at the B&B, my camera is the next casualty. Another guest helps me rescue my pictures, before it seizes up for the last time, following my phone out of existence. I read Agatha Christie and try to pretend I don't feel ill. But the next morning I can't get up. My landlord nobly drives me to the hospital where they give me antibiotics. I spend the next day in bed. Upper-class murderers and Vikings, and a hundred boat tickets, do a phantasmagorical dance through my dreams. I survive, but miss my boat and invalidate every one of my careful bookings for my journey to Iceland. There's not another boat for a week.

Erik's world seems to be repelling me with full strength. Not only am I in a town that didn't exist in his day, but I can't get out of it.

~~~

So I have a week to explore Stavanger. I move out of my B&B, which has queues of pre-booked, sensible guests, into a place called Folken. For most of the year, it is a music venue, but it has been converted for the summer into 'a unique sleeping quarter where you can still sense the vibes from the concerts'. I sign a disclaimer agreeing not to complain about 'sound leakage' from more concerts, downstairs, or theft of my possessions.

The 'sleeping quarter' turns out to be a black painted, black-floored room, complete with black stage and empty bars, lit only by glowing paper floor lamps. Across the floor, about forty camp-beds have been set up, only a metre or so apart from each other, labelled with laminated numbers. There are no showers, but you get a ticket for the local gym where you can wash and, if you feel like it, go to an exercise class.

At least I don't need to worry about dripping water on the carpet.

～

I find a museum for canned sardines. Around a century ago there were seventy-odd fish-canning factories in Stavanger. This can't have left space for much else.

In Stavanger, the sardines were smoked before they were canned. I try a fresh smoked sardine, first twisting its head off as instructed. It is amazing how much it tastes like the sort that come in tins.

It is amazing how much easier sardines are to think about than the rest of my journey.

I buy a sandwich and sit in the plaza between the cathedral and the harbour, munching. Evening sun is making the few clouds glow. A tiny, sparrow coloured bird – I wish I could identify birds - jumps up onto my bollard. It bounces around it, feet together. I toss it some bread and it turns its big brown eyes suspiciously towards me before plucking it up and leaping off the bollard to eat it at a distance. Then, so suddenly it's a shock, I am in a storm of seagulls. Black-headed birds zoom straight past me. There's a yellow-beaked sort that swoops more lopsidedly. Pigeons join in, tentatively, at the edges. I clutch my sandwich protectively. Then, as suddenly as they came, the birds are gone, and I watch the pattern they make as the performance is repeated a few metres away.

Later, a very well-dressed tramp raids the bin next to me, selecting only half-empty bottles. Leaving everything tidy, he moves on across the square. Drifts of volleyball players, tourists, and locals out to enjoy the evening pass by.

～～

'Ideas grow. Potatoes multiply. Local commerce is as healthy as our produce. The region of Stavanger is thriving. Thriftiness is combined with innovation, cutting edge technology and our international orientation.'

The oil industry, I realise. The modern Stavanger. I puzzle over this while sitting on my campbed, tidying my scraps of paper and notes, trying to maintain a mental link to Erik. There are three of us here now. The girl from Korea gave me a sweet, but I haven't seen her again, only her tidy mattress. The Berliner, Franziska, appeared in Folken a couple of days after me. She was buried under a giant rucksack, hands filled with a selection of supplementary bags. She has tales of the far North where she spent last winter. '*Kalt und schrecklich*' she describes it. 'Cold and horrible…it is never really light: well, from twelve till two it is less dark… it rains a sort of rain that's half snow, half rain, and you just don't want to go out. And getting up in the morning it is so hard, you have no motivation at all.

'But,' she pauses, 'you do make up for it in summer. The midnight sun – it is amazing to stand outside at 1am and see the sun.'

∾

Gradually, I feel better. I call my parents, first to enlist their help in my state of sickness and then to reassure them that I'm alive, well and in perfect health to continue the trip. I can hear my mother's unexpressed doubts, and I ignore them systematically. I send emails, make phone calls and, after less hassle than I had imagined, the tickets are rearranged. I email an Icelandic archaeologist to delay an interview. I squeeze the Icelandic itinerary into a shorter time, so I can still use my tickets to Greenland. I replace my camera, praying to the gods of travel insurance that I'll get the money back.

~~

Another evening, it is raining, hard and fast and heavy. The twenty or so hippies, goths and indie-rockers of the town assemble, quietly sitting down with their cups of beer. The music is soothing, ballads sung by a red-clad redhead accompanied by a man with a black guitar.

Later, everyone sits outside, smoking and snoozing. These guys are from Saltdal, to the north. We compare countries, and places, and childhoods. Erling, neat and serious, has a fact for me. 'Did you know that rats are Norwegian? The Latin name for a brown rat is *rattus norwegicus*.' We try to think of other Norwegian animals. 'What about Norway lemmus?' Erling suggests. '*Lemmus lemmus*.' I am puzzled. 'Lemurs? You have lemurs in Norway?'

'No, no, not lemurs,' someone corrects, 'lemurs are nice, everyone likes lemurs. These are just rodents, small rodents.'

'What do they look like?'

'About this long, and… and…' She pulls a face, teeth to the fore, hands raised and curled over, nose wrinkled.

'Rats?'

'No, more like hamsters. And every four years, everywhere you go there are suddenly hundreds of them, everywhere you look.'

'Not - lemmings? I thought they were only a computer game!'

'No, they are real. And there are so many, they all follow each other: wherever one goes the others follow. If it falls in water, there are hundreds of swimming lemmings until… until there aren't. So the computer game is right!'

Erling grins. 'So that is Norway's gift to the world – rodents. Great!'

'And boats, and Vikings' I add, to cheer him up.

~~

Meeting a modern Erling reminds me about Erling Skjalgsson. On my last day, I make the effort to visit his memorial. It turns out to be a huge, slightly bulging cross carved from stone, with runes scratched into the surface. Erling's dates are about 975-1028, so he would have been born around the time Erik and his father left for Iceland. He is credited with bringing Christianity to the area, and he died in battle, fighting alongside King Canute.

What I like most about Erling is that he is real. This stone was probably put up in 1028-30 – or so deduce local historians. Their argument is that the inscription criticises Erling's opponent in that battle, Olav, who was made a saint in 1030 – and that after this date, such criticism would have been dangerous. If the historians are right, the stone testifies to Erling's existence, and part of his story, only two years after he died.

This is much better than anything existing for most saga heroes – Erik included. I feel satisfied just looking at the cross. It is as if I have finally met a person from Erik's day. Erling actually, definitely, existed.

Going on what is said about them in the sagas, Erik would not have been in favour of Erling. Christianity was not a religion he approved of. I consider building up some dislike for Erling out of loyalty, but somehow, in the sunshine, it all seems too far away.

~~~

United in the face of the hostel's strangeness, Franziska and I have made friends and, as we are both going north to Bergen, we take the same boat. But as it buzzes out of the port, I'm not much company. I am looking back at the shore, trying to imagine away the town, its wooden wharf-houses, its cathedral, and to picture the gently hilly fjord that lies beneath it. Maybe there are a few stone houses, by the shore. There are farms in the distance, widely scattered. This is not the peaceful land of today: kings are regularly doing battle over parts of it. Erik and his father are leaving because of some killings. I imagine they are not travelling alone, but Erik's mother is there too, perhaps brothers, sisters.

It was already a land with history. Though none are visible from the boat, Bronze Age burial mounds will have suggested a population reaching back in time – or who knows, perhaps something more mythical.

I sprawl out on the deck, and giggle with Franziska at a small girl with polka dot tights whose mission – thwarted by her mother – is to push a plastic chair overboard. Modern Stavanger reappears, in far better focus than its past. I try to think what the two visions have in common, and all I can come up with is rats, lemmings and gulls. Yet somehow, unplanned, through a series of coincidences involving fish, boats, tin cans, oil and human beings, one has grown from the other.

~~~

I huddle up in my jacket, watching the clouds for glimpses of sky. A wide metal bridge crosses the fjord above our heads.

Then there's a stretch that's just forest, and rocky islands covered with pine trees, and rocky islands that are just rock. A red house stands alone amongst the pines.

Islands, hills, eventually sunshine. The slopes get steeper and craggier. Still pine-covered, they rise in odd, lumpy shapes around us. Another town, and another, and once, inexplicably, we change boat. But then we come to a place where the hillside is encrusted with houses and sparkling glass. In the foreground, to my left, a zigzag of roofs over yellow and red wooden buildings. And on shore, the main streets are filled with balloon sellers, so pink and blue dolphins, winnie-the-poohs and dalmations dance against a backdrop of hills and houses and sky. Bergen. My last Norwegian town, the place where I can catch a boat to Iceland.

～～

We're staying in a flat belonging to someone called Audin, a connection of a connection, perhaps of a connection, of Franziska's. But he is not here.

One wall of the flat is covered in clocks, none of which tells the right time. There are paperchains. In the middle of the floor is a traffic cone with a scarf wrapped around it. A corner is filled with a giant rainbow flag, which says PEACE. I'm thirsty and the world is a little wobbly from too much sun.

Franziska reports that she in the same state. The others are on their way to a party. Then they go, and a green bookshelf arrives. At some point, I am not sure whether before or after the bookshelf, or even before or after the flat, I go to sleep.

When we leave the next day, I leave Odin a thank-offering of whisky. I could do with some gods on my side.

~~

I am a week behind, and more and more frustrated that I'm not in Iceland. In imagination, I'm sailing already. To go with my sea voyage, I have chosen the longest seagoing book I could find, *Moby Dick*, and Melville's Ishmael is at the mast-head:

'a hundred feet above the silent decks, striding along the deep as if the masts were gigantic stilts, while beneath you and between your legs, as it were, swim the hugest monsters of the sea... There you stand, lost in the infinite series of the sea, with nothing ruffled but the waves. The tranced ship indolently rolls; the drowsy trade winds blow; everything resolves you into languor.'

Ishmael is in the South Seas, but ships like his went all over the earth, doing frantic battle against creatures bigger than their own boats, in a quest for glory and riches. Often, claims Ishmael, whalers reached the unknown ahead of explorers.

Stories of early voyages to Iceland are as rich as those of whalers. Iceland was for centuries the edge of the world. Irish monks set out there before Vikings, searching for seclusion. Medieval Europe kept these tales alive. St Brendan, most popular, set off with seventeen companions in a curragh, a small sailing boat made of ox-hide on a wooden frame. They left Ireland with a fair wind, and when it dropped away they began to row. They rowed and rowed, and soon the rowers were exhausted, so Brendan gave instructions that they should halt, and let God blow them where He chose.

God chose that they should float for forty days on the sea, before finding land. And after this wait, He led them to a series of miraculous islands. On one, a chorus of birds sang the Lord's praises. On another, the monks lit a fire, only to find the island sinking and swimming away. Another was a rocky, treeless place flowing with hot slag, and populated by vicious, hairy smiths. On the monks' approach they were pelted with burning slag, which landed in the sea and made it bubble and boil. St Brendan rallied his monks: 'Soldiers of Christ, be strong... we are now on the confines of Hell. Watch, therefore, and act manfully!'

That Hell, many consider, was Iceland. Another island might have been Greenland – a 'column in the sea' made of clear crystal and topped with silver-coloured canopy. A glacier? An iceberg? Who can tell?

Less legendary monks, their less dramatic adventures described in a ninth century work on geography – Dicuil's *De Mensura* – brought back tales of a land where the sun never set. At midnight there was enough light, they said, to pick the lice from their shirts.

~~

Bergen is still sparkling in the sunshine, despite its reputation for rain. I wander up and down the Bryggen, with its red and brown warehouses. I visit the fish market, where there are model trolls for sale, and seal pelts, and possibly some fish.

But I want to be afloat, voyaging onwards on the rolling waves, heading for unknown lands. I want to be in the place between, where there is no land ahead or astern, to port or to starboard. I want to feel the might of the sea, the weakness of humankind.

Moby Dick is getting stranger and stranger, and more and more compelling, and through various accidents more and more bedraggled. My copy of the Sagas containing Erik's story is only a little bit neater.

Suburban Norway has done its best to trap me, to distract me from Erik with oil and sardines and student flats. But I am about to make my escape.

CHAPTER 3

THE OCEAN WAVE

From the Norröna's Deck 7, the world goes on forever: fjords and fjords and fjords. Above us the clouds are in eiderdown formation, and the sea, in every direction, is solid grey.

A man in ship's uniform is feeding the gulls. They flap against the wind, legs all over the place, to snatch bits of bread out of his hand. Sometimes he throws a piece down, down, down towards the water and they swoop and swerve to catch it, becoming distant black and white v-shapes far below us.

First to left and then to right we leave the fjord behind. She's a quiet ship, only a gentle be-re-be-re-be-re disturbing the evening. Finally we are among islands. The hills are a distant silhouette, layer upon layer, the furthest off mottled with snow and merging with the clouds. Soon the land is just a line separating sea and sky. We are out of the islands, heading for Iceland, and the ship acknowledges our arrival in the open sea with a little more movement. I can smell the fishy saltiness of a voyage.

Somehow, from up here the view is all about sky: streaky mackerel sky, pink-tinged and bright cream on blue-grey.

I must be at mast-head height on this deck: banish the ship and replace it with a sailing boat, and the view and the gulls would be the same. Maybe another longship on the distant horizon. After all, Erik's journey to Iceland was not astonishing or unusual. He and his companions were travelling about a century after the island was first colonised and its entire population had already crossed this way from Norway. 'And went to Iceland' is the description of his journey in the Saga - it was not remarkable enough for more.

What would the boat have been like? Viking ships came in a range of shapes and sizes, but the most sensible choice would have been a cargo ship, broad, high-sided and robust. To set up a farm in the new country, Thorvald – Erik's father – must have been wealthy enough to make the investment in animals and building. My guess is that, rather than travelling as a passenger or boat hand, he could afford a share in a boat.

The advantage of a ship like this was the luggage allowance. *Skuldelev* 1, a Viking cargo boat excavated in Norway, could be sailed by a crew of six, each of whom could then have six and a half cubic metres of cargo, weighing up to four tonnes. (That's two hundred times the airlines' standard twenty kilo allowance.) Of course, it might be prudent to take more crew in case of piracy or sickness, but the transport potential would still be good. Cows, pigs, sheep, horses and possessions could be put in the hold. Everything needed for the establishment of a new farm could be brought from home. And it was, presumably, door-to-door transport if you lived on the coast – unlike my route, which will involve a bus or so after this ferry to get to Erik's first Icelandic home.

Erik's journey can't have been comfortable. Later Norwegian medieval laws state that 'a ship which requires bailing three times in 24 hours will be declared seaworthy for all kinds of travel; but if they so wish, the crew can entrust themselves to a ship which requires more frequent bailing'.[2]

I am very glad to be on a ferry.

~~

On the bright blue metal deck, I mentally check through my baggage, comparing it with Erik's. No electronic kit, of course: no camera, no phone – I am very protective now of the replacements I bought in Stavanger, each wrapped in its individual plastic bag. No glasses – I'd have been completely useless as a lookout, or at hunting. No timepieces. No books, or pens and pencils. No technical gear: no sleeping bag, no quick-drying polymer fabrics. Instead, furs and woven cloth. No penknife – instead, probably an axe and maybe a sword.

And a completely different set of information in my brain.

2 This excerpt is from the lawbook Grágás as translated by Arne Emil Christensen in his article on ships and seafaring in Fitzhugh and Ward's *Vikings: The North Atlantic Saga*. (2000)

Just as Erik would be lost in my world, I would be lost in his. I can't farm, or fish, or sail, or build a house. I can't use a sword or even an axe. I can't ride a horse. I would die within weeks of trying to establish myself on a piece of cold, hostile, unsettled land. Would Erik die as fast if he found himself suddenly in modern London? So much would be strange: the vehicles, the buildings, the tarmac streets, the noise and smell. Food would come in plastic packets from buildings, not from hard labour in the fields. The dangers would be moving vehicles and pickpockets, not bears and rockfall.

But it's not only the survival instinct that is different. My head is also full of a thousand years' worth of human history and discovery. I think about everything differently. I know how my body works, roughly, the heart pumping blood, taking oxygen from the lungs around the body. I know that we are the product of millions of years of natural selection. I can mentally rewind the evolutionary story, putting humans back in trees, getting rid of opposable thumbs, watching birds stop flying, amphibians creeping back into the water, life getting simpler and simpler until only a few cells are reproducing in a hot pool. I can go further, reducing the complex carbon molecules that make up our cells to their atomic components. I imagine the Earth swirling back into the mass from which it, the planets and the Sun emerged. I see the Universe sucked backwards into a big de-bang.

However Erik saw his world, it wasn't like that. The legends from his period may not be related particularly reliably, but they paint a picture of the Earth shaped by a race of gods, the Æsir, and a race of giants. When Gefiun, one Æsir lady, put her oxen to the plough near Denmark, she caused Zealand to detach itself from the mainland. Thunder was because the god Thor was using his powerful hammer. A rainbow was a bridge to the home of the gods, the red part burning fire to stop the giants getting across. True or false, this is a vast distance from plate tectonics, electric discharges and light rays bent elegantly through hovering droplets of water.

And even the worldview isn't the limit of the differences between Erik and me: the workings of his mind, the way he remembered things and learnt things must have been different. A fellow traveller's complaint of a few evenings before has stayed with me.

'They just take photos, endlessly. They don't look, or remember, they just take photos. And what do they do with all these pictures? Show their friends, once, then store them on their computer! They won't remember the place, because they didn't look at the time. And they will forget about the pictures. And then what was the point?'

We can record and communicate the essentials of a place through making 2D images of it: exact replicas. And to do this, to record so much information, we do not need to use our brains at all.

Erik and his local contemporaries had to rely on words. Harder still: spoken words. Writing had not reached them, or only very minimally in the form of curt runic inscriptions. Printing, and paper, were unimagined. My brain has a heap of half-remembered truths that I know I can verify – or falsify – in a book, or in my notes, or online. Erik had no such resource.

All human knowledge was living knowledge. It died with the last person to remember it. A person, or an event, might be recorded on a monument, in a few lines, or described in a story, one of the sagas told in quiet moments, passed on from teller to teller for hundreds of years. When the story was forgotten, when it went untold, the characters within it were lost forever.

Stories mattered.

~~

Stories still matter. Everyone on this boat has a story to tell, especially – I like to think – those of us travelling couchette-class. Rightly, this might be called sardine-class: there are nine bunks in each cube-shaped unit, stacked in threes and butting onto each other like pieces of a jigsaw. You could complete the puzzle by putting three more bunks in the space used for people to get in and out of bed. Couchette-class would be cosy, except that there is always someone snoring, and there is too little space to linger.

It's a long walk from the gangway, and soon after boarding there's a trail of backpacked couchetters wandering confused through the lower decks. For the couchettes are in the very bowels of the ship, where the stairs are no longer carpeted, where the sea's movement is felt the most, and where the first class passengers will never venture.

~~~

I meet a very young man who reminds me, in the best of ways, of a hobbit:

H: This couchette, it reminds me of the isolazion I was in this weekend.

A: Sorry, the what?

H: Isolazion. I-so-la-zion.

A: Um, so why were you in isolation?

H: They put me there. The police in my town are very aggressive.

A: (laughs nervously) what had you done wrong?

H: Oh, nothing. And my friends knew I had done nothing. They said I was making trouble and told me to go away, and

I did, only I went back to shout for my cigarettes. I was very drunk. We were all very drunk. And so they put me in isolazion.

A: Um, how long for?

H: Oh, only a night. But I was not lying down, I was like this [He sits up, fidgets, mimes biting his nails]. The police in my town are very bad. Ha! And there is a police training place there too, so all the new ones come, wanting to get points.

A: Oh! But you got to the boat in the end.

H: I have a job in the Faroes. I am working as a landscape gardener. And you?

I wonder, vaguely, if he really means landscape gardening, and who it is who landscapes gardens in the Faroes. I explain about Erik.

H: But I think he did not go on a luxury boat like this! Ha! But you can tell about all sorts of Norwegian traditions on this ship. Like duty free. That is a good Norwegian tradition.

~

I meet a man called Tom from Florida. Like Erik, he's an exile – but from choice: he never stops anywhere long enough to owe tax.

T: Say, this boat reminds me of a boat I was on once. We were laying cable.

A: Cable?

T: Yeah, fibre-optic cable. In the fibre-optic boom. They were laying cable everywhere. Some of those boats go north in winter and it's real rough. You're shaking up and down, up and down.

As he talks I get an image of a ship filled almost entirely with a roll of cable – being unrolled, like a ball of thread, to stretch right across the ocean.

A: So what did you do, what was your job?

T: Oh, I was with the submarine team. Basically there's a submarine that goes behind the boat, digging the trench for the cable. And we can dig it deep – some of those things go more'n a mile down in the ocean floor.

A: Why?

T: Fishing trawlers. And anchors. That's basically why. Also you have to be careful about sharks. The cable makes an electric field which attracts them, they think it's food and they bite it. They put shark armour on the cables these days.

A: So you were down there steering it?

T: All remotely. We're sitting in our cabins, controlling the thing. I used to dive, but I haven't for ten, twenty years. Fixing oil pipes, deep down, five hundred feet or more. That was dangerous: coupla guys I knew of died.

It seems there are many modern livings to be made at sea.

Another thing Erik didn't have was a compass: along with maps, they hadn't been invented. The sagas are full of people blown off course, sailing the seas for days on end, sighting strange lands along the way. Latitude – distance North-South – could be estimated using the position of the sun or stars, if they were visible. Longitude – distance East-West – could not – there was no way to establish longitude at sea until the eighteenth century. When sailing up and down the coast, navigation was by landmark, and this method was extended as much as possible to the open sea. For instance, a slightly later set of directions suggests:

'From Hernar in Norway one should keep sailing west to reach Hvarf in Greenland and then you are sailing north of Shetland, so that it can only be seen if visibility is very good; but south of the Faroes so that the sea approaches half-way up their mountain slopes; but so far south of Iceland that one only really becomes aware of birds and whales from it.' [3]

Despite all this, the oceans weren't empty. The sagas are full of journeyers, however lost. Getting lost seems to have been pretty important to a good voyager – a major way of discovering things.

~~

3 Excerpt from *Hauksbók*, translated by Sveinbjörn Rafnsson in his chapter The Atlantic Islands in Peter Sawyer's (2001) *Oxford Illustrated History of the Vikings*

On our second day at sea, I get up early. We have overtaken the sun, which last night was glowing ahead of us: now it shines through cloud onto the water behind. Otherwise, there is nothing in view. We are in a soft grey world, clouds above and beneath them slightly darker water. On deck, people are walking about wonkily, unbalanced by the strong wind.

I'm told there were dolphins in sight yesterday evening.

As the day goes on, the horizon gets closer and closer, and the greys of the sky and sea become more and more alike. By lunchtime, it is hard to tell where they meet. It is hard to see anything but mist. The ship's horn phooooooonks.

There is really nothing to look at, so I curl up on deck with a book.

～～

I've not been trying hard enough to learn Icelandic. Usually, when I visit a country, I make at least a start, a few words and sentences to make it slightly less embarrassing that I end up speaking English with everyone I meet. This time, I think because I am visiting three countries – Norway, Iceland, and Greenland, each with their own language, the challenge was overwhelming. But the fog has left me with no excuse not to try.

The list of Icelandic pronunciation challenges is long. There are two letters – Ð/ð and Þ/þ – which aren't in any other language. Both of them are pronounced th but they are different. The good news is that we have them both in English: þ is th as in thing, thermostat, Thor, therapy; ð is th as in the, this, rather.

J is pronounced y. Hv is to be pronounced kv. Rs are to be trilled. (I consider giving up at this point - I can't roll my rs despite years of trying.) There are some accents too, to give plenty of options for how to pronounce vowels. Acute accents lengthen vowels – Reykjavík is pronounced Reykjaveek.

And there is something mysterious going on with double Ls.

Words are more fun. I can immediately understand Faðir, dottir, sonur. *Koma frá* means come from. *Góðan daginn* is good day. *Hafa* is the verb to have. A *gistiheimili* is a guesthouse. A *sjúkrabíl* is a sickmobile, an ambulance, a *sjúkrahús* is a hospital. *Smjör* is smear, or butter. My favourite word, *Bless!* means Goodbye! (the same as the archaic meaning in English – goodbye is short for god be with ye).

Then there are words that sound like North Country or Scottish words: *tjörn* is like tarn, which means pond. *Kirkja* is like kirk – church. *Barn* is like bairn – child. And of course there are words that are completely unfamiliar: *staersti* means biggest, *foss* is waterfall, *eyja* is island, *vík* is bay, *eldfjall* is volcano. *Takk fyrir* means thank you. I commit that one to memory.

The similarity makes sense – English and Icelandic are closely related languages, Germanic, like German and Dutch. And it is English, not Icelandic, that is the rebel child of this family. Since the Norman conquest, English has absorbed bits and pieces of other languages: that's why we say hospital, not sickhouse and – later adoptions admittedly – ambulance and hotel, not sickmobile and guesthouse. To confuse matters, we've not just adopted words from French, Indian languages and other non-Germanic tongues. Bored of such exotica, we have words borrowed 'back' from the Germanic family. Butter comes from a nearly extinct Germanic language, Frisian, spoken in a small region of the Netherlands.

While I would struggle to communicate with an English speaker of the year 1000, Icelandic has not changed so drastically in this time. Icelanders can still read the sagas in the original Old Norse with only a little study. If I should happen to meet him, Erik would probably understand my Icelandic – if, that is, I pronounced it right. *Góðan daginn, Eiríkur*, I might say… but the conversation would not be very deep. Not unless I get very fluent, very fast.

Another Icelandic habit, unchanged for centuries, is their use of patronymics instead of surnames. Icelanders don't have surnames. The phone books are arranged by first name. If extra detail is needed, they are known as their father's son or daughter: Bjarni Einarsson, Leifr Eiriksson, Jónas Kristjansson, Freydis Eiriksdóttir, Laura Þorhalsdóttir and so on.

Objecting to this blatant favouring of the father over the mother, I am relieved to find that nowadays you can choose to be known as your mother's son or daughter. However, few people take up that option: it is tantamount to disowning your father or suggesting you don't know who he is. Some people go for putting both parents' names.

My conversation with Erik gets more interesting.

A: *Góðan daginn!*

E: *Góðan daginn! Hvað heitur þu?*

A: *Ég heiti Alexandra. Alexandra Anthonysdóttir. Nei, Alexandra Anthonykristinasdóttir. Nei, Alexandra Kristinaanthonysdóttir.*

E: *Útlendingar! Bless!*

Probably if I want to sound properly Icelandic, I'm going to have to change my family's given names as well.

~~

I get absorbed with talking to Erik, and it's a while before I look up. When I do I start: the view has finally changed. Between the cloud and the sea is a strip of green, hemmed with small stone walls. It can only be the edge of a Faroe.

Our ship feels large as we edge our way into the port, Tórshavn. Eager, raincoated photographers click away from the back of the boat. In my notebook, I write 'Turf roofs!' Chunks of hillside cover red, wooden houses of all sizes.

H leaves for his landscape gardening, never to return to our couchette. Three of us who are making the longer voyage leave the boat together – Tom, the tax exile from Florida, Stephanie, a pigtailed German woman, and me. The stopover is only an hour and a half, so we are focused. Stephanie and I are looking for an impression of the Faroes, and their wildness, possibly including sheep on isolated hillocks. Tom is looking for toothpaste.

First, we visit the town, navigating up and around the sloping streets. We find a white church, with its tower curved at the top, in its own little piece of meadow. Its doors are closed.

The group splits: toothpaste is not to be found in the wild spaces Stephanie and I are seeking. We find a little park with a stream running through it, a proper stream, not a town stream, and damp grass sprinkled with buttercups. We find a huge Thor's hammer, a war memorial. We twist the map around, working out how to get to the coast.

Inevitably, we pick a route through the most industrial area. We comfort ourselves: here, even the sheds are surrounded by grass rather than tarmac.

Finally, behind someone's tractor, we glimpse the sea, grey and misty with a mistier boat just visible. A footpath leads down a slope, past more buttercups and rusty tin huts. There are even some sheep – these ones not isolated, but trying to cross the coastal road. A man picks one up and throws it bodily back into its field. Meanwhile, other sheep escape.

Then we come full circle and climb up by the lighthouse to where we can see our ship, filling up with caravans and motorbikes.

~

I grumble about the mist and the short stopover to Tom, who is cheerful – his requirement for toothpaste has been satisfied.

I wonder about H, and whether his new boss will hear about his night in a cell.

As we draw away, the clouds are moving up and up the slopes, revealing a few houses. Opposite, the outline of an island looms.

And then, as we leave it behind, I realise that the island is not the only one in sight. Another is close on the other side of the boat and as I watch, more and more huge mounds rise from the sea. A glance at a map soon shows me what's happening. The Faroes are an archipelago and Tórshavn was on the edge nearest Norway: now we are passing right through the middle.

The islands shake off veils and then shreds of mist. They are massive; hulks; glorious green, flat topped, spikey topped, striped across with narrow bands of cliff. As they come clearer, I can spot wind turbines on one, and a group of houses at the foot of another. Cliffs and steep slopes plunge straight into the sea.

The furthest Faroes are still blue-grey silhouettes, a background for the bright greens and browns of the nearest. Light on the clouds throws them into contrast.

Slowly, we turn, moving now between the islands. The wind on deck is so strong that I am fighting to stand up, holding tight to the rail. It blasts through my two windproof jackets and my jeans, freezing me. I return to the cabin, shivering and violently jumping up and down, but as soon as I am warm I am out there again, staring and staring, trying to fix in my memory something, at least, of these islands.

Ahead now, in the distance, the mist is all that is visible, a glowing strip on the horizon. To left and to right we are walled in by islands: we are in a valley of islands.

And then the last mound has come into colour, shown itself in its grassy, rocky, hummocky glory, and returned to silhouette. The Faroes are fading, the colour seeping away. The odd outline floats above the clouds. Now there is only one outline, spiked like the back of a stegosaurus. Now there is only mist, rolling closer and closer, and our turquoise-and-white wake stretching out and vanishing into it.

～

Fog, fog, fog, fog, fog, fog, fog. I come inside, stare at my hair in a mirror – wind-ruffled, salt-glued – and head straight for the buffet. Here there are bikers and hikers, evening-dressed cruisers, families and parties. Both the cheapest and the most organised of us have run out of food by day two of the voyage.

By the next morning the couchette, always hot with the radiation of nine bodies, is starting to smell – not badly, but gently, as if to say 'Perhaps it's time to go'. At about 7.30 there's a radio announcement: we must leave our cabins. There are legs wherever I look, as nine people try to get up, pack, escape. I dress in the better-scented showers, and go on a hunt for breakfast.

～

Popping my head outside, I glimpse something. I step out further. The wind is blowing so hard I have to turn my back on it to do up my coat. Sea-spray, sharp, half-frozen, spits in my face. The gods don't want me out here, but I think I can see a hill so the gods will just have to be defied. Tightly gripping the banister, I climb on. At the top of the stairs is a rippling puddle of water to step over, then a fight against the wind to the front of the boat.

The wind is still pushing me backwards. There's a man a little way ahead of me whose coat is inflated with it, so that he looks as if he should be tied to a string and floating like a balloon. I put up my hood, as more icy spray hits my face. But the struggle has been worth it. I was right, there are hills, but not only hills – I can make out patches of snow, and further off is what might be a glacier. As my nose starts to burn with cold, and I hug myself against the spray and wind, I am fumbling for words to describe the place in my notebook. The Faroes were magnificent, but this is more than that, wilder, more rugged. These hills are awe-inspiring, at some level faintly terrifying. I have run out of adjectives. Could I justify the word almighty?

~~

I warm up for a moment inside. When I can feel my fingers again we are closer in, and the wind, blocked by the sides of the fjord, has died down. The deck is filling up with raincoated travellers, getting in the way of the view. But now I can see waterfalls, plummeting down the slopes from the snowline. The greens have separated out into grassy, and coppery-grey, and reddish.

A house, blue-green, stands alone at the foot of a slope. The waterfalls are everywhere. On the skyline are a selection of weird and wonderful shapes. There are hilltops like silhouetted hedgehogs. There are round-shouldered mounds, rising to nipple-shaped peaks. But for all the water and apparent growth, there is something missing. Nothing is bigger than shrubby. There are no trees.

Anoracked, we tourists stare. We watch the gulls circling around us, until one passenger gets frustrated with our ignorance and explains that they are not gulls, their grey-mottled wings and heavy build making them fulmar. The ship's horn hoots long and loud, and echoes longer around the valley. Eventually the fjord closes behind us, the open sea far beyond the hills.

Ahead of us, a sprinkling of red and blue rooftops is Seyðisfjörður.

~~

A thousand years ago, Iceland was different, or so the sources say. Ari the Learned's *Íslendingabók*, historians' favourite text, begins at the beginning of the island's Viking story: the Norse Settlement. The Vikings, he says, found a virgin land inhabited only by a few Irish monks, and covered with forest. Ari wrote in the early twelfth century, two or three hundred years after

Settlement, a few generations after Erik and his father arrived. Already, as he wrote, these days of wooded slopes were in the past.

The story of these vanishing woods is much told these days, and Ari's version has been added to. Having terrified such Irish monks as may have been there, Norse settlers in their thousands set up farms. They brought cows, pigs, goats and sheep, never before seen in Iceland. They also set out hunting the walruses, and the auks, puffins and other birds that lived around the coast. Archaeology has produced traces of these activities, alongside burnt twigs that suggest that sites for new settlements were cleared by fire.

All this was happening long before Erik arrived. By about AD 900 there is archaeological evidence that the landscape was being changed. Pollen samples show that there was far less pollen around – so far fewer trees. Further evidence suggests increased erosion. There are ample possible explanations. Pigs root up plants including trees, cattle and goats eat their bark and leaves, sheep will eat anything, even small trees. Charcoal-burning and cutting of wood for building and for ships could have done more damage. Where the trees were gone, the soil would be more easily washed away by rain and snow. Life got harder.

It was harder for newcomers, too, because much of the best land had been taken. Erik and Thorvald settled Drangar, in a remote part of the Westfjords, that uneven, wild peninsula on the far side of Iceland, nearly on the Arctic circle. They probably sailed straight there, or they may have called in on contacts first to find out where there was land.

My route, rather differently, has been decided by ferry and bus companies. Landing on the east coast, I am about as far from Drangar as it is possible to be in Iceland. Not only that, but I have a pretty hazy idea of how to get there. Although there are buses for the first few days' journey, they run out well before Thorvald's choice of isolated bay. Over the next week or so, the challenge is to make my way there. And it should be fast, because I'm still a week behind schedule.

It would be a good start to come ashore.

ENCOUNTERS

CHAPTER 4

LANDNÁM

I hand over my passport, beaming at the big blue-uniformed official. My mind is already busy with thoughts of dinner, sleep, washing and bus passes, and all the things that suddenly need doing. I want to explore Seyðisfjörður. I wonder how many of the crowd coming off the boat will remain here, and how many will disperse.

Meanwhile, the customs officer is flicking through my passport. He stares at my picture and shows it to his colleague. They chat. I wait, impatiently, as my fellow travellers walk past. Surely, surely my photo looks enough like me for me to pass through?

'Do you have any alcohol?'

'Yes.' I am carrying a little single malt whisky, in case I need to make offerings to any more gods.

'How much?'

'A small bottle. Half a litre, I think.'

'Step through here, please.' He motions me to a curtained-off area of the office, and helps me lift my bag onto a wooden shelf so I can open it more visibly. Inwardly, I groan. Outwardly, I try to look delighted at the thoroughness and efficiency of the procedure.

'Why are you in Iceland?'

I hesitate. The question is a little abrupt: I stammer out something about travel writing.

'You write a guide?'

'No, um,' How to explain that I'm following a Viking because I want to imagine his life? I'm not sure where to start and it feels madder and madder as I explain it. I try another tactic. 'Here's the alcohol.'

He waves a hand, uninterested. 'Okay. What else do you have in there?' He stands over me, peering into my bag. Embarrassed, I rummage through the chaos.

'Er, clothes, sleeping bag, more clothes...'

'You have any food?'

'Er, jam, biscuits, chocolate'

'Any cheese?'

Suddenly, we have left the realm of normality. For a while there I was intimidated by this large, government-authorised man, with his abrupt, stern manner. Now he wants to know if I am carrying any cheese.

'No!' No cheese, no cannabis, no cocaine. But he is not appeased: he is still looking critically at my suitcase.

'Any milk products at all?' He looks severe. 'That is not allowed'

The thoughts drift across my mind: do I look like some sort of milk-smuggler? What does a milk-smuggler look like?

And is this really a problem for Iceland, the import of foreign milk? They must severely lack proper social problems, but it is small comfort. I am carrying some milk chocolate, which may prevent my coming ashore. I hesitate, then admit to it. To my relief, it is forgiven: perhaps the health-giving cocoa and sugar cancel out the potentially lethal milk.

'Chocolate is allowed. You can close your bag now.'

For a moment, we return to reality: he is once more a straightforward customs official, no longer a figure in a Dahl-esque children's fantasy. 'So,' he continues, 'when are you going home?'

'I'm not, I'm going to Greenland. On the 27th.'

He harrumphs. 'There is nothing there, you know.'

I look doubtful and he relents, gesturing wide with his arms.

'Well, scenery of course, a lot of scenery. But nothing else.' He glances at my bag again. Now I have shut the main section, he can see another pocket, as yet unopened. He draws breath. 'What's in there?'

'Dirty laundry.'

Feeling, no doubt, that the pocket is an unsuitable shape for cheese or other illegal milk products, he decides not to inspect it. As I leave he smiles pleasantly at me, and I feel almost sorry that I haven't afforded him the excitement of confiscating some smuggled yoghurt. I step out into Iceland.

Seyðisfjörður is a small town on Iceland's east coast and the end of the line for the ferry. There's one road, maybe two, and it's quiet, so quiet. Tom and I are looking for the youth hostel. It's a little walk from town, and for the last twenty metres the road is gravelly and I haul my pack onto my back. Black grit crunches under my boots.

The hostel is pink, and peaceful. The single corridor is hung with pelts and snowshoes. From my window, I can see a little waterfall and blue and yellow flowers. From the kitchen there's a view over the harbour to where the *Norröna* is still lying. I sit and gaze, and Tom makes tea. I am trying to analyse the colours, to memorise the view: the deep brown craggy peaks, with snowy patches, then the brown and green grassland, with patches of bluer green something. Lower down there are lines of cliff. It must be houses high but from here it looks like a step. Then there's more green, and houses, white with coloured roofs. Everything is reflected in the water, slowly clearing of ripples after the ferry's arrival.

∼∼

Tom, with cup of tea: 'I really like this place. You know, I keep on thinking I should be going places, doing things, but maybe I don't have to... okay so I'm supposed to be figuring out retirement, but, well... well... maybe I'll just stay awhile.'

I grin at him and nod and think vaguely that he's right, and wrong, and right. I decide to watch the ferry leave, but by the time it does so I'm asleep.

~~

Later, it tips with rain. The world is still wobbling a little post-voyage, but we have moved from sleepy to hungry. Someone tells us we should try to get fresh fish from the factory at the far end of town. Along the road we tramp, water running down our coats. It's not a moment to admire the blue wooden church: we take shelter instead in the supermarket, scanning the produce for unfamiliar possibilities. I find flatbread, dried fish, skyr: skyr is Icelandic yoghurty cheese, a national product - perhaps, I think bitterly, the reason they defend against incoming dairy. We pass a technical museum with an astronaut figure just inside. More and more, there is a smell of fish. We pass a warehouse, peering at it suspiciously until we work out that the factory is the next building.

Inside, we climb clanky stairs and are met by a white-wellied foreman. Authoritatively, he summons a colleague. We wait, and watch. There's a constant grumble-clunk of machinery. Behind our broad-shouldered foreman is a production line: fish is being packaged. Women stand either side of a wide steel table. They wear tracksuits tucked, for the most part, into white wellies. Over the tracksuits are big white shirts, and over these, blue plastic aprons. Matching shower caps cover their hair. They take pieces of white fish and chop, chop, chop them to size. They stand on boxes, and a river of water flows beneath them and the table, across the stainless steel floor.

Another wellingtoned woman appears, and we explain our wish to buy fish.

'How much fish?'

'Enough for two for a meal' I say. 'Two or three meals' says Tom.

'Two people, two or three meals... you want whole fish, or fillet?'

'We want fillet,' says Tom, 'but we'll take anything'

'I think we can spare you that' she says, and vanishes. We wait. We watch the women, listen to the grumble-clunk. She returns, with a bag filled with white fish, and hands it to us. 'What sort is it?' asks Tom, but we don't understand her answer.

~~

Despite what I have been told, there are some trees, tall as houses, clustered about the village. It is not a profusion, but it certainly gives the lie to tales that trees can't grow at all in Iceland. The youth hostel helper beams at me when I ask about them.

'Oh but those trees are only twenty, thirty years old! And they were planted especially. And looked after. If you go to the mountains there are no trees. So much snow, so many rocks, they cannot grow.'

'So you've put a lot of effort into these trees?'

'Oh yes. We plant them and look after them and water them and pray please pleeeeeease that they grow. Otherwise there are no trees.'

~~

Tom is staying, I am going, but he has made me a fish sandwich 'for the road', with cheese as well as fish between the malted bread. At eight the next morning, I step out of the hostel into mist. The world feels hushed. Sounds take turns to come into prominence, first the waterfall outside my window, blending as I leave it behind into the rushing of other water, the pieu pieuus of birds, chasing each other invisibly.

I am catching a bus. Then I'll go over the hills and follow Iceland's main road around the south side of the island. The road will take me to Reykjavík, the capital, and then onwards, to the area Erik and his father settled when they first came to Iceland.

The bus – which is not a bus at all, but a minivan with a trailer – climbs up into the cloud. At every bend in the road, there are waterfalls; soon we come to patches of snow and moss. We reach some yellowed sheep. One rubs her head against the road-post. Then we are over the ridge, and there are slopes ahead of us, and a town squatting in the valley. One slope is covered in tiny pine trees, waist high.

~~

At Egilsstaðir we have several hours to wait. I eat my sandwich gratefully and wonder what Tom's up to, alone on our fjord. But I've found more companions and one, an Italian with a sunburnt nose, works out the best direction to walk in. We abandon our bags at the tourist office. This town may be bigger than the last, and have more supermarkets, but two or three minutes bring us to wide open fields, then to the wilder shores of a lake.

Underfoot, it's spongy: moss is growing through everything. But there are flowers too, thyme and orchids and cistus. There are even a few tiny pine trees. There are plenty more plants I don't recognise: thick succulent-looking giants and tiny white stems of flower. On the beach, where the lake is covering everything in white floury sediment, I spot huge daisies growing happily between the stones. Then there's the lichen, frothy-looking sponges of the stuff rising through the moss.

Iceland's climate is tough. It's cold, and for parts of the year it's dark for all but two hours of the day. It's windy. Occasionally, volcanoes erupt, spewing out hot lava and killing everything for miles around. But mosses and lichens are persistent. They can move into this almost uninhabitable territory. They can take being soaking wet, but can also dry out completely and survive at temperatures tens or even hundreds of degrees below freezing. They start to grow, on whatever surface offers them a hold. They catch the water, stopping it from draining away into the ground. Very slowly, they break down the rocks they cling to. Only later can other plants arrive, and then the process continues, the soil getting richer and richer and supporting a wider and wider range of plants.

Mosses and lichens, in other words, are even tougher than Vikings, even better at colonising new lands. What is more, to the new arrivals in Iceland, lichen and moss would have been omnipresent and useful, a packing material and a source of food, a factor alongside the hunting and fishing and grazing land that made the island a good colony.

~~

A view: the lake, mossy greenness, a wide field full of hay-bales and, a few hundred metres away, as if sprouting from the meadow, a group of tower blocks. A *pwit pwit pieu*: a bird with a long red beak is addressing the world, sitting on the hay. Later, I work out that its beak and its black and white plumage make it an oystercatcher. The lake sloshes, depositing more sediment on the beach. More birdsong: *pwit, pweet* and the occasional long trilling *prrrrrrrrrrrrrrrrrrrrr*.

~~

Some past travellers are easier to find out about than Erik – and their experiences were closer to his than mine will be. There was a rush of British visitors to Iceland in the second half of the nineteenth century, Victorian travellers who painted and wrote, examined and analysed, daydreamed and – universally – discussed the astonishing lack of roads. The more helpful of their many books provide a packing list: mackintosh boots above the knee for fording streams on ponyback; special boxes that will fit on the side of a saddle, to replace the more accustomed trunk. These writers praise the hospitality of the Icelanders who, when tourism was barely known, accommodated the often unannounced visitors in their own family bedrooms.

One of my favourite travellers is Miss Ethel B. Harley, later Mrs Alec-Tweedie, whose journey is a mixture of champagne, rebellion and curiosity. I suspect her of being a thoroughly terrifying woman: later in life, she was on a selection of committees including the Divorce Law Reform Union, the Eugenics Society, the Cremation Society and the Professional Classes War Relief Council. She spoke at the Paris Exhibition of 1900, on the Role of British Women in Agriculture. She was awarded a Navy League Special Service medal for war relief work: at about the same time she undertook a several thousand mile journey in the Middle East and Africa. She had two sons, both of whom died in the Great War. But in 1886, all this was yet to happen. Aged nineteen, she refused to be put off by the advice of a family friend that a journey to Iceland would be 'too arduous an undertaking for a lady' and persuaded her parents to let her, with her brother and three mutual friends, set off for a land that 'to Londoners, seems much the same point of compass as the moon.' In fact, this might summarise her reason for going: Switzerland, or Germany, more conventional destinations, would be no rest from the rigours of the London Season, since half London might be found in those lands.

Miss Ethel B. Harley's journeys to and from Iceland were simultaneously more luxurious and more strenuous than mine. She travelled by cargo boat – the only option in those days – and the captain made clear his disapproval of female travellers. On the return journey, the cargo was six hundred and seventeen ponies, packed so close together that they could not lie down. During the six day journey, the 'poor ponies' changed from healthy, cheerful beasts to emaciated skeletons, and eleven died: Harley comments on the skill of the sailors in extracting the dead animals from amongst the rest and throwing them overboard.

It would sound miserable, except that it clearly wasn't. 'How inconsistently some people dress on board ship!' Harley writes of the few other women aboard on the journey out. 'The girl wore a huge white sailor hat, covered with a profusion of red poppies, and her whole time seemed to be occupied in holding it on her head with both hands to prevent its blowing away. But it would rain, and the red from the poppies silently trickled all over the hat, and gradually formed rivulets on her face.' The main problems of the journey were that the wind and the smut from the funnel made oil-painting very difficult and, later, in rough seas: 'the soup landed in my lap, and a glass of champagne turned over before I had time to get it to my lips.'

Because of the roughness of the roads, Miss Harley defied Victorian convention and rode 'man fashion' rather than side-saddle around Iceland: this was radical enough to require four pages of justification. And when taken on a tour of a farmhouse, she felt faint at the stuffiness, a mix of fishy smells, human smells and smoke from the fire that filled the chimneyless room: she had to leave.

I'm sad not to be travelling by pony, but not very. Harley even mentions her guide, an Icelander well-accustomed to ponies, tumbling off and rolling over and over down a slope. I have ridden a pony twice in my life – and both ponies tried to throw me off. And, if I needed another reason, here's William Morris (yes, that one), another who travelled to Iceland, describing the state of his possessions after a long ponyback trip:

'at Eyrarbakki we bought some wheat flour and put it in a tin box, the bottom wherof came clean out at Hnausar: at Hjardholt our tin case of mustard was found smashed, and the mustard all over everything; here the great mess is in the medicine chest: the chlorodyne has run into the citrate of quinine, and made some kind of chemical combination of it which looks like a kind of sweet-stuff 'rock'; and both these which appear to have 'gone off fizzing' have mixed with the sulphur ointment and made a slimy jelly of it; and the whole thing is peppered beautifully with red precipitate (louse powder, so please you). One of the boxes has a mixture of cocoa, grass-cut latakia and paper at the bottom of it, which it is quite a joy to turn out onto the stones here. As to the biscuit boxes, why tell how the whisky keg has danced a hole in one, and what a queer powder most of them hold now?'

The worst I've suffered – apart from my fall into the fjord at Stavanger, which had severe results for my phone and other salt-water-sensitive items – has been the explosion of a yoghurt pot: days later I am still finding crumbly yoghurt-remains between the pages of my book. On reflection perhaps this justifies that customs official's objection to my carrying milk products, but it's nothing to fizzing sulphur ointment. I dread to think what I would manage to do to my possessions if I had to put them on a pony and ford rivers.

~~

Apart from adventure, two things brought the British to Iceland: geology and the sagas. William Morris was there for the latter, composing poetry about the old stories. I have to admit I've not bought entirely into his motives. Back in England he was part of a movement that romanticised medieval life, condemning the Industrial Revolution, advocating a socialism that encouraged the workers to create unique rustic artefacts with joy. Beauty was everything. Heroism was to be sought out and admired, used as an example. With a century's hindsight it seems a bit idealistic, but each to their own – my motives are probably no more sensible.

In a similar spirit, W. Gershom Collingwood set out for Iceland in 1897. Collingwood was an Oxford graduate and a student of Ruskin's; he knew his geology and was passionate about all things Viking. His home was in the Lake District and, based on a study of the Norse origin of place names in the region, stories he had been told by locals, and some excavation, he had written a book for children set around Lake Coniston, its eponymous Viking hero called Thorstein of the Mere. He was a member of the newly-formed Viking Society and it was probably while working on a saga translation that he decided to visit Iceland, aiming to produce a book which would illustrate the landscape of these stories.

He did it, too: he published both a *Pilgrimage to the Saga-Steads of Iceland* (with his travelling companion and guide, Jón Stefánsson) and an illustrated version of *The life and death of Cormac the Skald*. But my favourite relic of his trip is the letters he sent to his wife and children, whenever he could find a ship to take them.

From the Faroe Islands, to his ten-year old daughter:

'This letter must be to you, being from a fairy island... Imagine (*you* can) a peeled walnut magnified into a range of mountains rather bigger than the Old Man [of Coniston] – and set in a blue sea – so all the crinkles and folds of the walnut are voes or long bays of the sea. In and out of them the steamer goes, winding about in streets as it were of mountains – with never a scrap of flat ground, nothing but basalt crags, grass slopes and sea water. And here and there in the ledges of the great peaked hills, near the shore are green spots, drained with lots of little dykes which are full of marshmarigolds, and rich with the greenest grass...'

And then, to his wife, on first sight of Iceland:

'It was a brilliant morning – and a strong east wind made even the little waves of the open roadstead white and blue – Such a blue sky, hard and clear: and half way round the panorama snow topped mountains. The straggling town of wooden and iron houses runs along a green promontory…'

~~

Back in the twenty-first century, I decide to sample some Old Norse foodstuffs. One: skyr, the yoghurty Icelandic tradition that I had spotted in various shops. You start by making yoghurt, adding friendly bacteria to milk so it thickens and sours. Then you turn it into cheese: you add rennet and watch it separate. At some point you do some pasteurising but the bacteria are still alive in the final product. Skyr these days comes in plastic pots with little spoons in the lid. It also comes in a variety of flavours – just like yoghurt. It seems to be mostly a dessert but I'm sure you could use the unflavoured version as a savoury. I'm sure Erik did. According to the Skyr website, the Norse settlers brought skyr-making knowledge from Norway, where it later died out. Vikings everywhere may have eaten skyr.

The first mouthful tastes yoghurty, but the texture is thicker, smoother. As I eat further and further down the pot, it becomes solider and solider until it has almost the texture of cream cheese. There's cream-cheesiness about the flavour too – it reminds me of fromage frais. At the bottom of the pot, I wonder why I feel so full and realise that maybe, as far as nutrition goes, this stuff is closer to cheese than yoghurt.

I feel quite happy for Erik and his contemporaries, until I try the dried fish. It doesn't look good: grey-brown shreds in a plastic packet. *Harðfiskur* is the Icelandic word. I try to bite off a tiny corner but my teeth won't go through it – it's like biting a piece of leather. The whole shred has to go in my mouth.

First, there's the smell of the seaside – the other smell, the less pleasant, old-fishy one. The stuff doesn't really have a flavour apart from that: it's a bit watery tasting. As I suck, the texture changes from leather to disintegrating cardboard. It is exactly as you would imagine eating old, dry fish to be. I swallow it as fast as I can, washing it down with water to be rid of the taste.

Nor is it the most revolting of the Icelandic repertoire: the worst, I am still getting up courage to try. 'Do people really eat rotten shark in Iceland?' I had asked a native on the boat, hoping against hope that this was that this was some kind of massive joke played on tourists. But the answer was yes.

'You should have the white stuff. The whiter, the stronger, you can almost predict.'

'Er, so if I want less strong, what colour will that be?'

'It gets more yellow. But the yellow stuff can also be strong. It depends also what part of the fish it is cut from, inner or nearer the skin.' His hands make slicing gestures in the air. 'But you should try the white.'

'I've read that it smells bad but tastes good, is that true?'

A slow grin spreads across his face. 'That would – not be a lie. But I think it is about thirty percent that like it, seventy percent not. You do not eat a lot. It comes in small pieces, maybe you have two or three with some *Brennivín*, that's an Icelandic spirit. An old tradition, very old.'

Another day. Today, with my fish sandwich and my skyr, I've had a very Viking meal. Especially if I forget about the chocolate biscuits and the Spanish orange.

~~

Four hours later, I am sitting on a suitcase in a car park in Höfn, a quarter of the way around the south coast of Iceland, watching out for a blue jeep.

It's been quite a journey. On boarding the bus I was impressed by the suspension under the driver's seat: half an hour later, I was envious. We were travelling on the 'ring road' that goes round the edge of Iceland: it is the biggest road for hundreds of miles and for some reason I had assumed it would be tarmacked and many-laned. In fact, road markings of any sort were scarce. The surface was bumpy and so muddy that the bus wheels brought up a dense spray, so we travelled inside a swarm of brown splashes. Every time the driver stopped at a town, he would hose down the entire bus, bringing the view from the windows back to his passengers. Twenty minutes further down the road, the mud was always back.

We started by sweeping through wide green valleys, full of grass and glowing moss. The odd sheep ignored us. The coach climbed over ridges, and twisted down hairpin bends to joyful cries of '*Bello, bello!*' from two Italians whose presence filled the bus. Then we reached the coast, and the road ahead seemed to have been cut from the side of a chocolate-brown gravel pile. To our right, reaching to the sky, was a mountain of mud and grit. In some places it had a covering of moss: in others it looked as if the surface was fresh. To our left, the slope continued down to the beach. It seemed a miracle that the upper half had not yet redeposited itself on the narrow horizontal interlude that constituted the road, making a single mountainside once more.

~~

The trouble with watching for a blue jeep is that I'm not good on cars. I can't really remember what jeeps are – is it a brand? Are they just big cars? Or do they have to be a particular shape? Luckily, travellers sitting on their suitcases are more conspicuous. After about ten minutes, a vehicle slows to a halt in front of me. A long, lean figure, the very opposite of the archaeologist stereotype I am expecting, unfolds from the front seat, smiles broadly and moves to shake my hand.

'Ms Fitzsimmons, I presume!'

Piling out of the now-identified jeep behind Bjarni are his team and his daughter, at first sight a chorus of four, identically clad. I realise later that this is because they have come straight from digging: when they change out of their company fleeces, warm trousers and hair wraps their identities, too, separate: Sandra, Bryn, Inga, Iris. For now I remain confused. We clamber back in and swing off down the road. I've been given the front seat and Bjarni talks intently to me, asking questions about my plans and genially swamping my tired brain with information about his site: Hólmur. But there is laughter too. It's Friday evening and the team have been digging all week.

It is hard work keeping my end up, talking to Bjarni. I have weaselled my way into meeting him through emphasising my archaeology credentials, but I am on a decidedly un-archaeological mission. Following semi-mythological characters is not what modern archaeologists do, and for good reason: archaeological history is full of bad deductions and even dishonesty arising from taking texts literally. I know of archaeology projects in Iceland, conducted admittedly many years ago, where a saga character's grave or house was 'identified' by no more than being in the right place. More famously, at the site of Troy (now in Turkey) the archaeologist Schliemann purchased local goods and buried them to stand for Trojan treasure. Taking early texts too seriously does not improve your credibility with archaeologists.

Because of this, I have just realised that my questions need to convey knowledge as well as curiosity. The trouble is, the knowledge is also lacking. The extent of my knowledge about Hólmur is that it's a site from roughly the period Erik is meant to have been in Iceland.

My strategy of not saying too much seems to be going OK. Bjarni is telling me about how he found the site.

'Nobody believed me, even the man from the local museum. So I made him a bet: I would dig, and if I found nothing, he would not have to pay, but if I did, he would. And a few months later I came, and we made a test trench, and we were digging and digging and we found nothing, and I always said 'dig deeper!' and at the end of the last day we found a loomweight. And so it all began.'

Phrasing it so as to sound like a refinement of detail within my wealth of knowledge, I ask what, exactly, has been found. So far, comes the answer, a longhouse, another building, and 'what I call the cult site.'

'Why do you think it's a cult site?' I'm swift with what I

know will be a good question. Cult activity in archaeology-speak is a notorious get-out. It can describe anything even vaguely religious and archaeologists generally use it to explain the inexplicable. Bjarni sighs, and the team, in the back of the car, giggle.

'That is a difficult question.' He pauses. 'It is a lot of things together. There is a lot of fire-cracked stone, this grave, a boundary suggesting an inside and an outside, with some objects only on one side, a lot of bloomed iron on the outside, a lot of different finds unconnected to each other in the pit-house. It is not a living space and it is not a working space. But you will see.'

I have forgotten, if I ever knew, what bloomed iron is, but it can wait. Other impressions dominate: we have left the road behind, and are bumping across grass. Bjarni halts the jeep in the middle of a field. We are on a low ridge across the opening of a valley, hills rising steeply in the distance. We climb out of the vehicle and walk across to a small mound with two posts in it.

Bjarni stoops to pick something up. 'This is a firecracked stone... and this.' He hands one to me. What was once a round pebble has been broken violently in two. 'When they are fresh they are very sharp, very dangerous, you would clear them away from a living area. But they were collected here' – he gestures to the mound – 'piled up all over the grave. It was maybe some sort of sanctifying idea.

'The posts mark the boundary. You can't see much any more because we covered everything up after we had excavated, but I put them in where we had found some post-holes. So, the grave is on the inside.' He turns around. 'And here, outside the boundary, there are these two child's graves. At least they are assumed child's graves – they were empty. I didn't even find a tooth. But that would be very rare in Iceland, the bones are so fragile. Also outside the boundary was a lot of bloomed iron, as if it had been thrown. Outside the sacred area. The separation is very interesting.'

I decide I need to know what bloomed iron is. 'Oh - it is the first stage in the manufacture of iron... later you beat it, refine it.'

Bjarni looks, I think, surprised by the question, but he turns again before I can respond. We re-cross the boundary, re-enter the area with the burials. 'The girls are in the pit-house.' And there they are, sitting in a row. It's a squareish hole, about a metre and a half long. In it were found, I learn, all manner of things: whalebone cutters, soapstone objects, beads, loomweights, a whetstone. There was a hearth too, and post-holes suggest a roof.

'Was the grave used more than once?'

'I do not know. We cannot tell. But some of the activities happened for a long time. One idea is that possibly the man buried here – we think it was a man – was the first in his family to die in Iceland. So this burial was different. And later members of the family were buried elsewhere. It could be a bit like – what's it called? – ancestor worship.'

I try to organise this information. This site is from the time that Erik is said to have lived. And here we have signs of day-to-day activity, something to do with a grave, something not connected with living or sleeping, maybe part of the adjustment to living in a new land. I think back to Norway, in the tenth century long inhabited and full of Bronze Age mounds and old houses. In contrast Iceland was a blank slate, a wilderness however great its possibilities. I can well understand how important a first grave might become: the start of a history, the start of a secure connection to the place.

~~

Bjarni herds us back into the jeep and takes us two hundred metres across the field to a second site – newer discoveries, part of this year's excavation. We wobble one by one down a plank into the trench, a large clay-brown pit cut into the grass. Bjarni gestures, and points out raised patterns on the floor of the trench - the very last remains of walls. 'Typical longhouse. Completely typical for Iceland. Except for this – there is a door at the south gable. That never happens. And here, you see, there is this channel.'

I nod knowingly over the south gable. My ignorance of longhouses is pretty thorough. I know they are Norse living places, and the shape of this one substantiates my assumption that they were, well, long. I focus on looking intelligent, and look carefully at the floor of the trench, as if hoping to identify the channel Bjarni has mentioned. After a while, and to my own amazement, I spot it: a u-shape of different coloured earth in the cut. 'We do not know what it was a channel for. But in this area there was almost no human activity. What I think is that it was an area for animals.'

'Which would explain the door!'

'Yes. I think it was a later alteration.'

I look over towards the walls and try to imagine the building at full height. It's shaky: what was the roof like? Where was the door? The animal-house at the far end is clearer than the living areas. I must find out more about longhouses.

But Bjarni's tour is quicker than my imagination can follow. A few steps from the longhouse is another excavation area. 'Here is a very small house – I call it the working area at the moment. You can see the wall...' – I can, a faint outline, I'm getting good at seeing the wall-shadows now – 'and we will excavate deeper so it will stand out a bit. There was a hearth too.'

'Have you found it?'

'No, but I know there was a hearth because there is so

much charcoal.' He smudges a black spot in the mud with his finger, and goes on: 'And here, this is very exciting. Do you see that white stone?' I do, just: something rounded, buried in the earth. 'That is soapstone. In Iron Age times there were no ceramics here, they used soapstone or wood or iron. But iron was very expensive. Soapstone was cheap, you could easily get it from Norway. And it is probably a vessel. We will excavate it. So this is why I say this was a working area. And this separation is very interesting. Work, social, and cult. It is true in many societies – we do it ourselves today, homes and offices and some people worship.' He laughs. 'I say some! Not all! Anyway, here they are very far separated.'

I'm distracted. No ceramics, I'm thinking, in shock. That's a missing technology as drastic as the Aztecs' lack of the wheel. In the Middle East, they had ceramics in the Stone Age: how did the people of Iceland manage for so many years without any? By carving soapstone, clearly. But still.

But there are so many differences between my and Erik's worlds that it's getting exhausting thinking about them. Bjarni's point is more interesting. Separation of work, social and religious life is a similarity between then and now, helping and not blocking my imagination. We can understand that even though this group were so very different from us, living in their turf houses with their stone dishes and a fire in the hearth, they were also at some level the same, eating, drinking, sleeping of course but – more, something about mind, not just survival – keeping spheres of life apart in a pattern not dissimilar to patterns we might see in modern times.

~~

Bjarni has one more revelation for me. I'm staring intently at the 'wall' he has pointed out, at present merely a change in pattern in the mud. I've realised it's made up of separate squashed-rectangular shapes in a row. They're turf bricks. Almost all houses in Iceland were made from turf, from Settlement until World War Two. It was the perfect material. It is very insulating, and pretty quick to build with. This wall in particular is interesting because it shows a different method of house-building.

'We always thought the turfs were laid lengthways, but here they are across – perpendicular to the wall. So whether it was just this family, or that everyone did it this way, we do not know. But these people knew it could be this way.'

My attention has been distracted by a pattern on the soil. Shown up against the brown background are brighter reds and whites, swirls and layers of different shades.

'That?' I have let up my guard and Bjarni is surprised I don't recognise it. 'Oh, that's tephra. From volcanic eruptions. This is tephra… and this… and this… that is how we see the separate turfs in the turf walls.'

He takes me across to the wall of the trench, where the team has made a cut a metre or so down into the earth. I do know something about the tephra: volcanoes erupt, they create a layer of ash over part the island, and this layer corresponds to an exact date. So archaeology found below the layer is from before that date: from above, after. What is more, if houses are made of turf, which in Iceland they were, and the turf of the walls includes the layer, the walls can be part dated. There's a very famous layer from about AD 871 – the Landnám layer – which is especially useful for dating Norse settlers.

'That layer we do not see in this part of Iceland. We are too far away from the volcano. But this layer is very familiar.' He points to a grey line in the soil: when he rubs his finger on it it crumbles like dust, or the ash it is. With awesome precision, he declares: 'This is 1783. And,' pointing to another, 'this is 1362.'

~~

Before leaving, Bjarni sends me across to drink from the stream that runs through the site. He tells me that the water is the best in the world, and the team, laughing, tell me not to argue with him and chivvy me on. I jump between big hummocks of grass. Distantly, I can see the small mound of the 'cult site'. Close by is where the longhouse stood, where people would have lived and used this stream close on a millennium ago. All around rise snowy mountains.

I scoop at the stream with my hand: it's slow-flowing, crystal-clear, fresh. The wind is blowing hard and cold and I soon make my uneven way back to the jeep. The wind is driving more than me away. Wind wears away the soil, and destroys archaeology. 'In fifty years' says Bjarni 'this site would be all gone. We have protected those we have excavated a little, but the rest – they will just be worn away.'

CHAPTER 5

TRUTHS AND TERNS

'Does anyone know where we are?'

Bjarni likes to challenge his team and I feel I've been adopted for the day. Following my tour of the site, which required extreme concentration, we have been playing Spot the Tourist on a speedy tour of Höfn which encompassed the supermarket, the wool shop, and the sculpture (singular). The town – population less than two thousand – is a lobster and fishing centre, but also an easy stop on the ring road. 'Tourist!' 'There's one!' 'Tourist!' And we've played guess the nationality too.

But now, away from the centre again, Bjarni has stopped the jeep, and we are staring out across water.

'When it's clear, this is one of the most beautiful views in Iceland.' Bjarni seems a little despondent that he can't share it. We stare at the mist, and at the hundreds and thousands of swallow-tailed birds, flying fast and straight above the water.

But it is not the view that has brought us here. Someone answers Bjarni's question, and he explains further. We are parked on top of a very ancient grave. Bjarni points across a narrow channel of water at an island. 'There, I think there is another farm.' This man can read the Icelandic earth as I would read a book. He suspects that the grave we are parked on is part of another, larger site. This time the farm and the grave are separated by water: 'again, this separation.'

I move to get out of the car, so as to see better, but there are cries of 'stop, stop!'

'If you get out of the car, those birds will attack you.' Bjarni says it straight and the team laughs at my bewilderment. Someone has mercy on me and explains further.

'They peck your head and make holes in it. Especially at this time of year, they protect their young.'

I decide to stay in the car. I ask about the birds, trying to figure out their English name. It is my first encounter with Arctic Terns – but it won't be my last. 'They have very small feet, they do not like to walk. But they fly very well.' One sets course right in front of the car, almost scraping the bumper, as we bounce back along the track. I flinch. 'Oh, it will be fine. They do that all the time.' A voice from the back: 'They like extreme sports, these birds.'

~~

As we arrive at the dig headquarters, I know I have to ask Bjarni about archaeology and sagas. I pull together a cautiously phrased question: how are the texts regarded by archaeologists in Iceland? To my relief, Bjarni neither explodes nor looks despairingly at me. He answers that even today, when most archaeologists are cautious about saga-related statements, the sagas remain too central. 'But it must change, otherwise what is the point of archaeology? We are a separate discipline.'

I wonder what Bjarni is going to do about his cult site, though. After all, he can hardly start talking about tenth century religion, and ancestor-worship, without referring to the religious practices mentioned in the texts. He admits it's complex and won't be drawn: the paper is being written. I dare to ask the crucial question: does Bjarni believe in the sagas?

'I do not believe in these precise points in history. 874, they say the land was first settled. But the Landnáms-layer is absolutely from 871. And there is cultural material before that.'

'Is it Norse?'

'Very hard to tell. But these points in time are legends. A few hundred years later they were trying to write a history of Iceland, and they chose this date. It is quite likely that people came to Iceland, one or two, a few more, maybe it was used as a hunting-ground and well-known, then a big group came across and it is this that is remembered and not the few before.'

And Greenland?

'It might be the same settlement story in Greenland, and in Newfoundland. It was not really Erik and Leif and Thorfinn – some people visited and used the places, and then some others.

Maybe Greenland was a hunting ground at first. If you went there and found a walrus, you would go back. You would get very rich. Walrus tusks were white gold.

'People did not just write history: they had motivations. It is always political. Snorri, for instance, who is one of our important sources in the thirteenth century. He was a very rich man, writing words that would please people, maybe the king, that would benefit himself. We do not write this kind of history these days.'

We do, but it's true that at least we consider it wrong. History as an unbiased, factual account may be an invention more recent than the sagas. Stories were important. The right story must be told. A people must be given a history, the right history. At any rate:

'These stories of first settlers are legends, origin-myths.'

My training says – as it has been saying for a long while – that Bjarni is right. There was no Erik, or if there was he was just another guy. My search for him is fundamentally flawed. I don't want to believe it though. Perhaps Bjarni notices something in my expression. As we leave the jeep and walk towards the building, he points out that, for fairness, I should also ask someone on the other side of the debate.

That evening, we sit by the window talking archaeology until the light dims at nearly midnight. Exhausted by all the knowledge Bjarni has shared with me, I'm still muddling the team's names, although out of their kit they all look different and all have totally different lives. Is it Brynn I rhapsodise with at length about chocolate covered raisins? They come in huge tubs in Iceland, I've never seen so many. And there's whisky.

'Oh, I miss the light.'

'Summer is over.'

Separable they may be but it's almost a chorus.

'It's only July' I object. 'There's still all of August. And it's still lighter here for longer than it ever is for me at home.'

'No. Summer is over. Summer is over in Iceland when the light begins to go.'

~~

The next morning the whole group sets out on an expedition. Archaeologists accumulate from the ends of the Earth – or Iceland, at least – in the small port of Djúpivogur. The journey there is hazardous: we have to travel back along the ring-road again. Bjarni is keen to add to my anxieties, telling me how often the road must be rebuilt as the stones from the slopes slip onto it. The route, I learn, is credited with criminal reform:

'There was one man, very tough, who was working on this

road alone... the hill slipped and he slid with it to the bottom. He survived, but after that he was soft as a lamb – he took a turn for the good, changed his life entirely.'

At Djúpivogur, the archaeologists pour onto a small motor boat. Kitted out in orange lifejackets, they cling to the rails around the back. 'Let's see who will not be seasick!' cries their leader boldly, as the boat starts to rock.

'Hald ir fast! Hald ir fast!' I hear the captain shout as the vessel speeds towards open water. The day is calm, but the boat is rolling and swerving over the waves. I am holding fast to the rail, but the rail is metal and my hands are starting to freeze. I tuck one in a pocket, clinging with the other and trying to bend my knees to rock in sync with the rocking of the boat. Sea-spray hits my face, and my hair is full of wind.

Behind is a half-circle of enormous, geometric mountains, one almost tetrahedral, poking above the mist. Ahead, there are rocky islands, and we slow, lurching only gently. There's a shout, something in Icelandic. 'Fat seals asleep!' is the translation and yes, there are round shapes on an islet. A few plop into the water and the silhouettes of sealy heads are just visible, before they dive. A small child – not an archaeologist – is brought out of the cabin to look at the seals: he stares intently while his parents hold tight to him and to the boat.

The boat creeps round the seals, before shooting off into yet rougher waters. There are more islands; they are left behind, and then there is just one ahead: Papey. Steep grey cliffs are covered with black and white birds, and splattered, streamed and striped with their excrement. The noise can be heard over the whole island: squawking and skrawking, *kuck–kuck–kuck–kuck–kuck*-ing. On top of the cliffs, though, is a grassy paradise, thyme-scented, soft, rolling hillocks. And a lighthouse. There had to be a lighthouse.

This is an archaeologists' pilgrimage and investigation in one. They follow a small path round grassy mounds, and walk across a plain of rounded rocks. 'Ah, Kristján!' they cry as they descend on a small wooden house. Here, only decades ago, lived the Archaeologist who Became President, Kristján Eldjárn, while he was excavating just before his election. President for twelve years, he won his 1968 campaign and stood unopposed in the next two elections, only standing down to continue with his archaeology. I love the idea of a country where an archaeologist can become President.

There is a chapel too, though nobody lives here any more. Behind white palings, the little black building with its red roof and white cross looks small but brave. It's sixteen square metres, and when it was built there were sixteen inhabitants. The priest came twice a year. The inhabitants of the island would go to the mainland about as often, for provisions in exchange for the feathers, eggs and fish that they could collect. So strange everyone must have been to one another, living apart so much. But it was a hard journey to make: today it took forty minutes in a motorboat and that lurching sea was what passes around here for calm.

Papey makes archaeologists curious because it, too, has a legend hanging about it. The name suggests that it was once home to those Irish monks who floated to Iceland in their curraghs, in search of seclusion. Certainly they would have found that. And on Papey they could have lived, off the birds and the plants. So far there is no real evidence that they were there, but there are a lot of ruins. The archaeologists peer and poke and mutter.

Puffins line the precipices that edge the island, sometimes making an attempt at flight, legs splayed, wings flapping. 'They are the commonest bird in Iceland but tourists get really excited about them.' Well, they have stripy beaks. The captain picks wild horseradish and offers everyone a leaf. Then the time comes to pour back into the boat again. It's rougher: the archaeologists watch the waves, leaning into them, frantically concentrating to keep their balance, once squeaking in chorus as a particularly large swell lifts everyone off their feet. The water froths and foams and there are white heads across the surface of the sea. The boat is rolling over them. The puffins and the ruins have their privacy again.

As afternoon stretches on, we rush back along the coastal road. Bjarni fills some unknown gaps in my knowledge: there's the residence of an English Lord to spot, and he has stories of the celebrities who take refuge in Reykjavík. I learn about the jasper and malachite in the mountains, and the tourists who came in vans to empty the hills of pretty stones until the government forbade their export. I learn of another human import to Iceland: in the eighteenth century reindeer were introduced, for hunting, but the hunting was too successful and they only survive in the heaths of the south.

I ask Bjarni what he thinks about the trees. 'Scholars think the country was partly wooded at Settlement – not everywhere was woods but much more than today. Now it is less than two percent.' But tree-planting, he goes on, does not find favour with everyone. 'It is like an epidemic – they think it will cure everything! Sometimes it is fine. But they do not think it through. For example, they plant trees also on archaeological remains, and that will destroy them forever. Also, I do not want to lose the view. This is my homeland – I do not want to turn it into a Scandinavian forest.'

I surprise myself: I can see what he means. I am uncomfortable with the idea of reforesting those wild hills: something important and empty would be lost, as surely as the forests that went before. Ari's text, about the trees that used to be there at Settlement, has its echo in the present day news about rainforest destruction. And yet –

On a misty day, I continue my journey westward. I've bidden a sad goodbye to Bjarni & Co, but I'm still thinking about archaeology, sitting in the bus. But then we round a corner and my thoughts jolt away from ancient peoples. Ahead is the blue and white of ice.

~~

Jökulsarlon is a glacial lagoon, formed where the glacier flows out into the sea. Icebergs float, jaggedy and weird, on smooth blue-grey water. The sky is blue-grey too, and the shore is made up of dark pebbles: on this dull day the ice glows, brighter than its surroundings. But this ice is not just white. In some places, it is an unreal blue. In others, it is snowy. In others, it is streaked and marbled with black volcanic rock it has collected on its long journey from the glacier.

The shapes of the bergs are as mad and varied as the shapes of clouds. Behind the crowds of spikes, ledges and lumps, I spot a giant blue pair of pepper pots. In the foreground is a speedboat, black-hulled with a white cabin, floating serenely out to sea. It will never get there: it is already full of bubbles, like half-melted sorbet. Even a little way downstream there are no icebergs left, just ducks – or what look like ducks – swimming happily in the freezing water.

As we move west, the bus is slowly filling up. Jökulsarlon, and the view of the glacier that feeds it, are definitely on the tourist trail, and guide-booked tourists quote guide-book nuggets at each other. 'Oh, you've been to Seyðisfjörður! I'm so jealous. I hear the houses are flat-packed, brought over from Norway. And there's a little blue church, isn't there?'

Between stops I'm glued to the window. We're passing through a gravelly plain, covered in moss and blotchy black-and-white sheep. Streams run through it, adding to the impression of sogginess. The view is almost the same in both directions, gravel - just ending in water on the left and in mist-covered slopes on the right. Cables march through the landscape next to us.

An hour beyond the lagoon, we are still in sight of the glacier. The bus stops briefly in Skaftafell: this area has been deluged by floods again and again, road and bridges swept away when volcanic eruptions under the icecap cause it to melt from below.

Grassland, moss, boulders. At the town of Kirkjebaejarklauster (a name I relish) I experience my first Icelandic traffic jam: the caravans are going round a roundabout and slow us down. At Vík, I eat a smoked lamb and pea sandwich. Next to me on the bus, a man called Mick from Nottingham explains intrusions and alluvial fans and volcanic plugs.

Another glacier, and a wide, high waterfall appears and vanishes. The fields are back, the road gets wider, and the bridges more solid. Even our new bus driver is more urban, with an earring and a shaved head in place of his predecessor's sensible short grey hair. The bus gets hot. There are more farms, more petrol stations, more houses and little red-roofed churches. The soggy East is all gone.

I start to think the emptiness is behind us: then we turn inland. For a while we are in a wilderness surrounded by black mountains, only lightened by the moss and lichen on their lower slopes. Clouds lower but the bus is still hot. I am beginning to sweat, and to feel tired and fidgety.

Then, on the horizon, I start to see tower-blocks and cranes. We pass a short forest, and a brown lake, and the road widens into two lanes each way- then three, a shock. There's a flyover, and fields and trees and warehouses, and more and more apartment blocks, and I glimpse what might be the cathedral before I am deposited, blinking and sticky, in Reykjavík Bus Station.

CHAPTER 6

THE BIG SMOKE

'It's twenty two degrees – we're having a heatwave!' My Reykjavík landlord wears, for the whole time I am staying at his hostel, a Liverpool football shirt. 'You should have come here, not gone to the foggy East!' My room-mates, Kiwis from London, are keen to discuss the mayor, commuting and house prices. They have been round the country in seven days and 'I think we've pretty much seen everything' one announces.

As snobby as Miss Harley about Londoners abroad, I get up early and go exploring.

Reykjavík may be Iceland's capital, but it has the atmosphere of a seaside town. The houses are clad in corrugated metal or smooth concrete, painted white, or beige, and with pretty wood-framed windows picked out in dark blue or red. The roofs are coloured too, and some of the houses are ornately decorated: one has an onion dome, with a criss-cross balcony round its base.

Water is all around. The harbour is packed with boats - tough-looking green fishing vessels, neat ferries and day-trippers, decorated restaurant boats, dinky sailboats. In the centre of town is a well-behaved lake, surrounded by buildings, where birds cluster on a round island. The whole place has a continental, tidy note. On the main street most people are dressed smartly – or at least, smartly enough to make me feel scruffy.

Above the town rises a white pine-cone spire, belonging to Hallgrímskirkja, the great white church. It stands in a wide square. Flanked by slopes of white columns, its outline points Concorde-like to the sky.

I have come here deliberately, but not for the church. In front of it, Leif, son of Erik, strides out in green bronze glory on the smooth white stone prow of a longship. Eyes aloft, his hair blows out behind him from under his helmet. In his right hand, clasped to his chest, is a small cross. His left hand, by his waist, grips the head of an axe. He wears a tunic: maybe wool, maybe chainmail, and a sword hangs from his belt. His cloak streams backwards in the imaginary wind. The muscles of his arms are emphasised: this is a figure of strength, power, boldness, determination, dream-fulfilment. This is a man who could have done anything, and he chose to visit America and to bring Christianity to Greenland.

I'd like to say I feel inspired, gazing upon this man who was so closely related to Erik, but mostly I am busy harrumphing. Harrumphing over why Leif got a statue and not Erik, harrumphing over the heroising image which clashes with what's in my head.

I walk around behind him and find an inscription inside the prow of the longship. It reads:

LEIFR EIRICSSON
SON OF ICELAND
DISCOVERER OF
VINLAND
THE
UNITED STATES
OF AMERICA TO
THE PEOPLE OF
ICELAND
ON THE ONE
THOUSANDTH
ANNIVERSARY
OF THE ALTHING
AD 1930

Sniffily, the first thing I notice is that they have spelt his name wrong. All the Is in Eiricsson are most Scandinavian and accurate, but the C is the American spelling sneaking in. Eiriksson, Eriksson or Ericson – no compromises please. And confusingly, Leif is a memorial for the foundation of the Icelandic Althing or Parliament. But he had nothing to do with its foundation (which took place over a hundred years before his birth) and his most well known connection to the parliament is that a local branch of it exiled his father. Hardly the stuff of the American Dream.

It seems bizarre to me, that the Americans were so keen on the rhetoric of this story. Later, I am amazed to find that this was not the first statue of Leif built by Americans. In 1887, one was put up in Boston. In 1901, Chicago got another. There are now ten or twenty Leif Eriksson statues spread across Norway, Iceland, America and, recently, Greenland. A special society – the Leifur Eiríksson International Foundation – coordinates and fundraises so that the number shall continue to grow. There is even a Leif Erikson Day in the USA, on October 9th.

This particular statue really was a gift from the American people - an Act of Congress decreed it and then a competition was held for the design.

It is only much later, reading up about Icelandic emigrations to the Americas, that I start to understand this obsession. When those British tourists were exploring Iceland, at the end of the nineteenth century, times were tough. For years the temperature averaged two degrees, and a particularly devastating volcanic eruption left a deep ash layer. Emigration was a really good option. By 1930 there were nearly twenty thousand people of Icelandic origin in Canada and about seven thousand in the US Mid-West. That's about a quarter of the number of Icelanders in Iceland at the time.

There had been just as much emigration from other Scandinavian countries, and it was a Norwegian origin senator who placed Leif's statue in Reykjavík. All these US immigrants were pioneers – just like Leif and Erik. They were Scandinavian – just like Leif and Erik. And Leif was a pioneer from Scandinavia in America. And a Christian.

I wonder if Erik would have been annoyed that Leif had a statue and not him.

~~

Also in Reykjavík is a centre for followers of Ásatru, the modern incarnation of the Old Norse Faith. With some trepidation, I ring up the 1100-strong Icelandic branch: I want to work out what Erik – very much not a Christian – might have believed. I meet up with their former president, Óttar Óttoson. He declares immediately that he is no expert on the mythology. 'What I am an expert on is, I would say, the practise of Ásatru nowadays and who are these crazy people who follow it,'

Óttar is emphatic that there's no one Ásatru – and no clear rules for practise. The gods I've heard of – Thor, Odin, Freya, Frigg – could be central for some, irrelevant for others. The stories – like the idea that thunder is caused by Thor's hammer – could be taken literally or metaphorically. Óttar is also emphatic that it's nearly impossible to work backwards from the modern faith to what someone like Erik might have actually believed. '...It is very hard to find out what this old religion was. The sources are valuable, but we have to be sceptical, they are written by Christians, and an Arab. Everything remains very misty for us.' And as for ceremonies: 'The sagas and eddas were written down on dried skin. They would not waste skin on trivial things everyone knows – how to brush hair, how to cook. So they don't put the detail, just that they had a ceremony.'

We talk about the conversion of Iceland to Christianity – or as Óttar describes it, the abolition of religious freedom. The story goes that by the year 1000, there were two religions in the country: Christianity and Ásatru. This was causing problems because they had different rules for living: if disputes arose, which set of rules should be used? So the question was brought to the Icelandic Parliament. The Lawspeaker considered the matter deeply, lying under his cloak for a night. He returned a verdict that Iceland should be Christian – but that pagan practices might be continued in private.

Erik's own family – apart from Erik – converted when they were living in Greenland. Erik's wife, Thjodhild, even refused to sleep with him when he refused to convert. So it's frustrating not to be able to understand what Erik was holding on to. Óttar does have one recommendation: that I read the

Elder Edda, a set of religious texts with slightly hazy origins, compiled a few hundred years after the Lawspeaker's verdict on religion. 'Not Snorri's *Edda*. The *Elder Edda*. Snorri did great work, trying to put things in a system, but he was Christian and he had to make links to that, and to the Ultimate Truth.'

Cattle die, kindred die,
Every man is mortal:
But the good name never dies
Of one who has done well

The *Elder Edda* is a collection of poems. Their verses range from the starkly practical:

A man should know how many logs
And strips of bark from the birch
To stock in autumn, that he may have enough
Wood for his winter fires.

And the cynical:

No man should trust a maiden's words,
Nor what a woman speaks:
Spun on a wheel were women's hearts,
In their breasts was implanted caprice,

To lists of the names of dwarfs:

Nyi and Nidi, Nordri, Sudri,
Austri and Vestri, Althjof, Dvalin,
Bivor, Bavor, Bombur, Nori,
An and Anar, Ai, Mjodvitnir,
Veignr and Gandalf, Vindalf, Thorin,
Thror and Thrain...

And descriptions of the end of the world as we know it:

Earth sinks in the sea, the sun turns black,
Cast down from Heaven are the hot stars,
Fumes reek, into flames burst,
The sky itself is scorched with fire.

I see Earth rising a second time
Out of the foam, fair and green;
Down from the fells, fish to capture,
Wings the eagle; waters flow.

The above are all quoted from Auden and Taylor's translation of *Hávamál* and *Völuspá*, the two most comprehensible of the *Elder Edda*. *Hávamál* is Odin's advice on living life well. *Völuspá*, on the other hand, is a sybill's prediction of the future:

she describes the world's beginning and its end.

Völuspá has me hypnotised for a while. Perhaps it is the images: glittering dragons fly across the sky with corpses, the gods play chequers with golden pieces, fields of wheat grow where none were sown. Perhaps it's the familiarity of the ideas. All those dwarf names have meanings, from Docile and Clever to Corpse, Colour and Oakenshield. It is a poem that takes getting to know: the first time I read it, only parts made any sense. But the endless questioning of the sybill holds it all together – each time she describes something new, she asks:

Do you still want to know more?
Do you still want to know more?

~~

I wander through the clean streets, pondering Óttar and Ásatru. It's classic: the faith, which I feel I have glimpsed rather than understood, may have something in common with Erik's beliefs, or it may have nothing. The mystery is deepened, not solved. Even Erik, I remind myself, may or may not have existed.

Later, I pass the hostel, and am accosted by a pink-eyed hippy sitting on the steps.

'Hey, can I sing you a song?'

I pause, about to refuse, but he goes on. 'Hey, can you sleep here? I can't sleep in all this light, I just sit here and go to the bar and eat and sit here some more.

'Let me play you a song. I made the Chinese Ambassador cry by playing a song, and tomorrow I'm moving in with him. He said: I've got a big house, empty rooms, you should move in. I love this country. I sold everything to come here. I have a degree in finance and I'm richer than you, but people think I'm homeless. But I can't sleep. I can't sleep.'

An Icelander is sitting next to him, in painty dungarees. He finishes his cigarette and goes back in. I listen to the song and wander on.

~

Fifteen minutes later I walk into a tenth century longhouse.

It's two metres below the surface of modern Reykjavík, and was excavated in 2001. Now it's preserved, spotlighted, in a dark underground chamber. Needless to say, the entire longhouse is not to be seen, just the first few layers of turf bricks and a long hearth running down the centre. Post holes suggest to archaeologists that the turf building was lined with wood, and show that it had a roof.

The longhouse was probably in use from 930-1000, so would have been here for the whole of the period Erik is supposed to have been in Iceland. He could even have come here. This was a good area so it was settled early, well before he arrived. There are hot springs nearby, there was plenty of driftwood, there was grazing land, and there were birch forests which could be cleared for more farmland, or for building wood, or to make charcoal to smelt iron. Hammers and crucibles have been found, suggesting that smelting was going on. There were eider ducks, with their warm, collectable feathers. There would have been plenty of other birds, a self-replacing larder from Great Auks to puffins.

The museum is attended by a team of knowledgeable people. I learn how the house was divided into two areas, along its length. 'On this side there were probably benches, and it was for the master of the house. On the other side of the fire was the working area, and also where the slaves slept.'

I'd forgotten about slaves. A fact not often discussed: Vikings were slave owners. Erik certainly was, while in Iceland. The slaves were often of Celtic origin, kidnapped in raids.

'How do you know what happened where?'

'We know there was a bench because there is no trampling on that part of the floor: people did not walk there. And we know from various places – written sources – that the other side would be the area for hospitality and so on.'

The lack of privacy is what I think I'd have found hardest. It's possible, of course, that there were firmer dividing lines in the house that have left no trace: curtains, for instance. But it must have been darker too: harder to see from the slaves' area to the other half. I wonder how dark.

'How was the house lit?'

'The fire, that would produce a lot of light. And in daytime light would come down the chimney. And they had their fish-oil lamps – they are surprisingly bright.' I've seen a fish-oil lamp in the displays of finds and been excited to learn that the wicks were made from Arctic cotton-grass, cotton-wool puffs on the end of long stems that shine whitely in damp green places. But my guide is expanding:

'But this darkness is something that almost no-one living today has to contend with. You could not keep the fire burning at night, these houses were extremely flammable. When you woke up in the morning in winter it would be pitch black. We do not experience this today. When you wake up there is usually something – a streetlamp maybe – something that gives some light. Then, if you went outside, you could not see a foot in front of your face.'

He holds his hands up, demonstrating the distance. The darkness almost had substance, it was so impenetrable. In winter, the light comes only three hours each day.

'What is interesting,' he continues, 'is that this darkness is rarely mentioned in the sagas. In some few, it is a twist of the plot, a person stumbling around in the dark, but mostly not. It must have been just a fact of life. But I think the darkness really explains all the beliefs in elves and fairies and trolls that people had. If you cannot see anything...'

He pauses, and the gloomy image expands in my mind. 'It must have got cold at night, too,' I add.

'Yes, and it was worse in later periods. The fires got smaller, eventually they were lit only in the kitchen. They kept warm basically with clothing.'

'Was that because the wood ran out, because the trees were gone?'

'Yes. And also the climate was colder. Those first hundred years of settlement, they were good times. Then it got tougher.'

～～

I have been distracted by a label:

Butter was not salted but became sour and could keep for years under a thick coating of mould.

Urrgh is my first response: then I remember that cheese like Brie is also preserved in mould. There's a note about skyr too, kept in barrels.

'Yes, skyr is a very good preserved food. What you buy in the market is diluted with milk. So skyr is a concentrate, the barrel will make three times its volume of skyr.'

'And as a concentrate it keeps?'

'Yes, for months. Basically, the three main foodstuffs of this country for centuries were skyr, butter and dried fish. Very high protein. They only really made bread on special occasions, although there is a flat stone in the centre of the hearth here that was probably used for baking. Grain was hard to grow. Barley was grown, but more likely used for porridge where you could add something, like seaweed or Icelandic moss.'

Another label says that food was preserved in lactic acid. It sounds a bit technical until I realise that lactic acid is whey, produced when milk is separated to make skyr or cheese. Fish and meat were preserved in more barrels, in this liquid.

'They valued fat. You cannot live on protein alone. That is why fish and whale were so important. For the oil.'

'For lights too?'

'Yes, but that oil is from the liver. You boil it up, then the oil comes to the surface and you skim it off. You can eat the liver afterwards. Shark livers are very good for oil, they are huge.' He spreads his arms wide. 'About a third of a shark is its liver. They are almost all liver. And...' returning to archaeology all of a sudden, 'they have found fishhooks here that are far bigger than you would use for normal fish.'

I've remembered the dreaded Icelandic delicacy.

'Did they eat rotten shark here too?'

'Oh yes. Because you cannot eat shark meat, it is toxic, but they were not going to pass up on so much meat. They had to find a way, and they did. Have you tried it yet?'

'Not quite.' And now I know it's a Viking Age food I have no excuse for evasion.

'Well, there are two rules. First, do not breathe through the nose. Second, drink plenty of alcohol with it, to numb the tastebuds.' He smiles at my obvious horror, and hastens to reassure me. 'No, no, it is good, it will not make you ill.'

Reassuring.

~~

I wander the exhibition for an hour or so, playing with the reconstruction computer, peering at the glass beads that travelled here from Europe or further, wondering what games would have been played with the decorated circular playing-piece that was found at a site nearby. Games like draughts and chess were big in Viking times.

On the way out there's a row of turf chunks in Perspex boxes. I'm walking past when my guide, keen I should not miss it, appears again. He picks up a fresh turf and holds it out to me. 'Feel this.'

It's cold, squashable, muddy.

'That's why turf walls are never very high. They fall over. Now feel a one hundred year old turf.'

This one is hard, solid, a bit crumbly.

'And after a thousand years there is no living material in the turf at all. So when you dry them out, they just crumble like dust. So we preserve them with chemicals.'

He produces a chemically hardened turf: it's almost plastic-like.

Something occurs to me.

'Can you still see the layers of tephra in the preserved turf? The Landnám-layer, for instance?'

'Yes, yes of course.' He rushes me back to the main exhibition and points out the light-coloured streak running through some of the turf bricks.

'Here. It is like the earth making time markers for us.'

On my way out, climbing the spiralling staircase, I pass a step coloured cream, and labelled Reykjavík 871^{m}2. I'm rising through the tephra of the Landnám-layer, returning from Erik's to my own time. I wonder who lived in the many years of settlement between us.

The simplest answer is: not many people. And you could add that life was much the same here as in that longhouse until the twentieth century, when various events forced the population into industrial modernity, swelled the cities, and connected Iceland to the rest of the world.

Reykjavík was not particularly important for most of this time. Towns didn't really happen in Iceland: the population lived on isolated farmsteads or in very small trading communities. The Church was powerful for a while: monasteries flourished, to which we owe the preservation of a large number of Icelandic manuscripts. The country was taken over by Norway; Norway was taken over by Denmark. Intensive trade restrictions came into being, cutting Iceland off even more from the rest of the world and making market towns pointless.

A census from 1703 shows that Reykjavík was a large farm, with an associated church, and six outlying farms. Sixty-nine people lived there in total. Enter, fifty years later, industrialist Skúli Magnússon. Iceland was still part of the Danish realm, and Skúli persuaded the Danish government to let him start a process of industrialisation. Reykjavík was to be the centre of the textiles industry.

Skúli's plans didn't really work, and fifty more years later Reykjavík would have sunk back into rural obscurity, except that it didn't. The reason it didn't was that during those fifty years, Reykjavík had somehow become the seat of a bishop, the seat of the court, the home of the Latin School, and the site of Iceland's only jail. The trade restrictions had been slackened and Reykjavík was officially a market town. By the time the 1801 census came around, there were three hundred and seven inhabitants. In 1836, there were about seven hundred.

Iceland in the nineteenth century was unusual because almost everyone could read, but there were almost no schools. The population was mainly rural, and widely dispersed. But this was also the time when nationalism took a solid form. Iceland's national parliament, which had closed for a while as all decisions about Iceland were moved to Denmark, re-opened – with limited powers – in Reykjavík. More and more trade took place in the town. By the end of the nineteenth century, the population of Reykjavík was about four thousand. The High Victorians visited: Collingwood described it:

'the modest cathedral and parliament house; the turfed square with its statue... the foreshore with its two slips and range of wooden warehouses; the four or five streets of shanties and shops, with corrugated iron a good deal in evidence, and ponies standing about everywhere; a town that strikes one as rather forlorn and hardly picturesque, though interesting to the newcomer with a kind of worlds' end interest – Ultima Thule reached at last.'

Miss Harley was more practical:

'There are two small inns in the town, as well as a club house, post office and stores, besides a druggist, photographer, and two or three silversmiths. As to vehicles, there were none, and the silence of the streets reminded one of Venice.' She also mentions visiting a hospital and a museum.

After the turn of the twentieth century, the town just kept on growing, and life got more and more modern. More schools, the Welfare State, a University arrived. In 1944, Iceland finally got her independence from Denmark, a freedom that was hastened because Denmark was captured by the Nazis in 1940. This much sought-after independence had a side-effect: the island was both vulnerable and strategically critical for Britain and the US. From 1940 onwards there has been a fairly continuous presence of British and then US troops, including a base in Keflavík, very close to the capital. Iceland became less and less isolated. The capital city offered more and more work. Now more than half of the population live there and in the satellite towns – about a hundred and fifty thousand people. One worry of country Icelanders is that the young people all leave for Reykjavík, sometimes because they want to but sometimes because they feel they have no choice.

Life has changed in the two metres or so of time since those turf walls were laid in newly-colonised Smoky Bay.

TRAVELLER

CHAPTER 7

WITCHERY IN THE WILD WESTFJORDS

Reykjavík bus station, eight fifteen a.m.. I have bagged the best seat in the bus, right at the front, and am eating Icelandic Noi Sirius raisin-filled chocolate. I am also entertaining myself by playing Spot the Tourist with an entirely unjustified sense of superiority. There's a matching couple in orange raincoats who stride determinedly across the tarmac to a bus, only to be sent off back again. Another couple, sturdy hikers from the last century, have their socks pulled up to their knees above their big boots. A nervous-looking woman, clearly a reluctant part of a camping holiday, queues hesitantly to stash her karrimat-festooned backpack.

The locals are obvious, in ballet-slipper pumps and straightforward slip-ons and carrying actual handbags.

We drive north. This trajectory will take me to the Westfjords and the bay, Drangar, where Erik first settled. It's good to be getting closer to him again. But I'm also nervous about it:

How are you going to get to Drangar? There's no transport for the last hundred kilometres of road. And the road is famous for being bad. And after that there are no roads and you have to find this mysterious boat for the rest of the journey! You can't do it!

Maybe I can walk. Erik did it when they hadn't got any roads at all.

Don't be daft. He had a horse, probably, and a boat. And was stronger. You can only go about 10k with that pack. And you don't have a tent. What, are you going to sleep under the stars in this weather?

Um, maybe someone will give me a lift!

Yeah right, because it's such a busy road! And that's hitchhiking. Dangerous, remember?

Well, I have to try, don't I? I'm going to follow my friend Matt's advice. He said 'just start walking.' If I don't start, I'll never make it. If I do, I might.

Your friend Matt is a bit tougher than you.

To add to this worry, I have no accommodation in Hólmavík, the town at the end of the bus route. I suspect there is no accommodation free there. I called the only number I had, and they were booked out. But as the bus is a twice-weekly affair, and my time is not infinite, I have decided to risk it.

~~

Drangar, where Erik and his father first settled, is in the far north-west of Iceland. This area, known as the Westfjords, is frilly-edged, the few roads desperately wiggling up and down and around the edges of the steep coast. Hornstrands, where

Drangar lies, is the northernmost section, almost touching the Arctic circle. It was one of the last parts of Iceland to be settled, and one of the first no longer to be farmed: nowadays its only visitors come for the birds or the hiking.

~~

We pass some more wilderness and a lagoon, crags and mounds, fertile meadows, a lava field and a mountain shaped like a whale. We round it and pass gravel piles and pits along the road. The landscape smooths out and we plunge into a cloud. Now there is nothing but mist and mossy dampness: to left, to right, ahead, behind. The windscreen is spotted with tiny droplets. We crawl. We stop: some damp people are mending the road. We crawl on.

~~

As we drive, geography blurs and Iceland gets mixed up with the American mid-West. At Brú, there is a gas station. In the gas station, staff in green aprons serve fries and burgers. They also sell Pringles, popcorn, and fuel. There is pumped pop music, and there are plastic chairs. A child, with a storm of curly hair, cries.

Brú is not a place, it is one of the Waiting Rooms of Life. I give in. I eat fries. I wait for the next bus.

~~

This bus keeps leisured time, but when I and a check-shirted couple and a bundle of newspapers have been safely stowed, it proves to have magical mist-clearing properties. Blue-green water appears on my right again. This must be the north coast of Iceland now, so in the far distance that water is the Denmark Strait and eventually the Greenland Sea. But across the fjord are fields right down to the water's edge, and farms. There's even a tiny village.

All of a sudden the road quality reduces. I try to take notes, but the pencil is out of my control, jiggling and joggling illegibly. We are right by the water, so close I can spot ducks swimming. The other side of the fjord is retreating, its slopes getting steeper. Above us, blue patches of sky send bright patches onto the sea. I keep watching the other side of the fjord, getting steeper and steeper until suddenly it runs out and the sea goes on to the horizon.

Our road keeps changing its mind. Sometimes we are taken high up the green slopes, watching blue sea and clouds sitting on the hills. Sometimes we go right down to the shore, almost amongst the seaweed and driftwood. Sometimes we cut inland between scattered rocks in a carpet of thyme, mist blowing around us.

Someone is collecting driftwood which is piled in ordered heaps. We pass a cluster of red roofs, a cluster of blue. And then we draw up to a petrol station on a mound, above a bigger than usual group of houses. The driver stops and opens the doors. We are in Hólmavík.

~~

An awkward moment. The bus driver offers to take me to my accommodation, and I have to admit I don't have any. I try to look confident as he points out the tourist office.

It isn't far, and I throw my bag down gratefully a few moments later, stretching my shoulders out and looking around. My blasé approach to accommodation seems ridiculous, now I realise the size of the place. My only hope lies in the one contact I have here – a Jón Jónsson, who I've been emailing. He seems to know everything, but I am not sure he can conjure up B&Bs if they don't exist. Putting off the moment of truth, I spend some time picking up leaflets, and contemplating the Icelandic hand-knitted gloves and the small carved and painted birds that are on sale.

Eventually, I approach the counter.

'Um, is Jón Jónsson here?' I ask.

It turns out that I am speaking to him – and also that his

organisational powers are close to magical. Tonight, Jón's wife will put me up in her guesthouse a little down the coast; Jón will drive me there himself when the office closes; from there I can visit the sheep-farming museum; here and now I should visit the Witchcraft Museum. Jón points it out, and the path to it across the village; he exudes optimism about my onward plans and assures me that I should get to Drangar and back easily, with his help, soon enough to catch the onward bus in five days' time.

Obediently, and gratefully, I set off. The Witchcraft Museum – could anyone refuse the chance to visit a Witchcraft Museum? – is the turf-roofed building, down by the water. Still high above it, I pause by a clump of bright purple thistles and survey the village. There seems to be a lot of bunting about. Someone has been painting stones, too – by the side of the road, some are decorated with flowers and patterns. I decide to explore a little before going to the museum: inhale some of the cool, fresh-smelling air after my bumpy bus ride.

I'm distracted by a mad construction, a criss-cross of long driftwood logs. Drying fish are hung from it, strung like rows of beads. Tassels of fish-heads dangle from corners. Above a string of fat specimens, a long and scraggy one leers towards me. Fascinated, I stare into its eye-sockets. This is a far cry from the sanitised plastic-packaged chunks of dried fish that I tasted a few days ago. Finally I touch the true, wild, ancient

Iceland, I think. Up here, they are closer to the Old Days. Fie on supermarkets, fie on national distribution. This is the Real Thing. This is how the Vikings did things.

~~

'Are you Alexandra?'

A wild-haired, wild-bearded man is nursing a cup of coffee in the sunshine on the bench outside the museum. I nod. Given that the telephone exists, I can't put it down to magic – but still, it's organisational powers that come close.

'Jón said you were coming. I am Siggi. Would you like a coffee?'

I decide to go straight in. 'There are no broomsticks,' explains Siggi, as he directs me to the first display. 'Nothing like that. It's not witchcraft as you understand it: it was different in Iceland. But you will see.'

It is altogether more sinister than broomsticks. I take the proffered audio-tour, and a slow, deep, hoary voice reads the English translation of every sign. Normally I am a skim-reader and a skipper: I avoid upsetting passages, I don't read the more revolting sections. But here I have no choice.

'A spell for a common man to find riches... mark the sign on the skin of a black tomcat with the blood of a menstrual virgin. Then catch a sea mouse in a net of virgin's hair, and keep it in a wooden box with the sign carved over it. If it is kept trapped you will find wealth. If it escapes, there will be a terrible storm...'

The museum is light, but cold stone. In one corner, a rune-carved strip of wood is clenched in the jaws of a giant, dried-out fish-head. The voice echoes on in my ears.

'The necropants must be made from the skin of a dead man's legs, dug up from a churchyard...'

'Mix the blood from a raven's heart with blood from your thumb...'

'Spit communion wine on a rib dug up from a churchyard...'

'To find a thief... to raise a ghost... to bring a dead man to life...'

A grotesque vision of life in the sixteenth-century Westfjords fills my mind: small evil ghosts, living dead creeping around at night, men drawing money from the scrotums of their necropants. I am feeling a little queasy.

'But of course, we do not know that anyone was actually using these spells,' Siggi's gruff voice brings me back to now. 'This area is mostly known for witchcraft, but the people here aren't the ones who said that. It was always other people. In the sixteenth century, most of the persecutions were here, but there is much more folklore in other parts of Iceland. There was one family that persecuted and persecuted. And many of them were educated in Denmark and Germany where there were many persecutions. They must have thought it was a useful idea!'

The museum's collection of grimoires is covered in signs and symbols, and nearly illegible Icelandic writing. Siggi translates some more spells for me. There are spells for everything, from nasty rape enchantments to charms for making a cat have kittens without a tom. 'This one is to find out what you want to know,'

'And how do I do that?'

'Oh, it is in secret writing. They often are. Only the headline is readable... sometimes they write out the whole spell and only the last word is in code, the word you have to say aloud. Very annoying!'

One spellbook has been copied and copied and copied, right up to the twentieth century. 'Icelandic people copied the gospels and so on,' Siggi explains 'But also more sinister things, like these, in secret.'

A museum of witchcraft does not have obvious relevance to the life and times of Erik, but I don't really care. The museum's last exhibit, however, has a direct link. I am shown a rounded, hollowed rock. It was found a few valleys north of Hólmavík. Here, in Goðdalur, folklore tells of Goði the Viking, a ninth-century pagan, first inhabitant of the valley. He is supposed to have built a farm and a temple and cursed the place against further building. A later inhabitant – who lived in Erik's times, and could have been one of his neighbours – is said to have been a very devout worshipper, maintaining the temple: pagan rituals may have continued here in secret for many centuries after the Conversion of Iceland. Recently a couple living in the valley unearthed this rock.

'Well, the story is that we had this stone and the police, the forensics, became interested. This lady was working on a technique for detecting blood at crime scenes. And she used the technique on this stone, and it showed there was blood.'

There is a poster made for a police show in New York about the blood: it describes spraying the rock with luminol and fluorescin, 'both of which showed a positive reaction in the region of the bowl.' although 'the presence of blood is difficult to confirm as there might be local factors that influence the reaction.'

Siggi defends his exhibit:

'You can never be completely certain. You have to say there is doubt: it would not be professional not to. But it is most likely blood. Now, we do not know how old it is – that we cannot detect with this technique. But the shape of the cup is very convincing. It is very like the shape of a cup in a ritual performed in one of the sagas. And local folklore says there was a temple in the place where it was found. There has been no archaeology in the area yet – but perhaps there will be. And if it is this sort of cup, it would be the only one that has been found in all Iceland. It is probably horse blood, you know, not human blood.'

~~

Interlude: two more stories about how the world goes round:

First story: trolls in the Westfjords.

Humans and trolls have always been enemies. Long ago, the trolls wanted to separate the Westfjords from the rest of Iceland, to create a land just for themselves. They began to dig a channel, and, just for fun, decided to make islands with the waste soil.

On Breiðafjörður, in the west, two trolls made lots and lots of tiny islands.

Up here in the east, the third troll had much less success, because the bay was so deep.

All the trolls got so engrossed in their digging that they lost track of time. Slowly, dawn was approaching. Trolls can't survive daylight – they turn to stone. The Breiðafjörður trolls suddenly realised what was happening and ran for home – but made it only to the shore, at Kollafjarðarnes, where they were turned into two stones that survive to this day.

The troll digging from the east managed to get to the shore

at Steingrímsfjörður. She turned back to look at her work – and was annoyed to see how few islands she had produced. She thumped her hand on the rocky shore, and a lump broke off. This made Grímsey, the large island in that bay. Then the light reached her and she, too, turned to stone.

Siggi (joking, I suspect): We are thinking of doing troll-watching for tourists, you know. Far easier to set up than whale-watching, none of these government regulations, you can touch them, kiss them, whatever you want.

Me: You should, I'd go, definitely.

Second story: a long voyage

In the Witchcraft Museum, upstairs, in a cabinet of magical artefacts, is a *Lausnarsteinn*. It's flat and rounded and would fit perfectly in the palm of my hand. It looks like a huge squashed conker.

Lausnarstarnir are found on the coast of Iceland – and Britain too for that matter – but are very rare. They are travellers: their story is about ocean currents. Lausnarstarnir are from Central America, west Africa, Columbia and the West Indies and arrive in Iceland after floating across up to eight thousand kilometres of ocean. The journey takes at least a year.

In the beginning, they are the seeds of a massive rainforest pea. This plant can climb up to twenty-five metres through the rainforest canopy – the equivalent, if they grew in cities, of nine storeys of tower block. The seeds are produced in pods sometimes over a metre long. This is a Jack and the Beanstalk plant.

The pods break up into segments and as each seed ripens its segment falls. Some land on fertile soil. Others land in water, and are carried off downstream or out to sea, at some point losing their segment of pod. After a year's travelling, the seed can often still grow, should it land somewhere less chilly than Iceland. In Iceland, *Lausnarstarnir*, picked up on beaches, acquire instead a mythical power. They are held holy in folklore: if you clutch one during childbirth all should go well.

~~

Jón picks me up at five. He is also picking up his four children, who are scattered around the village. We make the round in a little yellow car, which seems perfectly happy to climb slopes that would make my legs protest. He still has no news of a lift northwards. I ask him about the drying fish I saw. He looks at me, concerned.

'But it is not real. Siggi put it up as a sort of symbol, because the building next to it is for fish processing. You are not allowed to dry fish in a village, because of the smell.'

I feel humiliated, a romantic tourist, an ignorant city dweller. The smell – of course.

'But is that how it's done?'

'Not really.'

Oh.

'You use a much bigger frame. And you can only do it if you have land outside a village.'

'So you could do it, on your land?'

'Yes, I could,'

But he doesn't. Oh well, modern times take us all.

'Look, down there,' Jón is pointing to a structure by the shore, wooden poles in a line. 'That is where you dry fish. And you see that shed there? That is for shark. They come to the fjord sometimes, and you have to hang them up for several weeks, otherwise they are toxic.'

I cheer up.

~~

Westfjords folklore is about ghosts, elves, magic, trolls and sea-monsters. That evening I sit attentively on a stool in Jón's study and listen.

Ghosts in Iceland, I learn, are different from ours. For a start, they always follow one person. Family ghosts can live for three hundred years, or nine generations. Almost always, a magician has woken the ghost, to set it on a family he doesn't like - but sometimes a ghost returns through its own choice, for revenge. Some ghosts kill people. Some just follow.

Elves are also important in Iceland's stories. There aren't so many stories about elves in the Westfjords, but there are plenty of cliffs and outcrops where people believe the elves live. And parts of the land are under their protection. Elves are not fairylike, or delicate: they do not dress in green and wear pointy caps. They are like humans, but a bit bigger, and usually invisible. They are to be respected. If they are not respected, they can be dangerous: they kill livestock, they may even harm humans.

'But you must not mix up elves and *huldufólk*, hidden people,' Jón adds.

'What's the difference?'

'Elves look a little different: bigger. *Huldufólk* you cannot tell apart from humans.'

A story about *huldufólk*: often, if one of their womenfolk is having difficulty in childbirth, they will borrow a human woman to help. After the labour, an ointment is rubbed in the baby's eyes. The human woman steals some, rubbing it in her own eyes. The ointment is magical, making *huldufólk* visible to her even after she returns home. But she can't tell them apart from humans, so when one day she spots a thief in a shop, and shouts, she gives away her secret power. The thief spits in her eye and her power is lost again.

Some people have a special gift and can see elves. Jón's grandmother saw elves, often. They would be going about their business: cutting grass for the sheep, making hay, fishing, farming. And there was one year when the whole village heard singing from the elf-church: it was a funeral.

The Icelandic trolls of the legends are huge and female: the males died out long ago. Many of the stories are about female trolls trying to get menfolk, trying to stretch male humans and feed them to make them into husbands. The Westfjords were the last part of Iceland where trolls lived. Everywhere else they were gradually driven away by the sound of pealing church bells. Men chased by trolls were advised to sprint for the nearest church and ring the bells: the troll would then run off, covering its ears.

Then there are the sea-monsters. *Skrimsli*, who are covered in shells, and who jingle so you can hear them from far away. *Fjörulalli*, who try to mate with sheep. *Fjörulalli* will also try to push humans into the water: they look like humans so you should be careful about letting people walk uphill of you. And there are people who live in the sea and can tell you everything about the future. And there are the *marra*, who give nightmares, and gloom: you might still say about unhappiness 'it lays on me like a *marra*'

'Do people really believe all these stories?'

Jón pauses. 'I think troll stories in Iceland have always been just for fun. There is always something suspicious about those stories – you can see an element of trying to get a good plot. Of course, that's just something I think: they seem that way to me. Elves? Sure people believe, certainly the older people do. The ghosts? Not all the ghosts, not the ones that attack you. But the ghost stories from this area are all small stories, about little things they did to different people.

'Round here the stories are all like that: some farmer knows a protective spell, or some little magic. There's no famous magician, just a lot of little stories about people knowing a bit more than they should...'

'Can we imagine these stories were around in Erik's day? Might he have believed in them?'

'Much of it is from Christianity. But I think much of it is from a storytelling tradition through the ages. Lots of these creatures are in the Icelandic sagas. But I don't know if people ever believed in it! Of course children did. A lot of stories in the folk belief are about dangerous places. Maybe at first they were told to frighten children away... then, after three generations, they become tradition and you don't know whether to believe or not. So safer to be careful.'

In the stories that survive about Erik, there are some ghosts and there's also magic. The ghosts are people on their way to being dead: risen corpses. There's an outbreak of disease somewhere in Greenland and a dead lady gets up and tries to climb into her husband's bed. He has to drive an axe into her breast to kill her properly. The poor man is greatly plagued by ghostly behaviour, for when his friend dies he also sits up again, and demands to speak to his wife. He predicts her future in detail and demands for himself a proper Christian burial.

In Greenland, after its settlement, there lives a prophetess and witch. She spends her winters feasting at people's houses, and telling them their futures. One year there is a famine, and she is invited to the chief farmer's home, to tell him when it will end.

She has to sit on a cushion stuffed with hen's feathers, and she carries a pouch full of charms. She is dressed in a blue cloak decorated with stones. On her head is a black lambskin hood, lined with white cat's fur. She has catskin gloves, too, and a staff with a brass, stone-studded knob.

She has a meal of goat's milk gruel, and hearts from a selection of animals. She eats this with a brass spoon and a knife whose handle is made from walrus ivory. Then she sleeps overnight at the farmhouse, and in the morning begins her rituals. Part of the ritual is a song: when it has been sung, the spirits are charmed and she can see the future more clearly.

We have talked for hours, but it's still light. At ten o'clock,

I wander down to the beach, bundled up as usual in layers of coats. I climb over rounded pebbles to where mussel shells crunch underfoot. The birds are making a racket too: *pieu pieu pwiu pwiu...* *pip pip* ... *cheeeew, cheeeeew, pirreeee, pirreew, chipchipchipchipchip* and the odd croaky *creaaawk*. I try to follow an oystercatcher that's leaving footprints in the sand.

The shore is covered in seaweed: little brown birds are pecking around in it. I spot bits of sea-sponge amongst the tangle of growth. I sit on a sun-warmed rock and put my hands in my pockets, counting sorts of birdsong.

pit pyot pweet, pit pyot pweet

pewoopewoopewoopewoo

Something flaps across in front of me and then dives steeply into the water.

I listen to the birds, the waves washing up on the shore, and my breathing.

I watch Grímsey, smooth and flat across the water, and think about the trolls who wanted the Westfjords all to themselves.

At midnight, the sun sets.

CHAPTER 8

NORTHWARDS AND NORTHWARDS

The next morning, there is still no sign of a lift. I suggest to Jón that I set out on foot, in the hope of hitchhiking, and he appears not to think this particularly daft. That's two people advocating the 'start walking' plan – though Jón is still optimistic that he'll find someone who'll drive me.

Not keen on carrying my pack if it can possibly be avoided, I decide to give it a few more hours. After all, I have to visit the local sheep-farming museum. Not only have I had firm instructions to do so, and a personal tour organised, it's also possible that I might learn something about growing and harvesting sheep, a subject on which Erik must have been expert.

~~

The sheep are happy to see me. They baa loudly and run across the road to head-butt my legs. I laugh at them, stopping so as not to be tripped up by this tangle of woolly love. There are only five of them: three are white with pink ears, one is mottled brown and the other is black. Inevitably, it is cupboard love, transferred immediately to Addi when he arrives.

Addi, cheerfully brown-bearded and brown-hoodied, is the sheep museum expert. While he fills bottles for the lambs – apparently that's what they are, but they are very big, woolly lambs – I wander the museum. Never would I have imagined that there could be so much gadgetry in association with sheep-farming. I can't even list names of objects, because so much is so strange to me: hundreds of mysterious wooden and iron tools, filling the room and covering the walls.

We take the bottles outside and the lambs slurp and suck at them. Milk gone, the lambs lose interest in us and we go our separate ways, they to walk aimlessly in the grass, we to inspect their history.

Addi zones in on the item he wants to show me first. It's a bit of dirty old rope. 'Now this, we keep for the smell,' he says, opening the glass lid of its cabinet. I reel back as it hits me. My dad used to have a jumper made of less than usually treated sheep's wool: this smells like that did, only twenty times stronger. Old, smelly sheep.

Addi grins at my reaction and explains that it's a ram's rope, that in its former life would have been tied around a ram's neck. 'Once we had an old farmer in here and he smelt it, and he said "ahhh, the Christmas smell." Because at Christmas the sheep are, ahem, making lambs and the rams smell so strong. You cannot eat them for about two months, because they taste like this too. But it is all hormones.'

Presumably, then, it's attractive to ewes: good evidence that I am not any kind of sheep as being close even to the rope makes me choke. I move on to my most important question: what's special about Icelandic sheep? I know they are all, or mostly, descendants of immigrant Norse sheep that came across with the settlers – so the lambs we just fed could easily be related to Erik's sheep. But how could I tell them apart from other sheep by looking at them, or by their behaviour?

Addi confirms some of my knowledge. 'They are related to sheep in Scandinavia, in Russia, in the Faroes and Orkneys.' He ponders a little. 'It is not the wool – they are not woolly like New Zealand sheep are, they have not been bred for that. I think perhaps they have shorter tails. Maybe their ears are different. I'm not sure – I was only in England for a week and I do not really remember the sheep. What do they look like there?'

I gulp. Despite numerous childhood holidays full of fields of sheep, I realise I can't even bluff an answer. I am guilty of sheepism: they all look the same to me, woolly with four legs, sometimes different colours. I stutter something irrelevant and fall back into silence. In my head, Erik frowns at my ignorance. I am a bit surprised to see him there. He's waving his axe rebukingly.

Luckily, Addi continues. 'They are very strong sheep. They can live for weeks without grass. Even today sometimes when they are herded one is not found, and then it is found weeks later, just lying there but alive.'

Then there are the Icelandic sheepdogs, small and nimble, light ginger with a distinctive tail, fluffy and curled around in a circle. 'They are very determined,' says Addi. 'Icelandic sheep are very determined, so they have to be.'

Sheep-herding happens once a year, in the autumn. The sheep live inside in the winter, in the old days in people's houses or in little shelters outside. In times past they used to be put out to graze even through the snow. Sometimes they are sheared but that's a new custom: sheep have usually been reared for meat more than wool in Iceland. The lambs are born in May, indoors, and the sheep are only put out to pasture later. All summer the farmer works fixing fences, putting down fertiliser, cutting grass for hay. In early October, the lambs are sent off to the slaughterhouse.

'There used to be slaughterhouses everywhere, but now they are closing down. Now we have to drive the lambs a hundred and fifty kilometres. For people further north it's two hundred and fifty. That's too far – the lambs get stressed.'

Times have changed in other ways, particularly in the last hundred years. Most of the gadgetry here is twentieth-century – in the times I'm interested in farmers probably just carried a trusty knife. Sheep used to have only one lamb each spring: now they have been bred to have three or four. As a result they often need more help with birthing and rearing, though it varies from farm to farm. Different farms have usually bred their own sheep through the ages so may have quite distinctive animals.

Sheep farming has declined, too. 'In the old days almost everyone in the area was a sheep farmer. The problem used to be that there was not enough grass. Now there's plenty for everyone. There are not as many farmers, though each one has more sheep. You might have six or seven hundred per family. In the old days, two hundred was a lot.'

We walk past more complicated tools, and Addi gestures at a bottle of *Brennivín* by the herding equipment. 'That's changed too. In the bars they try to make it like a shot, and they serve it cold. But they used to put a sock around it when they were herding, to keep it warm. They used it as medicine too.' Suddenly, his quiet features light up in a smile. 'Ah, and now we come to my favourite part of the museum.'

Unnervingly for that remark, we're in the slaughterhouse section. There are numerous complicated and less complicated gadgets for killing sheep: for instance, the *Svaefingurjárn* – Sleeping-iron – a metal spike to be put into the back of the neck, and – at the more modern end – a stun gun.

'I used to work in the slaughterhouse here, before it closed.'

I am not sure how to react to this revelation. 'What did you do?'

'We were taking out the stomachs. It was good.'

I think my expression betrays my horror and he shakes his head at my squeamishness.

'It is like any job – biff, boff, you just get on with it. It's the people you work with who are important. It was hard work sometimes – when the stomachs were fuller they were quite heavy. I don't know why some were fuller. There were lots of farmers working there, just for the season. On the last day we had a waterfight.'

He looks nostalgic. I ask what people did before slaughterhouses.

'They just did it in a field: built up a wall to hang the meat from.'

~~

Finally we come to the end of the museum, and the reason for all this hard work. Icelanders really did use every sheep product. The milk was made into cheese, skyr, cream and butter, cow's milk usually being drunk fresh. After slaughter, some of the fat was used for candles, and ram's stomachs were part of a – not altogether reliable – weather prediction system. Then every remaining part of the animal was eaten. I cringe as Addi describes some of the products: lungs, believed to cure alcohol problems if eaten, cooked, on an empty stomach; liver; heart; mashed brain; kidneys; testicles;

At this point I stop him. The other products had sounded familiar enough, if nothing I choose to eat myself, but testicles?

'Sour testicles. In meza, er, whey. That's one way of preserving meat.'

'Pickled testicles? Are they, um, nice?'

'Oh it's very good. Just extremely good. I can't describe the taste but it's extremely good… ' He thinks for a little. 'No, no, I can't describe it. It's very good.'

And then at the end there's *slátur*: blood boiled up with sugar and water, 'very good too' and anything leftover is thrown into the stomach, boiled, and given to the dogs.

'Or you might eat it yourself,' Addi adds, 'if times were very hard.'

～～

Addi drives me back to the village, and we chat about his visits to London. Somehow, we get onto traffic jams.

'I can't even imagine a traffic jam here.'

'No.' Addi laughs. 'I mean, even if everyone in Holmavík decided to go to the same place at the same time… there would be, maybe, a kilometre of spaced-out cars but still it wouldn't be a traffic jam.'

I'm wandering around the village when a black jeep roars down the road, swerves past me and draws up in front of me. Siggi's face appears from a window, and he gestures for me to get inside. 'We have found you a lift! We have found you a lift and he is leaving almost at once.'

Half an hour later, I'm on my way north again.

~~

Hafþor, a light-haired, smiling, slightly nervous man, is the Holmavík teacher and my lift. He is going to Norðurfjörður for two reasons: to check out a new museum, and to visit the school. Art is his subject, but he teaches at primary level so he teaches everything.

He teaches me about Norðurfjörður. There are thirty people living there, so the school has two pupils. In winter, the road we are driving on is impassable, so everything is brought in by plane. After they are fourteen, the children go to school in Reykjavík, boarding and coming home with the food supplies. It's a long way – but if they went to Holmavík they would be stuck there until the after the snow melted in spring.

Hafþor first came to this part of Iceland while doing research for a book, about Njalf's Saga. He gets very excited as he tells me about the places he visited. 'It is so precise. You can read that they came to this fjord, to Bjarnarfjörður - the next

fjord, to this waterfall, to this farm – and it is right for today.'
He points to a farm, a square white building surrounded by
heaps of hay. 'This farm is in the saga.'

He also points out eider ducks, a line of white along the
shoreline. 'It's the males you can see, the females are brown,
they're guarding their young.'

Then there are swans, a group of them in another little
fjord. 'Did you know they go to England for the winter? They
tagged some of them, so they could know precisely where they
were. If the weather is good, they can fly over in one day. But
sometimes they must stop and rest on the sea.' The journey
can take up to four and a half days.

We are climbing, now, the road leading us away from the
shore. The light is getting brighter and brighter: a dim day
is turning glorious. We reach the top of the slope and start
to descend. We are in a new valley, smooth and green with
a gentian-blue stream. There are little cliffs here and there,
russety-grey, but they are covered in growth except for on the
very steepest part. 'This is Bjarnarfjörður,' says Hafþor. I gaze.
We wind on down through the valley.

～

In Bjarnarfjörður is quite the prettiest museum I have ever seen, tiny and built half into the hillside, grassy on roof and walls. It is a sister of the Witchcraft Museum: 'Quite a new idea,' Siggi had said. 'We want you really to experience it, how hard life was for the poor people in the sixteenth century, why they might try a little magic to give them hope, hope that next week, next year things would be better. You see, there are two groups involved in the witchcraft trials, the wealthy – the 'nobles' as it were - and the poor. The first group is well documented: the second we know almost nothing about. We want visitors to go in there and really let their imaginations work.'

With the sun shining and the valley so beautiful, I am not sure it's going to be possible to identify with sixteenth century misery. I ought to have come in the pouring rain, or on a cold day in winter when everything is snow-covered and it's dark for all but two or three hours.

We open the door, and then shut it immediately, gasping at the smell. I take one final lungful of sweet, fresh air, open it again, and step inside.

For the first few moments, my senses are overwhelmed. I can see nothing: the only light comes through the low door. I can smell nothing but old sheep, so strong that I can't even remember other smells. It's quiet, except for whispering voices, muttering Icelandic words, telling stories.

The door closes. Later I notice that it's weighted down by a huge vertebra that I can only assume comes from a whale. My eyes start working, and I find I am in a small room. The floor is earth. The walls are hung with bundles: feathers, ropes. There is a box of skulls. At the one end of the room is the food store: a butter churn, dried fish, and to my excitement some chunks of dried, rotten shark, deep orange, hung from a hook.

In the other, dim room, I begin to make out the pattern of turfs on the walls: stripes of what was grass above the darker soil below. There's a place for livestock, who would have shared the house in winter. Hafþor mutters: 'I really cannot imagine having to live with the sheep.'

In the dark days, this would have been the whole world: this, and stories of trolls and elves and times past. Runes and symbols are carved on some of the beams: protective charms, circles crossed and decorated, eight lines made into a star. They keep knives sharp; protect sheep from foxes; prevent drowning; prevent theft.

Danger and hunger all around, who would be averse to a little enchantment? And who would not fear their neighbours, if they looked as if they could master a spell to break a horse's leg or worse?

~~

Blinking, I come out into the sunlit present. Hafþor is ahead of me, chatting to the museum's keeper. It is time to drive on.

That afternoon, the colours of Iceland shine forth unmisted. She is a jewel, glowing under the bright blue sky. As we come out of Bjarnarfjörður, the hillside gets steeper. Next to the sky, the slopes are topped with rocky needles and crags. They are dark, but in the scree below them are streaks of red and yellow ochre, as if some giant had dropped a box of pastels and let the remains crumble dustily down. Shadows stripe the cliffs, dark and light.

We come into the top of another valley, a fjord where nobody lives - russet mountains, sapphire water, emerald grass, and a waterfall sparkling white. We stop the car and wander a little. The waterfall makes the only sound, a background hushing.

Further north, in another fjord, there's a sweet hotel, beautifully kept, and an abandoned herring factory, wire mesh showing through its concrete cladding. Hafþor chats to the hotel's owner. I walk around, followed by the hotel's dog. He watches me suspiciously as I photograph a waterfall that comes straight down a cliff. I listen to it roaring, and to the gulls squawking round the old factory.

Soon after that, the road goes mad. We are going up and down, round hairpin bends, weaving around the contours. Often, we seem to be heading straight for the water, saved at the last minute by a sharp twist in the road. Once or twice this happens on a steep sandy slope. Once we meet a caravan on a blind corner: luckily, everyone is driving at about walking pace. Sometimes a chunk of rock sits in the middle of the road, and we bump over it. Hafþor says: 'When it rains a lot, the rocks fall on this road from the slope.' I am glad it's not raining.

Up above are more crags. All around are green slopes. Sometimes steeply below us, sometimes by our side, is the edge of the fjord. A little way out dark stacks stick up through the water.

~~

By the time we arrive at Norðurfjörður, I have almost collapsed from tiredness and hunger. The guesthouse is a bright white building next to two or three others on the shore. I can stock up at the little shop, and stow my possessions in a cosy room. I bid a sad goodbye to Hafþor, and watch him drive away.

A little later, after eating and resting, I look around the bay. *Only thirty people live here*, I keep thinking. There seem to be eight or nine buildings, the cluster where the guesthouse is, and where the boat comes, a little way down the side of the fjord, and a few more spread out across its head. All around are fields, green dotted with yellow. Above are red, rocky hillsides.

I walk along the shore to the other houses. The pebbles beneath my feet are pink and green and grey and brown, and there are pale blue mussel shells. The wind's up, and I can hear breakers washing the beach at the head of the fjord. When I get there it's sandy, dark sand with bird footprints all over it. A stream runs through the sand, pebbly-bottomed in its own channel. The colours are brighter underwater, brick reds and emeralds.

The creators of the footprints come back, a pair of sandy-coloured birds poo-weeing at each other. Their legs move so fast under them that their bodies look as if they are gliding free, a handsbreadth above the ground. There is a silliness about the busy legs and the floating bodies. All alone, I smile at them.

~~

Ever-so-slightly, the endless daylight is getting to me – this far north it is never dark. The next day I wake far too early to do any exploring, so I perch in the corner of my bed, wrapped up like a giant caterpillar in my sleeping bag, and write down the events of the last two days. I feel like a parcel in the post: helpful, competent people have been passing me from hand to hand for days. However easy it makes my life, it's unnerving to have so little control of my destiny.

Today, though, is my own. I want to absorb this isolated place. Northwards and northwards, I think, wanting to walk towards places in Erik's saga even though they are too far away, and I am catching a boat tomorrow. There's supposed to be a hot pool further up the coast. I dress, and ask my landlady for suggestions about places to visit. She describes something, but her English is not up to geological terminology and I am left with a vague idea about a tall rock. I don't really mind: I only want to wander. I don coat and boots, and step outside.

The only sounds are the rushing and trickling of water and the cries of birds. A v-formation of oystercatchers flies low over the water. The colours are still vibrant: after tramping up the road for a while I find it's too much to remember, and have to stop to write a list.

Glowing green – moss almost burying a stream

Silvery-grey – driftwood piled on the shore

Black – spiky crags jutting from the water

Brown and ochre – seaweed

Indigo – the sea

Yellow splashes – buttercups

Purple – a drift of thyme

Russet and blue-grey – the slope; bright white – a patch of snow

Brick-red and mustardy-yellow – streaks high up on the hills

Grey-green – fenced-off fields of drying hay

A red tractor

A sandy-gold gravelly path

Sparkling, rippling water

Creamy-white – sheep huddling behind rocks.

I tramp on. Now I am beyond what is practically the last outpost of civilisation. A few cars drive confusingly past me. The road leads nowhere – what are they doing?

The air is chilly and my legs are starting to resent so much walking. To my left, a slope's dark surface is freckled with white stones. I inspect them more closely and realise they are not white but covered in white residue. Water is trickling around them. Suspecting something, I dip my hand in and find it blissfully warm, perfect bathtub temperature. I track the stream to its source: it bubbles up a few metres from the path. Most of it has been tapped off, and a pipe leads to a swimming pool that I can't yet see, but there is plenty for me to examine and warm my hands in.

Hafþor told me yesterday that strange things grow in hot springs – strange, exotic bacteria. Certainly there's something weird in this one: a bright orange slimy substance. A bit nervous of bacteria that survive at extreme temperatures – they might be better at surviving than me – I poke it with a stick. It's bouncy, almost rubbery.

Further up the coast I find the swimming pool. I giggle: it looks as if a giant had put his square kitchen sink down on the beach, and then some humans thought it would be a good place to swim and added a changing room. There are no other buildings for miles, but there are six people splashing about in their swimming kit.

Next I come to a pebbly beach. A stack rises from it – it looks like a giant forearm with a clenched fist, reaching for the sky with one finger raised. My landlady's rock. At a distance, I think maybe I could climb it: close by, I realise that it's impossible. My head is only just above the elbow. Walking along the beach is hard work, the stones clunking around underfoot. I rest on a ledge.

For the whole morning, I've felt disconnected and confused. Several times I have laughed out loud, all alone, at birds or at strange landmarks. My notebook is my only companion and I am writing in it constantly, recording every detail of every scene, every inner thought. But, I realise, I am not doing it only to keep a record: I am doing it for company. Here, where there is almost nobody and where my phone doesn't even pretend to have reception, I have nobody else to speak to. It's unnerving. I can no longer judge my humour, or my sense of what is interesting. I wonder if I can have a conversation at all.

~~

I shiver. My isolation is self-imposed, but I wonder too about Icelandic life. Even today, there are lone farms, far from anywhere, their owners in touch with more sheep than humans. Perhaps it is not only the darkness that suggests elves and *huldufólk*. Perhaps, in the great empty landscape, day after day without hearing another voice, it is to be expected that company, friendly or not, would reveal itself, make advances, come to be known.

The scenery is majestic, and weird enough to be fascinating. Hot water comes out of cold earth. Twisted, contorted wood is brought up by the tide. I can see chunks of pumice, solidified lava, amongst the stones on the beach. I can find rocks that have been broken apart by the force of a frost. I can stare up the slopes and out to sea and feel that there is not another living thing for miles and miles.

I am small, and vulnerable, and alone. Landslides could rush down that scree slope. The sea could wash me away. Alone, I would not last more than a few nights in this landscape: it is a feat of human cooperation that I am here at all; that Norðurfjörður is supplied with food; that the thirty inhabitants stay on there.

I take comfort in some more Icelandic chocolate – Noi Sirius caramel, very good – and walk back to the guesthouse.

Later, I sit by the shore and watch some ducks splashing around. It is so quiet that I jump when a white motorboat whooshes into the bay. I go to meet it.

A group of colourful walkers gets off, bright in their raincoats, rucksacks and boots. Chatting noisily, they pile themselves into cars. A group of twenty or so stops, and forms a circle, holding hands. Puzzled, I stand around to see what they will do next.

'Are you Alexandra?'

A blond, round-faced man whose shirt has naval epaulettes has come up to me: Reimar, the boat's captain. I admit to my name, reflecting that Jón's powers of organisation are mighty.

'We leave at about ten, tomorrow.'

I nod, and smile, but I am still transfixed by the circle of hikers.

'Oh, they always do that. It is a tradition.'

At which point they all raise their hands and shout and Reimar goes to bid them goodbye.

~~

Later still, I wander around the harbour. I pass a small boat playing pop music all to itself. I peer into the water and see seaweed on the bottom of the bay. I walk up to the quay again. The motorboat has gone – there's just a parked car and heaps of limpet-encrusted wood. At the end of the quay, some birds are making a racket. Fifty plus fulmar, mottled grey, are swimming in circles. They swim with their wings crossed, so that the almost black wing-tips make an elegant V. Their grey feet paddle busily beneath them: occasionally, they dip their beaks in the water. As they glide around they make little squeaky grunts in their throats: *puck-puck-puck-puck-puck*. But then the peace is disturbed: two birds hunch their shoulders and flex their wings and open their beaks wide, aggressively *aaark-ark-ark-ark aaark*-ing in each other's faces. It happens again and again, with different pairs: if no one gives in they half-fly at each other until one is chased splashily a few metres away.

A day or so later, in the same place, they're quiet again. I wonder if they were sorting out some sort of hierarchy. Perhaps they only do it once in a season. If so, I feel very privileged to have watched.

CHAPTER 9

DUCKS AND VIKING BATHTUBS

There is nothing to see but murky grey mist, and the waves are shaking my breakfast. Even wrapped up in my coat, three jumpers, and my warmest jeans, I'm cold. My hood is pulled up over my hat. I look enviously at the group of elderly Icelanders who are also aboard: they are much tougher than me. Or so I believe, until one is sick over the side.

The lifeboat looks vaguely like an inflated dinghy and could not possibly fit all of us. I shall have to trust Reimar not to crash.

The elderly Icelanders are on a sightseeing trip. They have chosen the wrong day – we cannot see one pebble of the famously beautiful coastline. For what seems like hours we rock up and down, shivering and focusing on the horizon – or, for lack of that, the place where the mist meets the water.

I think about my destination. Finally, I am catching up with Erik again. Since I arrived in Iceland, I have not visited anywhere mentioned in his sagas. Drangar, however, was the place he and his father settled soon after they arrived. They must have approached, like me, from the sea, but their cargo of livestock was rather different from mine of sightseers, and it was the end of a long voyage. This is about as far as you can get from Europe on the island. Doubtless they had stopped off on the way, to eat and to sleep and to find out where land was not yet claimed. And they ended up here.

Nowadays, just one family lives at Drangar, and they only come in the summer. They are descendants of the last couple who farmed the land, fifty years ago – there are plenty of descendants as the couple had fourteen children. There has never been a road to Drangar. Once, that was not unusual. But as roads spread across the rest of the island, the bay became more and more remote.

I wonder how to explore this piece of coastline in the fog. I would like to speak to the family, and learn about how they manage there, but I imagine they will be hard to find. As I contemplate the problem, a cry goes up. 'Drangaskörð!' Looming out of the mist is the first bit of land we've seen since we set out: a zigzag of cliff emerging from the water, as if a dragon had fallen asleep with its nose in the sea. Wobbly people rush to the right side of the boat, in so far as it's possible without letting go of the railings. There is too much mist and sea-spray to take pictures, even if I wanted to shed – and probably lose – my gloves.

Drangaskörð is the beginning of the Drangar bay. The boat is chugging closer to the coast now, and a little land is visible below the cloud. It's – in familiar style – very green and buttercuppy. It's flat nearby but with a glimpse of steep slopes further off. We come to the innermost part of the bay, and I can see a half derelict barn next to the mooring-place, and a tall white farmhouse behind.

Reimar's mate is lowering the lifeboat. I watch puzzled until I realise with shock that it's not, in fact, a lifeboat: it's a dinghy. I am meant to climb off the back of the big boat and jump into it. The sightseers are exclaiming at my decision to leave the boat in the middle of nowhere. Securing my camera, and making sure my rucksack is properly closed, I go backwards down a few steps, and their helping hands make sure that I land in the boat and not the chilly water.

I hold tight, sitting on the black rubber side as the motor revs up and we speed towards the landing place.

~~

We bump gently up against it: dark, damp, slimy wood; figures looming out of the mist; a hand held out and gripped; a scramble; words of welcome:

'We are mostly here for the ducks.'

Three sturdy, raincoated, wellingtoned men hand me up the slippery wooden slope to the shore. They exchange words with the mate, agree when I am to be collected. Another man, in what looks like an orange boiler suit, crosses our path and walks off through the deep grass, saying something in Icelandic as he goes.

'Ha!' laughs one of my companions. 'If you wait fifteen minutes and then follow that man, you will see a naked man swimming in a hotpot.'

I really have no idea what is going on. I should have guessed, though, that Jón's efficient plans would not have me simply wander around a remote cove. This seems to be a welcome committee. I focus on the immediate.

'Is there really a hot spring here?'

'Oh yes, and a very old bath, probably Viking.' This gentleman has a green raincoat, a black knitted hat, and a broad grin.

'I'd love to see it, but maybe without the naked man?'

'No, no, better with... a far more real experience. A Viking in his bathtub.'

My guides, who so far I can only distinguish by the colour of their raincoats, but without whom, I am beginning to realise, I would be spending a very damp and unprofitable few hours, are leading me up towards the house. As we pass the barn, Sveinn – blue – brings up the ducks again. Not the birds, so much, but their down.

'This is eiderdown...' He picks up a bundle of grey fluff from a mound inside, and holds it out to me. 'In spring, we make holes and fill them with hay. Then when the ducks come and lay their eggs and put feathers over it, we take half' – he scoops with his handful of feathers – 'and replace it with hay.

And if it rains like this, we take the wet feathers and put back hay.

'In this bay there are about five thousand nests. And we take about this much from each.' Sveinn holds out a big handful, about the size of the A5 notebook I'm clutching, and Ingi, his green-coated companion, chips in: 'To make a kilogram you need about seventy nests.'

We're getting damp: the mist is raining on us. The men lead me on up to the house. As usual, I am suffering from information overload: I don't know what to ask about first. I lapse into silence as we walk through thick, deep, damp undergrowth. 'You brought the wrong boots,' says Sveinn, as I stop to tuck the ends of my jeans into my hiking boots. It doesn't help: I am soon wet up to my knees. 'We all wear rubber ones. You see, there have been no sheep here for forty, fifty years. All this grows back. And it gets very wet.'

～

But the undergrowth helps my imagination. When Erik and his father brought sheep here, they would have been the first sheep ever to reach this place. The ground would have been thick with plants, luxuriant with them. Maybe there were even trees, although this far north trees would never grow as well as in more southern parts of the island. Certainly there were birds, useful not only for down but for eggs and meat. And seals and maybe walrus, rich pickings.

The travellers would have had no welcoming committee, but drawn up the boat, emptied it, pitched tents, made fire and food, and started the business of living. Arriving in spring would be best, in time to make hay, storing up food for the animals for the winter. They would need to build shelters too, digging turf and piling it up expertly to make walls. I wonder, with all the work, how much time they had to celebrate their arrival in a new place; whether womenfolk were of the party; how many they were. I wonder what thoughts they had of supernatural help or hindrance.

~~

This family have not been here since Erik's time, and the legend of their arrival is almost as good a story as his. When the farm was set up, everything, animals, people and tools, arrived by sea in an Icelandic version of Noah's Ark. Later, the wood-fired range was brought here in pieces and assembled by some of the brothers. Everything that does not grow here came by boat.

In the kitchen, the conversation has a momentum all of its own. People chip in enthusiastically, adding to each other's stories, taking over and continuing, words bouncing across the wooden table. More friendly faces have appeared, and joined in, and I am barely able to take in one idea before another is proffered.

'All our wood is driftwood, from Siberia. It mainly comes from the big rivers there. And the ice brings it from the North.'

'Sometimes the ice comes all the way here in winter. Many times when I was young.'

'With sometimes a bear, a polar bear.'

'Yes, often it happened in the old days. I have never seen one but I found a dead one once.'

'There might be one here now you know. We would not know. They come over, they cannot get back, they try to survive. The farmers killed them in the old days.'

'You need a good gun.'

'My grandfather killed one.'

'So the polar bear is maybe our terrorist. We do not have other terrorists, just polar bears.'

'Ha!'

Someone gives me tea – 'English ladies prefer tea!' – and I sip it gratefully.

~~

The world is getting bewildering again. Somehow everyone here knows I am following Erik, and the stories rain down. I try to concentrate, to take notes on the veering conversation, catching phrases, losing their context, giving up and drinking tea.

'So, Erik the Red... I must show you our Viking ruins.' Sveinn, who is one of the fourteen children, and knows everything about the valley, starts to say. But he is interrupted by one of his brothers or brothers-in-law.

'A while ago a man came here, his name was Erik the Red. He did it all the Viking way. Viking cooking, in a huge pot... he had a small boy with him, too. He stayed about a week, came by sea and went away by land. He went away carrying that huge pot. And he had no proper shoes, only Viking shoes. He must have had sore feet.'

Somehow we get onto the old farming days. 'Oh, it was just an ordinary farm. Sheep and horses and goats. And we hunted seal too.'

'How?'

'We used nets.' Sveinn pulls a wry face. 'It is a cruel thing to kill a seal, but then it is a cruel thing to kill a sheep. And we all do that. But we don't hunt them any more, there are fewer and fewer. We used to sell them for their skins but they have no value any more.'

'Brigitte Bardot,' someone cuts in. 'The price went down overnight. Do you know Brigitte Bardot?'

I don't, and he sighs. 'Too young. A famous French film star. The price of skins was high but she was against them and overnight the price fell.'

'And the Greenpeace movement too.' As another voice adds to the story I look around the kitchen, where everyone is serious for a moment.

'It was okay for the Icelanders, but very bad for the Greenlanders. They lived in small villages and there was nothing else for them to do.'

'Now we collect eiderdown. Then it goes off on a big ship to Reykjavík. It is there now. They clean the down, take the hay out. Then they sell it to Japan... Thailand... Germany. Mainly Japan, rich Japan. One kilogram costs eight hundred or a thousand pounds in the end.'

'Of course we do not get that much!' There are smiles again, laughter lines on faces. Sveinn takes up the story once more.

'It's big money and you don't have to kill anything except gulls and foxes and mink, to protect the ducklings. A fox can take twenty ducklings.'

'They say the fox came from Greenland many thousands of years ago, he was the first mammal. We believe the mice came with the Vikings, and definitely the rats. Definitely the rats. We have to show you where Erik the Red kept his ships!'

I want to know more about this: 'Are there actual ruins?'

'Yes, but they are deep down. You have to wear a helmet.'

'A helmet?' I imagine a deep cave, with rocks falling from the ceiling, but:

'Yes, you need a helmet because of the terns, the arctic terns. They will attack you.'

~~

I'm still nursing my tea and enjoying the warmth: it's not time to visit the ruins yet. More and more people keep arriving in the kitchen – there are ten members of the family here at the moment including three of the grandchildren. I want to hear about the valley's stories. Are there any ghosts?

'Ghosts?' Ingi jumps and spills his tea. 'See, there are ghosts here.'

'The farmer who lived here before us believed in ghosts. He saw them everywhere.'

'And the old lady who lived near here said they were everywhere too. It was always a strange smell... the smell of bread, the smell of pancakes... there must be a ghost. And she said this really from her heart: she believed it.'

Sveinn is looking thoughtful. 'A bit away from here there are two stones and the dwarves lived in those stones. My mother said 'don't talk loudly walking past those stones because dwarves don't like noise."

'And you believed her?'

'Yes… yes.' He nods slowly.

'Ha!' Someone grins at him. 'I think you believed in them just in case!'

There is a pause, before a newcomer speaks. 'And then… there is the family ghost.'

Gloomy nods all round. 'This farmer from nearby, he made a ghost from a drowned boy. He is still following us, even in Reykjavík.'

'I was once sleeping, in the south, and he tried to kill me!'

'How?' I am startled, still not accustomed to the idea of ghosts that can touch, hurt, kill.

'To strangle me.'

'What did you do?'

'I fought him!'

No-one but me is much perturbed by this revelation.

'And then there was the photo… we were all there for the family photo and someone said 'What we want now is Mori' and when they were developed they were blank. The photographer said never had such a thing happened to him in all his career, many years. So there is no doubt he was there.'

'What does he look like?'

'He's a young boy, in clothes made from brown wool. Maybe not so beautiful because he has been in the sea for many days, he was drowned. So if you see him say hello from us!'

Ragnheiður, a tall, motherly lady, helps me spell the ghost's name.

'Mori means dark brown. It is a common name for that type of ghost. If you're drunk you get a Mori too, a hangover.'

'After drinking you can see ghosts better.' Ingi again. 'There are holes in your aura, they can get in.'

The family, explains Ragnheiður, are here from mid-May until the end of August. They bring up a lot of provisions, but then they stay put, mostly, although some groups only come briefly, to visit. They have a refrigerator nowadays, so it's getting easier to keep food. There's even a solar generator, Sveinn adds, so in winter there are at least lights. I ask about winter: how cold is it? Sveinn shrugs.

'It's like anywhere else in Iceland. Sometimes it snows, sometimes not. Not when I was young, but in the old old days, it was hard. The ice came year after year and you couldn't get enough hay for the sheep and cows. When we lived here it wasn't so bad, it was a good period. But ice in the sea is like ice in a glass, it cools everything down.'

~~

Ragnheiður lends me Wellingtons and waterproof trousers. Feeling stupid, I also accept a large white builder's helmet, doing it up firmly. Sveinn puts on his jacket again, and picks up a large purple umbrella: this too is for tern-defence.

As we parade, helmeted and umbrella'd, across the meadow, I'm wondering how much they are winding me up: the family definitely have a sense of humour and I can't tell if they believe half what they have told me. After all, I must seem pretty strange: an ill-equipped foreigner asking about ghosts and Vikings. The terns are real enough though. I check the helmet's fastening. Meanwhile, my jeans, under the waterproof trousers, seem somehow to be getting wet. The undergrowth is knee-deep and getting deeper.

We are walking into a cloud of terns, a storm of terns. They sound like a whole display of those squeaky, shrieking banshee fireworks. Sveinn walks straight through. He points to a ball of fluff in the undergrowth to our right: 'a baby one' and strides on. I am having difficulty keeping up – nearly waist deep in plants by now I don't want to trip and fall.

Then we stop. Sveinn, whose umbrella is making me think more and more that I am in Narnia, turns to me and props its handle on his shoulder. He gestures with his free hand towards the shore, twenty metres or so to my right.

'The coast was much further in at that time. And this is where they kept their boats. Three boats, three very big boats, each in its own place.'

He waves his arm at the mounds of vegetation. 'Can you see? All around here!' He gesticulates, drawing long thin u-shapes in the air. I can't see, peer as I may, anything other than very healthy plants. Particularly, there are some large hogweedy-looking things.

Sveinn walks a few steps forward – and down. Now, only a metre or so away from me, his head reaches up no further than my waist: I am looking down even on his umbrella. Oh! Suddenly things connect. I'm standing on top of one of the walls, which stretches away to my left before bending and returning behind him.

'So they're turf walls?' I ask

'Yes, big turf walls. And it was clearer when there were still sheep here. We should not let this stuff grow. It breaks up the turfs – it will destroy these walls.'

He pauses for a moment, deep in thought and undergrowth, as the terns squawk above his umbrella. I watch him, standing in my bright white, ill-fitting helmet and my borrowed boots. Here I am, I think, way up north, following in the footsteps of a semi-mythical character, asking the locals to show me where he kept his boats. Somehow the moment is so surreal that when Sveinn looks up and speaks again, I can't tell whether he has a twinkle in his eye or not.

'Yes,' he says, 'Yes, certainly Erik the Red kept his ships here.'

Later, I email Bjarni the Archaeologist to ask about boathouses. He tells me that none have been excavated in Iceland, but that a lot have been found in Norway in the right period.

Some further reading reveals, primarily and unsurprisingly, that boathouses are hard to date without excavation. One way to make the attempt is to look at proximity to coastlines (which move, making a sensible distance a different position in different periods). Unfortunately, varying weather conditions between sites, and varying perceptions of what is sensible, make this an unreliable method.

More helpfully, reconstructions of boathouses across many periods and places broadly agree. Sveinn's ruins are the right sort of shape and size to be boathouses: while they remain deep in the vegetation and under a tern colony more cannot be said. Probably they will be eaten by plants before anyone gets a chance to investigate.

But if this was a boathouse, the walls enclosed a roughly rectangular space, which would quite possibly have been roofed. At one site in Norway, from a few centuries earlier, the earthen walls were wood-lined: perhaps these walls were, too, although wood is much scarcer in Iceland. A slipway would have led from the shelter to the shore. At this site, three such buildings stood next to each other, suggesting three boats needed to be moored at once.

Returning to the farmhouse, we pass more arctic tern chicks. Sveinn picks one up and lets me stroke it: it is soft, downy. 'Funny that something so cute turns into something so vicious!' I remark.

'These? Oh, but they are such beautiful birds. Annoying, but beautiful. They are just protecting their young, you know. I can understand that. They do not want us here.'

I mutter that they're not doing that good a job, with all these chicks lying about in the undergrowth. Sveinn continues.

'These birds fly every year from the South Pole. They are here all summer and there all winter. They arrive here on May the eleventh. They are very precise. On the tenth, or the eleventh or the twelfth, you will see four or five terns, looking around. The next day there will be many hundreds or thousands.'

He leaves me with directions to the Viking pool – I have decided that, as I'm soaked already, I might as well do all my exploring at once. I'm to follow a path to a stream and the stream to a path and go left and right and over the bridge. Or something. Luckily, Ingi appears out of the vegetation and leads the way. We cross a stream and walk on up another, the path getting closer and closer to the steep edge. 'Sometimes the river is much higher, and it takes away its banks,' explains Ingi. This is the old route: there's another path for tourists who want to go bathing. In fact, there's another pool they have built for the tourists, closer to the shore. As this is the house bathtub, it seems only fair.

Just as I am wondering whether we will ever reach the place, we cross a precipitous bridge and Ingi points upstream. The first thing I see beneath the mist is a yellow bucket, with soap and shampoo piled in it. Next to it, there's stream – and a beautifully built rock pool. It is about bathtub depth and I think it would fit two comfortably. When I put my hand in, the water bubbling into it is bathtub temperature.

'This bath,' says Ingi, 'has been used for a thousand years.'

~~

Hot springs, nowadays, are a novelty. Hot springs before central heating must have been a luxury that brought washing up to royal standards. And they crop up all over Iceland.

The reason they are everywhere is the same reason Iceland is volcanic: she is sitting on a plume of hot magma welling up from the gap between the American and European continental plates. Underground, Iceland is hot, hot enough that Icelanders can be eco-friendly with no effort by using geothermal energy for most of their heating needs. Parts of Iceland produce hot springs at boiling point and above.

Even in the parts furthest from the magma plume, Iceland is warm all over beneath the surface. It is also very damp, and as the rainwater falls it is absorbed, seeping through layers of rock and taking up that warmth. Eventually it hits a layer of rock that it can't pass through, and instead runs along it until, still warm, it reaches the edge of a hill and flows out into the world again.

In my opinion, the Icelandic pioneers, Erik included, chose their new home well. If I were to be stranded on a lonely island, I'd choose one with a hot spring.

~

Despite the mist, its wetness creeping through my helmet and into my hair, I love this place. From September to April, almost nobody comes here. Any birds that want it can have it to themselves – foxes allowing. And because it's barely tended – the Drangar eider-farmers make a little hay, but nothing more – the undergrowth is reclaiming the land. So after a thousand years, or thereabouts, of sheep-farming, the work of those pioneers who cleared the land is finally being reversed.

Somewhere up behind us in the clouds is Drangajökull, another great glacier. All around, the steeply sloping hills are full of arctic foxes. I wish I could stay to watch the mist clear, but it might be days and days.

Ingi leads me back to the house, past the camping place for such tourists as are hardy enough to come here. We pass more ruined turf houses. 'How old are they?' I ask.

'Oh, those are quite recent – they were for sheep, or storage.

In the old days there were many huts along there for the sheep and every day you would check on them in winter. And they would send the children, sometimes two or three hours in the snow.'

Another one is half tumbledown, near the landing place. 'This is the oldest one in Drangar. They used it for shark drying. And they used to keep shark liver in here. It brought in a lot of money, the oil, in the old days before gasoline.'

'Are there shark in the bay?'

'No, they had to go a long way to find it.'

Sveinn adds to this later: 'It is completely dark in there, there are no windows. The oil was kept in barrels and if it gets in the light you get the fishy smell.'

Back at the house, I remove my wet clothing, and borrow yet another pair of trousers as Ragnheiður dries mine out on the range. I drink more warming tea and, as my toes and fingers tingle back to life, feel pathetically grateful. Curling up in a corner, I spot some knitting, beautiful soft brown and grey stripes on their way to being socks. I admit that I have never learnt to knit, and Ragnheiður is shocked. Knitting is compulsory in school, she tells me, 'You take sewing, knitting, design… they are practising it now.'

And they are: the three children show me their creations. Then they show me all round the house, the eight-year-old taking his telescope to keep an eye out for the boat that will pick me up. I see a photo of their grandfather – or great-grandfather – a grey-bearded man in a triangular hat against an almost entirely white background: Drangar in winter. Proudly, they show me a picture of the fourteen children.

My boat doesn't come for a while, so I accept some bread and cheese: beautiful oaty soda bread, baked fresh. I ask about other Icelandic foods. I hear about soups and stews, the solid staple recipes that are the same the world over and different in every cook's version.

'Salted lamb in a soup with beans and things… you probably use pork, we use lamb, in Iceland it's always lamb. Then we have the meat soup. That's sort of like Irish stew. Everyone has their own recipe. Most people put in carrot, onion, cabbage. I put in leek and celery and sometimes sweet potatoes. Some people put in turnips.'

My guess is the settlers ate a lot of stew, but it's only a guess, and I'm certain they didn't use sweet potatoes. Ragnheiður pauses before coming up with something completely different. 'Lots of Icelandic people do really good fried fish balls. Each person has their own recipe. You eat them with cucumber, boiled potatoes, cut up some tomato…'

Sveinn and Ingi and I walk down to the shore. A few curved bones, which I imagine to be ribs, lean up against a pair of old wheels, and I ask about them.

'A few years ago there was a whale here, on the beach. Those are some of the bones. An artist came and took the rest, he made Viking carvings out of them, or something.'

'What kind of whale?'

'Ooh…' Sveinn says the name in Icelandic. 'This sort!' He draws a square head shape. 'With a lot of teeth!'

'Er… killer whale?' I guess, badly.

'No, much bigger.'

Ingi intercedes. 'It is the sort that is in *Moby Dick*.'

'What, the great white whale?'

'Yes. That is such a good book… there is so much about whaling technique in there. And the captain, his fight with the whale is so… so…personal!'

I stop him: I don't want to spoil the ending. Sveinn asks me if I have seen another book, *Icelanders*, in which he and his family feature. I haven't yet.

'You must. There is much in there about my childhood.' And there is: I learn later that he and his brothers trekked two days to school in the postman's footsteps; that he can mimic the bark of an arctic fox well enough to fool one.

'It is a good book,' says Ingi. 'They interviewed crazy people from all around Iceland.'

'Yes, some very crazy people,' agrees Sveinn.

'And they interviewed you!' adds Ingi

Sveinn grins for my camera. 'Yes, they interviewed crazy people all around Iceland and I am very proud to be one of them!'

The tide is out and we clamber over rocks to a place where the boat can pick me up. Ingi helps me as I slide down onto the seaweed, and Sveinn hands me from mound to mound, and into the little rubber boat. I call out 'Takk!' and 'Bless!' and they call out 'Safe journey!' and the sightseers haul me up into the main boat. Swiftly, swiftly, we are away. We pass the sleeping dragon again, and go out onto the rough grey sea.

I stand holding tight to the rails of the boat, looking back.

~~

Erik's father lived in Drangar until the end of his life; Erik left it again to marry. Erik's marriage was seen as a good thing: his wife is described, at that point, only in terms of her parentage. The marriage took him south, to a far less remote part of the island.

Erik's other, more renowned, interaction with the legal system, was soon to follow. The site of the Assembly at Þorsnes, where eventually Erik was sentenced to outlawry, is my next destination. But, yet again, I'm going the long way.

I wait for a few hours in Norðurfjörður, until Reimar brings another boatful of jolly walkers. Amidst a lot of laughter I meet my lift, a Reykjavík engineer who had been hiking. Clearly, it was a tiring weekend: his companion sleeps through the journey.

We leave Norðurfjörður behind. Out of my window, rocks jut from the sea like sharks' fins. The sun is setting, turning the clouds pink and yellow. A troll with a grassy head stares at me from the roadside. Holmavík is ninety... twenty-five... nineteen kilometres away.

'Have you heard that Christopher Columbus came to Iceland first on the way to America?' I haven't. 'Well, they say he came here, to find out how to get there. He sailed north from Portugal to ask the Icelanders. How else did he know it was there? In those days the edge of the world was a waterfall.'

The swans are spread out across the water of their fjord, fifty or so of them basking in the evening light. We round corners, go up and down and up and down.

My driver's mother came from these parts but moved to Reykjavík before the war. 'Everyone was moving. There were no roads. They were happy but it was a hard life. It was a six hour walk to the nearest farm. A hard life!'

At midnight, he leaves me outside my guesthouse and drives on to Reykjavík: two hours more at least. I pause and look out across the village, still lit up by the fading sun. With its population of six hundred it feels overwhelmingly huge. It is bigger than any village in Iceland from Erik's day.

CHAPTER 10

PUFFINS, PARLIAMENTS AND
ICELANDIC SWEETS.

Erik ate puffin. This fact is not specified in any historical document, but it's what any right-minded Icelander would do, and – this is the clincher – what any right-minded Icelander would imagine any right-minded legendary Icelander would do. Their stripey beaks are common, and were even more common in the days when Iceland was newly populated. Back in Holmavík, I track Siggi down again, at the Witchcraft Museum, and interrogate him.

'Oh yes, we definitely eat puffins!' he replies.

'How?' I demand. 'Fried?'

'Yes – with potatoes and vegetables.'

Not hard to cook, then. Erik, of course, would not have had potatoes, which are a more recently discovered vegetable. Time for the technical bit: 'How do you catch them?'

'They have a net, like a shrimping net. A round net on a long stick, three or four metres. And all they do is stand at the bottom of the cliff and – fwop! – catch them, twist their necks, and do it again.'

It sounds like something even I might be able to manage – technically, at least. 'So it's not very hard then?'

'No.' He sighs. 'But I don't catch them. They are so cute. I don't like to kill them. Eating them is another thing.' He grins.

'What do they taste like?'

He pauses, clearly enjoying the thought. 'Mmm… like puffin. Very good.'

Erik ate them, so I suppose I have to. In Iceland, there's no conservation argument I can pull – they are common. Holmavík's restaurant is serving puffin, pan-fried, and Siggi is keen enough on eating it to put up cheerfully with my interrogation for the course of an evening meal. There are all sorts of questions that I've been storing up. Dried fish, for instance. How do people possibly eat, let alone enjoy, dried fish?

He looks at me with the bewilderment of a connoisseur. Where to start? 'But it is not all the same. There are many sorts. Sometimes it can be too dry. What sort of fish was it?'

I don't know. Cardboard flavour, I felt, at the time. But I'm not quite rude enough to express this.

'Catfish is the best. You should try catfish. And it should not be completely dry. It should be a little chewy. And with a little butter…mmm.'

The butter surprises me.

'You had it without butter?' His eyes light up: this is the answer. 'Ah, that might explain a lot! You must try it again. The butter is very important!'

Siggi is explaining how to cook seal (just boil it and eat it) when our puffin arrives, beautifully presented on a plate of rocket leaves and potato croquettes. The pieces of meat have been fried and then sliced, revealing the pink in the middle. I push away the image of a cute bird with a stripey beak, pick a piece up with my fork, and put it in my mouth.

The taste is most like beef, at first, but more delicate, and the texture is quite different, much finer. There's a very slight fishy edge to the flavour, especially in the browned meat. It's good, and unlike anything I've ever tried. Mm, puffin, I think, and: Erik and Co weren't doing badly, if this was part of their diet.

∼∼

Earlier in the day, I walked up onto the hills behind the village. I breathed in the smell of thyme and sun-baked earth, and gazed across the ridges and ridges of mountains that came into view at the top. I let the dizziness of the height overwhelm the dizziness of movement and experiences of the last few days. The flowers were alpine: I found patches of tiny bright blue gentians, matching the colour of the fjord in the distance. It felt summery, southern, although the wind pounded through my clothing.

Tomorrow, I'm off again, taking the bus in a loop around the Westfjords. I am to go west first, spending a night at Ísafjörður, the largest settlement in the area. From there the bus continues south, to Breidafjördur, in time to meet the boat that will carry me across the water to Stykkishólmur. Stykkishólmur is within walking distance of the site of the ancient parliament where Erik was expelled from Iceland – the site that I'm aiming to reach.

~~

The bus takes me through a reddened landscape. There's a particular kind of grass, with red seed-heads, that is everywhere, and something about the light is showing up the same tones in the rocks. High up, snow has settled in wide stripes across the fellside.

In the middle of nowhere, we stop. The driver's small son punctiliously opens the door for me: he is the only other passenger. The two of them share a coke and I stretch and admire the view.

It feels empty. Where the road twists ahead of us, the fjord's head makes a sort of keyhole shape. In the centre, the water is a glowing blue: above, the sky is a paler reflection. The human traces are lonely: the road, stretching out behind us, a picnic table, and a signpost.

We carry on round the fjord. For a stretch, waterfalls run beside us continually. As the sun gets lower in the sky, the water sparkles more and more. I stop being able to take in the scenery: there is too much.

Our next stop is a little town, Súðavík, colourful houses and a futuristic petrol station. Motorboats buzz about on the fjord in the bright evening sunshine, white like the snow on the slopes above.

We wiggle in and out of fjords. We shoot through a tunnel, underneath a Toblerone-shaped mountains I spotted hours ago across the water. More winding road and then, just across the fjord, there is a tiny runway where a plane is landing; a lagoon; a town, Ísafjörður.

~~

Some of the buildings are four storeys high. Not sure I can deal with this level of urbanisation, I get out my town map before I walk to my accommodation.

But the place isn't big enough that my landlady doesn't spot the traveller and jump up to meet me. She tells me I have a choice of four – four! – restaurants, and that the supermarket is open until half-past eleven at night: welcome news. I realise that I've been wearing the same jeans for over a week, jeans that have been soaked through at least once.

I shower and change.

When I reappear, my landlady presents me with a chocolate bar. 'If you want to learn about Iceland, you should try Prince Polo,' she declares. 'This is what we all grew up with.' For context, she's in her fifties, white-blonde hair framing a round face, bustling and beaming. 'They have changed the packaging though, and I think the shape. It is not as good, we think, as it used to be. It is Polish, but I do not think they eat it in Poland, they make it just for the Icelanders.' Lest I should think Iceland too isolated, she adds: 'We had Coca-Cola too, of course.'

Actually, I find out the next time I meet a Pole, they do eat Prince Polo in Poland. But my landlady is expanding on the subject of Icelandic confectionary. 'We have a lot of sweets in Iceland. The liquorice, that is important – some are like throat pastilles and you have just one but some Icelanders are greedy and have more. Icelanders have too many sweets, I think - look at the shape of the nation! And we have these.' She offers me a Noi Sirius chocolate raisin and I explain that I am already an addict, and that they just don't come in big enough packets in the UK. 'That is no good at all,' she agrees. 'We have three sorts. This is one of the things Icelanders have to be sent when they are abroad. Another is a malt drink. It is yeasty like beer, but sweet. To look at it, it looks like Guinness, dark, but to taste they are so different, it is like black and white I think.'

It sounds foul, and reminds me to ask about dried fish. Since Siggi's revelations about butter I am determined to give it one more try.

'You can buy *harðfiskur* down by the harbour. Also in the kiosk and in the supermarket. But the supermarket is more expensive and less good.' She gives me extensive directions, involving mountains and paintings on buildings. Then she goes on:

'But have you tried beef jerkey?'

I have, once, but did not think it was Icelandic, more American.

'Yes, but they are making some experiments. They make beef jerkey and also whale jerkey. Someone who is an Icelander, but who was visiting, went and bought a lot. He tried the whale, but he bought more beef. Also in the town there is a perfume factory, they make perfume for men. The bottle is made of glass in the shape of a ram's horn. The top is very fine, made from metal. So it is a bit like a Viking helmet.'

Not sure what to say, I express my regret that I need no men's perfume.

She laughs at me. 'Yes, yes, I tell you only so you know some of the strange things you find in a town like this.'

In this town you are never far from water, and it is very still tonight. The mountains that rise to either side are reflected in every detail in the fjord. By the harbour, hulking and sometimes rusty boats are also reflected. So are the buildings, pretty in their neat rows.

Keeping the tall mountain to my left, as instructed, I walk down to a little red house where I eat a warming '*plokkfiskur*', a mix of fish, potato, onion, salt, pepper and milk boiled together. Then I wander across to the park, where I know there's an arch made out of a whale's jawbone.

It is a strange end for the jawbone of such a powerful creature. Stood up on its joints, it's been painted white, and a metal joiner holds the two sides together. There's a rubbish bin next to it, and a flag at the top, and petunias planted nearby. It feels like an amenity rather than a marvel of nature.

Despite the controversies and constant discussion of whaling in Iceland, it's not something that bears on Erik's story much at all. The Vikings didn't hunt whales: they were too big. They might well have used the materials they produced when the odd giant cetacean was beached on the shores of a fjord: oil, for light and fuel, meat. It's easy to imagine that the flexible bones, used for corsets and umbrellas in particular before the invention of plastic, might have been useful: the arched jawbones too. But there are no Norse tales of whale-hunting.

I stand under the arch and stare up at it. I imagine a whale around it, rising up through the ground so only its nose is visible, and so I am in its mouth. I'm rolling around with plenty of space to spare: the jawbone is nearly three times my height and six of me could line up across its base.

They are huge creatures. I can't imagine what it must have taken to fight one.

~~

The next morning, I open the door of an old blue shed, one of many near the harbour. The first thing I see is a yellow hose, with water running from it across the concrete floor. I call 'hello?' and a man in blue overalls appears and says something in Icelandic. I say 'har-th-fiskur?' trying very hard to pronounce it correctly.

'*Harðfiskur!*' he exclaims, opening a chest freezer and holding out a massive bag. I gesture small, smaller.

'2 kilo? Kilo?'

I say 'hundert gram?' but foreign pronunciation of English words is not enough. Luckily the man is cleverer than me, and produces a piece of paper. He writes on it:

500g?

I reply:

200g?

He looks troubled. He washes his hands in the hose and rummages in another freezer. Then he finds a piece and puts it on the scales.

'Exakt!'

I pay him and thank him and go off with my fish, which defrosts and smells all the way to Stykkishólmur.

~~

It is the same bus driver: he greets me with a big smile. In fact, he is the bus driver and the bus company in one, driving to Holmavík one day and on this route the next, with one day off each week.

Today the fjord is even more a mirror, the clouds perfectly reflected, the triangular mountains doubled so seamlessly that mountain and reflection look like one diamond. Then we climb away from the fjord, and suddenly we are in an outsize natural gravel pit, driving carefully around the sandy-coloured mounds. It is as if a young giant had been here, making piles with a spade. The road winds and wanders through them. There is water even up here, but it is hard to see because it is so full of reflected mountains. There's the odd patch of snow, and here and there a sheep. As we go down again, there are more sheep, and more grass.

And so, eventually, we come to another fjord. We stop for ten minutes by a waterfall and I step out of the bus, blinking in the bright light. It's two falls: one is wide and high, lots of little falls in a row; one is lower, frothier and wider still, a sheet of water crashing and foaming into a rocky pool.

Away from the waterfall, this fjord is gentle. We climb up the side until the water looks like blue ink in the distance: then we go over a pass and across slopes full of boulders. Finally we descend again, towards a new fjord. This time the water stretches for miles ahead of us, the mountains on the other side a thin blue, faded layer. There is a scattering of islands in the foreground. Breiðafjörður.

~~~

I climb up as high as I can on the ferry and stand facing out to sea. I want to see what's ahead – the site of Erik's banishment is just across the water.

But we won't be leaving for a while: the boat is still filling up. While I wait, I pull the packet of dried fish out of my bag, and extract a piece. It is stiff, board-like, not unbendable but reluctant. It is cream-coloured and vaguely patterned with squares, as if somewhere in the drying process it was laid on a criss-cross rack – unless catfish are criss-crossed inside, which I doubt. Confidently, I spread it with butter. Almost like smoked salmon, I think: just need some bread. I open my mouth and put it in and – clunk – my teeth meet on a hard, unchewable surface.

Not that way, then. I remove it and glare at it. Then I remember something else: tear it, don't bite it. I start to pull a piece off, my fingers getting covered in butter. It makes a ripping sound, the fibrous strands reluctantly pulling apart. I put the buttery shred in my mouth and begin to chew.

As I chew, a flavour begins to come out of the fish, rich and a little salty. The more I chew, the better it tastes. Perhaps it helps that everything smells a bit fishy here – that part is not overwhelming. But – I like it. On the down side, the stuff takes forever to eat and I have about a week's supply.

Still, a triumph. I chew and chew and feel very close to Erik as the boat starts moving across the fjord. It's not only the fish – for the later part of his life in Iceland, this was his nearest stretch of water. He lived on an island here for a while. He sailed away from here to discover Greenland, past Mount Snaefell – a mountain I can just make out in the faded blue shoreline ahead of me.

Mount Snaefell is a snow-covered volcano, a gently conical mountain at the end of a glacier. Everyone on the boat is photographing it as we get closer and closer: the snow on top is as neat as the icing on a fairy cake. Past it, I can see the way out to the open sea, to Greenland.

But Mount Snaefell is not all there is to look at. This fjord is full of tiny islands. More remarkably, some are arranged in rings: they are the edges of old volcanic cones, covered with grass and, on their cliffy edges, with bird-life.

The water is unevenly rippled, its surface textured differently in different places, making whirls and calm patches. Across this pattern move more birds, these ones black and skittering just above the surface. Sometimes they are flying, flapping their wings desperately as if they might fall down any minute. Sometimes their feet are in the water, kicking, but their wings are still working and they move like speedboats. Finally one or two manage to take off properly, and one swings towards the boat. I glimpse a stripey beak, white chest and red feet before it swings back. After that I keep seeing threes and fours of puffins, flapping and skudding above the surface.

The tourist in me coos, and the naturalist is impressed. But then Erik pops back into my head, this time carrying a large net. I remember I am a Viking explorer, down to the dried fish after a long voyage.

Mm, puffin, I think. Now, all I need is a frying pan…

~~

Stykkishólmur, which we reach in late afternoon, perches. It perches on little cliffs, perched on the edge of the peninsula.

The first I see of it, as the boat draws closer, is an island covered with people running, walking, jumping and picnicking on its steep grassy slope. The grassy slope is well above the water, balanced on cliffs that are orangey with lichen and finely striped up and down with basalt columns. Later, I sit on the island, watching v-formations of kittiwakes – identified with a new bird-book – zooming across the water, listening to the cawing of birds. The water is calm, the world is calm. At the moment, tired from travel, this quiet is exactly what I want.

Stykkishólmur has been a trading post for centuries, because it has a natural harbour behind the basalt island, but it was in the nineteenth century that the village became more important. Due to the enthusiasm of one official, Árni Thorlacius, it was home to the first two-storey building in Iceland.

This wooden house was imported – as, later, were the houses in Seyðisfjörður – timber-by-timber from Norway. Surrounded by turf houses, it must have attracted attention. Árni was progressive in other ways too: he kept the first continuous weather records in Iceland, pages and pages of charts covering about fifty years.

These were rich people, with elegant rooms, but according to the museum guide, the children – five of whom survived childhood – would have slept two or three to a bed, some sharing with their grandmother. When they had guests, even more squashing up must have been necessary. Morris stayed here once, and Collingwood also passed through the town, after Thorlacius' day.

~~

Þorsnes, the old Viking Assembly-place, is very close to Stykkishólmur: hence the proliferation of Victorians who wanted to visit it. On the map, the distance is not far, so I set out on foot.

Gradually, I realise I've made an error. This is a busy road, the only one in and out of Stykkishólmur. I'd assumed there would not be much traffic flow to such a tiny place, but the lorries roar past me. The road goes along the peninsula, directly inland. I can see my destination, frustratingly across the water on the peninsula next door. My legs hurt, and the mountains seem sudden and distant. The size of the sky makes me feel queasy. Or maybe, I think, slightly worried, it's something I ate.

Eventually, the peninsulas join, and I turn almost back on myself. My map suggests there is a footpath here, so I veer off the road and cut cross-country. Another mistake. I end up walking on deep moss and falling down gaps between piles of stones, traversing the sides of rocky mounds, climbing over fences. I try to return to the road, but it is far away. I think:

I wish I had a horse. And could ride one. I think: *Well, I have great respect for all those Icelanders who trekked far further than this to come to the meeting of their local parliament, before there was a road.* I think: *Bet most of them had horses, or boats.*

I find the road again, and tramp some more. But now I can see a farmhouse. A lopsided lamb, a black patch over one eye, runs out to greet me. But I am not looking for a farm. I'm looking for the site of an ancient local parliament.

A girl emerges from the house with a bottle. The lamb runs up to her, and a little later I follow. I'm feeling rather foolish: I don't even know what there is to see here. Where do you start looking for the place something happened?

'I'm lost!' I announce. 'Well, not completely, I'm looking for the Þingvellir.'

'You are in the right place!'

'Yes – but – where should I go?'

'Do you want to see the Bloodstone?'

I've not heard of it, but it sounds worth seeing. 'Yes please!'

'Okay, I will show you.' She calls up to the house, and slips on a pair of ballet pumps: she's wearing a sweater and calf-length trousers. She leads me down a path and across a field.

'You are lucky, we have cut the grass so you can see.'

And in the middle of the meadow there it is, a brown, weathered rock in an unshaven patch of grass, another equally large just behind it.

'This is the bloodstone! It is very old, it cracked at some

point. When they had their parliaments here and someone did not agree, they just used that stone to cut their head off. They cut off many people's heads here. You are meant to be able to still see the blood, but it is very old blood. I don't think you can.'

It is all covered in moss and lichen, but she rubs a finger on a particularly russety patch. 'This is said to be blood.'

We peer at it. It is entirely unconvincing. Undeterred, she points at the other stone. 'This stone is important too, it was also used for cutting heads.'

'Are there many ghosts here?' I ask. 'Oh yes!' But she doesn't want to expand. Then an arctic tern swoops at us, shrieking, and she ducks.

'I do not – like – those – birds.'

She returns to the house, letting me picnic in the field. Feeling profoundly disrespectful, I sit on the Bloodstone, the sun on my face, admiring the view onto the fjord, with its mass of islands, imagining the place in Erik's day. It is shortly after that that another tern speed-dives at my face, sending me precipitately across the grass.

Later, I try to find out about the beheadings, but I draw

a blank. Even asking Norse scholars, I draw a blank: the beheading story must be more recent than the sagas. But in a letter of W.G. Collingwood's, I find something even more dramatic:

'the Þingvellir of Þorsness... where Cormac and Bersi went – where the Thorstone is on which they offered human sacrifice.'

Human sacrifice! It's the same stone: Collingwood drew it and a hundred years later I can recognise it. In the saga he's recalling – People of Eyri – they describe a circle where men were sentenced to be sacrificed, and describe their backs being broken across it, and a stain of blood that can be seen on the stone. Collingwood is cynical about the bloodstain – 'a stain... not of blood, but of iron in the stone.' Yet he dug all the grass up to search for the circle, finding nothing. Then he pronounced:

'Whether men were really sacrificed here is doubtful, in spite of the word of the ancient writer. Human sacrifice was no doubt a part of the old pagan religion, but there are no records of it in Iceland and it is quite against analogy if we imagine a conclave sitting round an altar, and enjoying the shrieks of the victim. The more we get to know of the real manners and customs of the 10th and 11th century Icelanders, the more we find them like ourselves, and unlike the races which enjoyed cruelty and flourished in crime.'

Collingwood wanted to bring the old Icelanders to life:

to think of the characters as real 'figures from history' and as heroes for his time as well as theirs. It seems human sacrifice was one step too repugnant for him. Of course, he may have been right – but everything in the sagas is subject to doubt at some level.

But as his writings show, there's a real conglomeration of sagas round here. You can join them all together and practically reconstruct the population of the place in Erik's day. This Assembly was presided over by a dynasty of *goður*, each of whom has a legend attached.

It was one Thorgrim, known as Snorri, who was *goði* at the time of Erik's trial. His story is a tangle of foster-brothers, bluffing and cunning. At one point he travelled to Norway and stayed with none other than Erling Skjalgsson – the same Erling whose memorial cross I found in Stavanger. On his return from this trip, and not without difficulty, Snorri claimed his inheritance and his right to be *goði*.

Snorri is one of the few saga characters given a physical description. He had yellow hair, a pale face, and a red beard: he was slender and good-looking and of medium height. After he had claimed his inheritance, things were not all easy, but he showed his abilities in hanging on to his estate despite this. The saga – People of Eyri – describes a witch up in the mountains, blood-feuds, a ship sailing in from Norway. It also describes other happenings at the Assembly in the year of Erik's trial:

a case about a fight that had arisen over the sheep when they were collected together.

So there's context for thinking about Erik, at that moment. He had been getting in arguments for years now. He was living on Oxen Island, one of the larger of the cluster in the fjord. He had moved there, away from his first marital home, because of a fight, something to do with some slaves or a property boundary. Last winter he had lent his boat's bench boards to one Thorgest. This year, he wanted them back. When they were not given to him, he went to Thorgest's house and took them. Thorgest went after him, and they fought a battle. Some of Thorgest's sons and some others were killed. After that, the feud was open: both men kept a troop of fighters at home, three or more each.

At the Spring Assembly here, Thorgest and some others brought a case against Erik for those deaths. The Assembly was very crowded. Erik didn't come – he and his allies were fitting out a ship for his escape, away amongst the islands. Only one of his allies went to the Assembly, a man called Stir.

Stir asked Snorri not to pursue Erik after the Assembly, making a bargain that he would owe him a favour. So Snorri, after the banishment was pronounced, let Erik sail, although Thorgest and his followers went after him. Erik's friends rallied round to help hide his boats, and then they sailed with him away to the edge of the great fjord.

Then he put out to sea, past Snaefells glacier, not to return for three years. And this was seventeen years before the conversion of Iceland: it was in AD 983.

~~

So say three sagas, anyway: Eyri, Erik, and Greenland between them. I walk down to the shore, listening to the racket of birds, my hood still up to protect from terns. The wind is blowing through the feathery grasses around the edges of the fields. There's a faint smell of horse manure – I have passed many ponies on my walk. If I didn't know the stories, this rough patch of grass would be like any field, anywhere – admittedly a field with a dramatic view. Yet if the sagas are true, battles were fought here, passions high. Judgements were made, outlaws created. For years this was a central place.

The wind whistles on, and the birds shriek, oblivious.

~~

As I walk back, the nausea returns. I feel increasingly strange: a day later, when I am climbing on the basalt island again, I have an attack of vertigo and nearly go over the edge. My stomach hurts, increasingly, wrenchingly. Perhaps it is an ancient curse, a piece of magic set on followers of Erik by his enemies. Or else it's those Norse gods again, taking against my quest. I hide in my sleeping bag, until my landlady forces me out to the doctor's and he, ignoring my protests that all my possessions will be left behind at the hostel, puts me straight in an ambulance on a saline drip.

Vaguely, I notice that the road is bumpy and that we don't have to use a siren because there's no traffic. The next thing I notice is the whiteness of hospital, and I wake one day to the scent of death. I pull myself out of bed and go, with my drip-stand, to the window. I open it, but it makes no difference. I go back to bed.

Several doses of antibiotics later, I realise the smell is coming from outside. The hospital is clean, efficient, crisp: neither am I dead, nor do they leave the dead in the corridors. There is a fish factory around the corner. It stinks.

Antibiotics, and the staff of the hospital, work magic. Presumably, if I had caught this bug in Erik's day, I'd be very sick or dead. But the gods are still strong. After five days, a short walk leaves me needing half an hour's sleep. I'm forbidden to do anything strenuous for weeks: it's likely I'll be faint and pathetic for more.

I try to eat the food I'm given: liver pate with rice porridge.

I reflect that, like Erik, I've been exiled from Iceland. Possibly with the help of some angry gods. Only, in my case, going to Greenland is also a really bad idea.

Yet again, I call my parents. But this time there's no way I can carry on. I'm going to have to cancel yet more tickets and plans.

But this is just a postponement. I am not giving up on Erik.

CONNECTIONS

CHAPTER 11

EASY, TO SAIL TO AMERICA
IN A VIKING BOAT

My trainers crunch along pebbles made of lava, dark reds and blacks with holes through and through like honeycomb toffee. It is almost a year later, and I am back.

My last memory of Iceland is of a complex arrangement involving meeting my bag at the bus station, and a flight that ended in the corridors of Heathrow Airport. At home, my parents took me in and I slowly recovered: it was months before I felt really myself. It is odd to be back, and I am not sure I trust it. I don't want to be ill again and I still don't know what caused it: bacteria, but from where? What if it comes back?

Then, life has shifted. I did some sums, and realised that my attempt to live on writing alone was going to end in starvation or an infinite dependence on my parents. To my own shock, I found a job, in a company that designs museums. I have spent the last months in a design studio, thinking about the history of trains. My new colleagues seemed to take my need to follow a Viking well – and helped me get into the spirit with a giant good luck card showing me wearing a Viking helmet.

I try to concentrate on now. This is Keflavík. To my right, a road stretches past warehouses. To my left is a strip of bloated yellowy seaweed; beyond that, the sea, the shore curving round into a harbour. It's not overwhelming and my fidgeting is still at the surface, a feeling that things should go to timetable, plans should made and be set in stone.

The pebbles slide around under my feet. I smell the sea, listen to the water and the wind. The sky is mottled, a blanket of grey and white with bluer places. Two arctic terns chase each other across the bay, calling *pirurrrr ch ch ch pirurrrrr ch ch ch*. Lorries roll along the road, and an oystercatcher flashes black and white, circles me, cries *pweet-pweet-pweet*.

I am visiting this beach because, nearby, there lives a man who has sailed to America in a Norse longboat.

~~

At the end of the beach the land slopes away, and a square of it is enclosed. In the middle of this tiny field, proudly upright, sailing on air, is a Viking longship. *Íslendingur*'s mast is up, but there is no sail; waves no longer reach up her bows. She is one of the world's youngest Viking longships and I am saddened to find her in a field, because she has had adventures, crossing the Atlantic twice though only twenty-two metres long.

Her captain, and builder, is unimpressed with his own achievements. 'The person who invented this boat was very,

very clever,' he says. 'I just copied.' Gunnar Marel Eggertsson drove up in a large red jeep: he is wearing dark outdoor gear and a baseball cap, and is unfazed by anything an outdoor life can throw at him. He leads me up the steps on the longship's starboard side, and we lean on the rail, looking across the deck. He continues. 'She is an exact copy of the Gokstad ship.'

The Gokstad ship was found in a grave mound in Norway and has been dated to about a century pre-Erik. I look across the deck. It's several metres to the ship's other side, an expanse of neatly jointed boards. Halfway across, the mast rises thick as a treetrunk. To my right and left the ship narrows to animal-headed prow and elegant stern.

'How long did she take to build?' I ask.

'A year. Well, six months with me and a friend working and six months I worked on my own. But in the old days they would have built a boat in one winter. They were very skilled.' Later I find out that *Íslendingur*'s builders used electric tools in addition to the axes and saws that the Norse had available. 'But still it took us longer than them.'

I want to know what life is like on board. 'You need at least six to sail her... nine if you are going far. We were nine, sailing to New York in 2003.' He looks at me contemplatively, as if he can see into my mind to the difficulties I am imagining. 'You know, all this is much easier than people imagine today. To sail in a Viking ship to New York – you just do it! In fact, it is very comfortable, very steady. She never rolls very much… of course, you're always trying to sail downwind, she's designed to sail downwind but she'll sail up to thirty-five degrees from the wind, six to eight knots.'

I'm cynical about what Gunnar Marel considers 'easy' and 'comfortable' – I suspect that his standards are different from mine.

'What about when it rained?' I enquire. 'Did you have any shelter?'

'Oh yes – we had two plywood boxes, one here and one here.' He indicates areas behind and in front of the mast. 'One to sleep in, and one for eating.'

'How long did the journey take?'

'From Iceland to Greenland it was seven and a half days. But we had problems with ice around the southern tip of Greenland, and it slowed us down. Iceland to Greenland used to take three or four days in the old days, on a different route. Then from Greenland to L'Anse aux Meadowes, the Viking site in Newfoundland, took us another six and a half days. That was the longest leg for distance. But you could do it all faster than that. From here to New York, if you had a good wind… a week and a half? With the right wind, she starts to surf – I've seen twenty knots speed.

Gunnar Marel has sailed from Norway to Iceland too. 'You know, in about the year one thousand, one man arrived at

Þingvellir, the parliament of Iceland. He said 'Four nights ago I left the king of Norway.' That we proved was possible – I was captain on another Viking ship, the Gaia, in 1991, and it took forty-eight hours to travel from the Faroes to Iceland. And that's more than half way to Bergen, so four nights could easily do it.'

It's only about twice as long as it took me on the ferry. And Gunnar Marel is continuing enthusiastically.

'It took just sixty years to colonise Iceland. After that there were at least twenty thousand people there. At least fifteen thousand people must have moved in those sixty years. It was much easier to cross the Atlantic than we imagine…this is the thing I am always trying to prove. People imagine it was very, very difficult.'

~~

And this is Gunnar Marel's mission in life. I ask him how it all began: how he came to spend his life building and sailing replica Viking boats.

'That is a long story.'

I look at him, waiting.

'My grandfather had a brother. He was the man who was the first to get the Icelandic sagas ready for printing in Iceland. So my grandfather knew the sagas back and forth like he knew his fingers. He was also a shipbuilder. And when I was ten years old, I was in the shipping yard with my grandfather, and I heard a customer ask him if he really believed the Vikings crossed the Atlantic.

'My grandfather was very very angry and told the customer that of course they crossed, that they were more clever than he could possibly imagine. I was ten at the time and I felt – yes, I felt goosebumps. It lighted up a spark in me that has always been there since.'

Gunnar Marel worked as a sailor and a shipbuilder for many years, starting work as a sailor aged fourteen. 'And in 1991 I had a chance to be a part of the crew of *Gaia* and then they made me captain. Fourteen months I was on that ship, sailing from Norway to Rio de Janeiro. And when I came back to Iceland I thought it was really strange we had no Viking ships. We only exist because of them: our ancestors arrived in them. We would not be a nation without them. I took it on as my duty to change this.'

～

I want to find out about navigation. Gunnar shrugs slightly. 'Of course sometimes they got lost. But overall it went very well.'

'But they didn't even have compasses!'

'They had an instrument to measure the height of the sun, and work out where they were. I've tried it and it is a very good compass – if you have the sun.' He looks at me, and at the clouds above us, before going on optimistically. 'But they were skilled sailors, just as they were skilled craftsmen. I know two captains today who always know where they are on the ocean, even if they have no instruments. It is something that comes – a gift if you live your life in nature.'

He looks at me, to see if I am understanding. I must look doubtful despite my nodding. Perhaps it's a parallel to those people who always know where north is, or can always find their way home, pigeon style. It is not an instinct I share. Gunnar continues:

'I felt it myself: on *Gaia* in 1991 I felt it very strongly. In my bunk I felt it when they were not steering the right course – sometimes I'd have to get up and give them a hard time if they were messing around.' He frowns. 'It's a serious thing – if you're some degrees off the speed slows and you have to reset the sail. So when you're in charge of a ship you have to be always thinking about the right direction. And this comes to you.'

'But you did have a compass with you, right? Even if you didn't need it?'

Gunnar nods. 'Oh yes.' He smiles broadly. 'Yes, yes, all of it. GPS, the lot. We were not allowed to leave Iceland without modern instruments. The regulation system is terrible – I battled it for two or three years to get ready for this trip.'

I'm intrigued. 'What do they make you do?'

'Oh, lifeboats and so on. And we were not allowed enough crew.' A real longship would have carried as many as seventy, to row in and out of port, but the *Íslendingur* did not have space for enough lifeboats. 'I was really trying to be authentic, to do it as they would have done it, but it was just impossible. We were nine so instead of all those people to row there is an engine, and ballast. But we never used the engine except coming ashore.'

Gunnar Marel looks frustrated even remembering, but I am struck by the funny side, imagining Erik's voyages held up by health and safety. On the other hand the lack of lifeboats makes their voyages sound a bit less attractive. I wonder if Gunnar Marel ever captained the boat through a storm.

'We had bad storms in 1991. Fifty knots wind, waves sixteen to eighteen metres high.' He gestures: 'The mast is only eighteen metres high.'

My eyes open wide as I try to picture this. 'Did the waves crash over you?'

'No – never,' and his expression shows that this would have been disastrous. 'But we saw them breaking close many times.'

'How do you stay safe?'

'Steer the right course. Try to avoid bad seas, or stay on the right side of the wave. Often we could see the weather coming. Sometimes,' he adds, 'it's better to leave Iceland in bad weather than good.'

I ask why and he grins: he's caught me out. 'Because after bad weather comes good!' He goes on more seriously. 'Sometimes you can wait days or weeks for the right weather. But they were very clever and skilled, and of course there are so many clues in the environment if you look: birds, clouds and so on.'

We are both getting cold, despite our wet-weather gear and warm clothes. We walk away from the boat, and into the small building next to it. We pass a pile of round, colourful shields. 'Those are for fighting – but also like a shelter when you're sailing – they make the sides of the boat a bit higher.'

~~

There is something else I'm curious about. Gunnar Marel is said to be a descendent of Leif Erikson – and so, I deduce, a descendent of Erik, Leif's father. 'Oh no, that's not true,' he says, and mutters about the laziness of journalists. My mind is relieved: a thousand years seemed a lot to be able to trace your ancestry. 'I'm not a direct descendent and I am not related to Erik at all,' he continues. 'I'm related to Leif's mother. Leif's grandfather was my thirty-three times great grandfather.'

'But how do you know?'

'Oh, through the sagas. Every Icelander can trace his family back – it's pretty easy.'

~~

It's when I'm given a guided tour that I start to understand how tightly the ship is designed. We walk the length of the boat: as she widens out towards the centre everything, every piece of wood, broadens too. Each tree was chosen specially, so as to have knots placed where they give strength not weakness. Gunnar Marel points them out. I feel he knows them personally – 'this one here, this one – here.' The oak is from Sweden, the pine from Norway. 'Yes, they would have selected trees this way, and imported wood: there is not wood for this in Iceland.'

Five thousand nails, eighteen tonnes of wood. Gunnar Marel lifts up planks in the deck for me, so I can see the workmanship continuing in the space beneath. I peer through the oarholes, and turn the wooden covers that stop water coming through them. Special curved wooden catches hold the ropes that balance the mast. There is a dragon's head on the prow, mouth agape and white teeth shining, removable when approaching friendly coasts. 'It is not a dragon, it is a serpent.' One large, smooth tree-trunk provides a resting-place for the mast, which can be swung down and laid flat on the boards of the deck, or stand proud.

Gunnar Marel is imagining being afloat again. 'Up to twenty knots you can sail her, and the mast will be secure without any ropes. And this is the clever thing about the design – when you go through the water, there are bubbles under the prow, so she moves smoothly and fast. It is as if she is saying 'I want to surf, surf, surf – I feel it on her. I feel the ship almost speaking to me.'

We move to the stern of the ship and look over the side at the rudder. 'The rudder is seventy-five centimetres below the keel, but when the ship starts to surf it comes up out of the water. In three or four metre high waves the rudder can be more or less out of the sea.'

That doesn't sound good. 'How do you steer her?'

'You have to use the sail.' Gunnar Marel has a habit of lifting his baseball cap off his head and replacing it: he does so now, pensively rubbing his head. 'When I first found the rudder in the air I felt so stupid, because I had thought I was in control – and then I realised: the ship had taken over.'

'Isn't that dangerous?'

'It is if the wind's not straight from behind. We were lucky. We knew it could happen, but we were not ready for it. But surfing – that is a wonderful feeling. I don't know how to explain it.' His face has lit up: his blue eyes are on remembered horizons. 'It feels as if you're barely in touch with the sea, almost like flying. And there's such stillness on board, because you're going as fast as the wind.'

~~

One more time, Gunnar Marel tells me that the Norse voyages were not so difficult as we believe. 'They were just island hopping really. If you are high up, you can see from Norway to the Shetland Islands, Shetland to the Faroes. I've seen the Shetlands from a hundred and seventy nautical miles in fair weather – from sea level, so from a mountain you can see much further.' He goes on: 'From the Westfjords, you can see Greenland, if it's clear. From Greenland you can see Baffin Island. I think they probably saw where they were going. I actually think this was all much easier than people imagine today. People tend to imagine the past as full of difficulties. Erik – Erik wouldn't have left Iceland for Greenland without seeing it before. Yes, he had fights and so on, as the story says, but he knew where he was going.'

'How many crew do you think Erik needed for that trip?'

'Oh, at least twenty or thirty people. A guy like him had that many people around always – and it would be impossible to cross without them. And after Leif discovered North America they probably went every year to get timber. It wasn't so difficult – you just had to do it.

'They had the ships and the equipment and it's almost stupid to me to hear educated people say they didn't go further than L'Anse aux Meadowes in Newfoundland. I'm almost sure they went down to Florida.'

~~

Gunnar Marel offers me a lift to Reykjavík, and I have a chance to ask him about volcanoes. I am fascinated by his Westmann Island origins – even by Icelandic standards the Westmann Islands are volcanically active, occasionally producing whole new mountains. One island, Surtsey, was born there in 1963 when volcanoes erupted underwater. Ten years later, the town on the largest island had to be evacuated because of another eruption.

'Do you remember that? Where were you when it started?'

'I was sleeping. My father woke me and said: 'there are some serious things happening on this island." He grins. 'I just thought 'he's lost it' and went back to sleep.'

'Okay,' I say, wondering if that's the end of the story. 'Um – and did you stay asleep?'

'Five minutes later he came back and pulled me out of bed. He told me to look to the east, and I saw a lava wall coming out of the earth, about a kilometre long, north-east to south-west.'

'Were you scared?'

'No, no-one was scared. There were about five thousand people living there, maybe a few more. Luckily the fishing fleet was in the harbour at the time. Everyone went to the harbour and got on board and sailed away. The car came a few days later.'

Just an everyday occurrence, then, a mountain growing in the centre of town. It took about six months and about a hundred houses went under the lava, but only one person was killed – it seems because they went back when they should not have.

Gunnar Marel saw Surtsey's birth as well. 'I remember it clearly, because of the sparks. It started in November, a heavy thundering sound.'

'Were you scared then?' He was quite a small boy at the time.

'No. No-one got scared, they just continued to live.'

'Did you watch it grow, though?'

'Yes. Oh yes. These eruptions lasted a few years, till 1965. Now it's the second largest island of the sixteen.'

'Was there much dust?'

'Oh yes, clouds of dust. Sometimes the whole town was completely black. In '73 everything went under. About nine hundred tonnes just on one roof. My father had just built a new house and we had only been living there for six months, so we had to dig it out. Everyone worked really hard to get things ready again.'

'How soon did the grass and things grow back?'

'Pretty soon, after two or three years life was pretty much normal again. They brought turf in, and seeds.'

~~

Even before I met Gunnar Marel, I knew he was closer to Erik than me. He is related directly to Vikings, and grew up in Iceland: my ancestry is mixed and I grew up far away. But the difference is bigger than that.

Gunnar Marel expresses pride in living through and past whatever nature brings. Twenty metre waves are a challenge, but if you keep cool you can sail over them. When volcanoes erupted near his home, Gunnar Marel's family just got on with getting out of the way, then came back to dig through the dirt. It is a pragmatic approach: there are problems and solutions. Bravery and toughness are values to aspire to, because the storms will come whatever.

I think it's an attitude Erik must have shared. And being tough about challenges from nature, being used to dealing with them directly, must have been part of being an explorer. I breathe deep: maybe it's something I need to learn from.

In that spirit, or in the spirit of the sailor, Gunnar Marel thinks one voyage in the Vinland Sagas is more remarkable that either Leif's or Erik's: that of Bjarni Herjolfsson.

Bjarni set out from Norway to spend a winter with his father in Iceland, but when he arrived he found Herjolf had gone on to Greenland, with Erik. Winter was on the way but Bjarni was determined to follow, so he and his crew set sail again at once. There were three days' fair wind but then fog set in, and a northerly wind, and they drifted with no idea of their course. Only after several days did they see the sun again, and get their bearings. But the first land they came to was a low, hilly, wooded place. Bjarni declared it was not Greenland, for there were no glaciers. They left it to port, and soon came to another land, flat and forested. Bjarni would not let his men land. A third place was passed, mountainous and topped with a glacier. 'A worthless land' declared Bjarni. Then they sailed for four days more, through a storm, and landed in Greenland.

His was the first sighting of America, though he gets little credit since he didn't step ashore. 'They told him that he was not curious enough! But that voyage has never been bettered.'

~~

In Reykjavík, not much has changed though I'm staying in a different part of town. I sit by a hot spring for a while, watching the steam rise and enjoying the warmth of it, breathing in its slightly eggy smell. I read that this used to be the town's washing area, and that until the twentieth century women carried the washing there, about forty minutes' walk. Eventually a road was built so they could push the washing in wheelbarrows instead.

~~

A new day, a new mission. This time I have followed a long road past the Tjarn – or Pond – and a roundabout and the National Museum, to the University. I am looking for the Árni Magnusson Institute, where ancient Icelandic manuscripts are stored and studied.

I ring the bell, and am summoned into a booklined corridor, carpeted, muffled. A tall clock ticks, softly. A maroon-clad lady bustles up the corridor and welcomes me gently.

'They are letting us use the director's office,' explains Rósa Þorsteinsdóttir, smiling. Her brown hair bobs neatly round her spectacled face. 'Will you wait in there? I am going to get the manuscript. It is down in the vault.'

The director's study is also book-lined. There is an abstract painting involving blue clouds and green deer on an autumnal hill, and a wide wooden table. I sit, listening to the silence, thinking of what I have come to see.

Rósa returns, carrying a white box. 'So – here it is!' Carefully, she sits down and places the box on the table in front of her. Then she opens the lid. I watch closely as she lifts out a book, pushing the box out of the way further down the table. The book is modern. But then she opens the cover, and I find that it is only protecting something smaller, pieces of dark-edged parchment, small uneven pages held somehow together. Looking closer, I realise gradually that they are no longer bound: instead, the pages are propped in a cream card manuscript holder.

Rósa places the manuscript gently on the table. I hold my breath as she opens it, and turns a few pages.

~~~

These carefully curated sheets have two names: *Skálholtsbók*, and *AM 557 4to*. *Skálholtsbók* was made in 1420, six hundred years ago, probably by the son of a nobleman in the north of the country, but little is known about its early history. Two hundred and forty years later it had made its way to Skálholt, one of Iceland's two bishop's seats. There the manuscript crossed the path of Árni Magnusson.

Árni Magnusson was a man with a passion for manuscripts. Born in Iceland in the mid-1600s, into a family of clerics, he became the first Icelander to hold a Chair in any university, as Professor of Danish Antiquities in Copenhagen. A year later he was sent to Iceland to carry out a land census for the Danish crown, and he used this journey to collect antique manuscripts and scraps of vellum. At the time, the manuscripts of Iceland were often being put to more practical use than reading, and many were not as well cared for as *Skálholtsbok*, in its comfortable bishopric. One eleventh- or twelfth-century copy of a Greek text on science was found pierced throughout and being used as a sieve for flour.

After ten years of census, Árni had a large collection to take back to Copenhagen, *Skálholtsbók* included. Only a few years later a fire destroyed much of the city and many of the manuscripts, but *Skálholtsbók* survived. After Árni's death, the book and the rest of the remaining collection were left to the University of Copenhagen. Recently, parts of that collection have returned to Iceland.

Skálholtsbók is one of two early manuscripts in existence that contain the Saga of Erik the Red: the other, *Hauksbók*, is still in Copenhagen. Between them they contain the words that are translated in the scruffy paperback that has defined the route of my journey.

For at least half its lifetime, or since Árni Magnusson collected it, this book has been a holy of holies, a source of a near original saga written a mere four hundred years after the events it describes. I am awed to be in its presence, not daring even to ask if I may touch. The pages are covered in small, dark writing, a slightly gothic-looking script. They are unevenly shaped, one or two only about half the width of the rest, and some with holes in. I assume they have been damaged, eaten by insects or torn during the book's long life.

But Rósa corrects this. 'This book is made from the bits and pieces that are left over from other books,' she explains. To make this sort of parchment, a calfskin was stretched and dried and scraped smooth. Then large rectangles were cut from the centre to form pages. The pieces around the edges were also usable, but they were mixed sizes, uneven shapes. It is these scraps that were used to make *Skalholtsbók*. Looking closely, I can see the evidence for this: the writing flows around holes in the parchment and goes to the edges of each piece but not beyond. Though many pages are missing now through age, the unevenness of those left is an original feature.

Down the side of each page are neat piercings that were part of the system for ruling lines – and they have their effect, the dense text is tidily set out. There seem to be no crossings out. Partly, this is because the sign for crossing out was different, a line below and dots above. Partly it is because the scribe has made few errors. There is one problem though: the first letters of important paragraphs, where a larger letter or even an illumination might be expected, are nothing but spaces.

'That probably means they were planning to make the letter later.'

'Would it have been the same scribe?'

'No, not always.'

We look through until we find one that is vaguely sketched in: an outline of an O but not finished. Then Rósa finds the pages that contain the Saga of Erik the Red. I scan the text closely. I cannot read Icelandic so I do not expect to be able to read the Old Norse script, but I hope to find words that are the same – *Eiríkur*, or *Graenland* maybe. But I am brought up short at once: the letters are unfamiliar enough in shape that I struggle. Rósa explains that the words are often abbreviations, letters missing or combined or piled on top of each other.

Rósa can read it, though. She finds the important parts – 'Here is the first mention of Erik' and I can make it out: E – i – r – í – k – u – r, the first three letters on one line and the rest on the next, saving more space. We find 'Grænland' and the part where it was named, and a mention of Leif.

Rósa gently pushes the book towards me and lets me turn its pages. I am surprised by how dry the parchment feels, its slight roughness.

'What are you looking for?' asks Rósa curiously, as I look carefully at each page of indecipherable foreign script. I find I cannot answer. What is so fascinating about a book I cannot read?

~~

I think I was hoping for magic, for an opening of my mind to the story, for a new understanding from this object which has conveyed Erik's essence through centuries.

But Erik is not here. This book is revealing nothing about him or his life: for that, I am far better off with my translation. The words convey no ideas, no images. They are no more than patterns of shapes. This is only parchment, if much written-on, much cared for, very old parchment. It cannot speak to me, and even if it could, I have read its words already. Yet still I look.

~~

I ask why the edges of the pages, and patches of the pages themselves, are so dark.

'Light, and smoke. It means it was used. These saga manuscripts were to be enjoyed, by people at home.' Rósa describes other manuscripts: big beautiful books of laws with rectangular pages and fine illustrations, that are the same age but lighter. Many of the big manuscripts were made to impress, perhaps even as gifts for royalty. 'The small ugly ones – they were for people, and they were read. And I think,' she is looking at me steadily now, 'I think that makes them even more precious.'

~~

Rósa tells me how the focus of modern scholarship is shifting away from these most ancient texts. Until recently, research was about finding the 'original' text. The authors of my 1960s translation prefer *Skálholtsbók* to *Hauksbók* on stylistic grounds: because the scribes of *Hauksbók* seem to have tidied up the saga, it is not considered as authentic as the more carelessly copied *Skálholtsbók*. Forty years before, *Hauksbók* was preferred – precisely because of its neat, well-styled storytelling. There is a further suggestion that I should not look at either manuscript because the first two chapters, including much of the story of Erik's life, were quite likely lifted from another text, *Landnámabók*.

Nowadays, there's more interest in the reception of the sagas, and how they were developed. 'How does a nineteenth-century copy differ from a fourteenth-century copy? What has changed? And we're moving in the direction of thinking every text has something to say to us. Why did a nineteenth century person sit and copy this saga? How? What else did they copy? In the past it was presumed that recent copies were of no interest in the search for the original. This is changing.'

Rósa beams at me and tells me about more recent hand-copied versions of many of the sagas: thousands of them in the National Library of Iceland. There are twenty-five or more copies of Erik's saga there, painstakingly copied out on paper in the eighteenth and nineteenth centuries. Up until even the twentieth century, the way to get a new book in Iceland was to copy one from a neighbour. Since then the sagas have multiplied even further: there are all the printed editions and translations all over the world. Rósa is right: where, who and why are intriguing questions.

I apply them to the pages in front of me. I wonder about the person who wrote out the stories, and about all the hands that have touched the parchment in the six hundred years since. Did it always feel the same? How precious was it when it was new, a book in a world where there were almost none? How was it cared for in its original home, a turf house however large, full of smoke and people?

Skálholtsbók does not only contain Erik's Saga. What is left of it – a chunk from the middle – contains seven sagas and five shorter stories. The Saga of Gunnlaug the Serpent Tongue tells of a beautiful woman and the two poets who fight over her. Stuf's Tale is about a blind Icelander who wins a passing king's respect through intelligent conversation, poetry and cheek. The Saga of Hallfred the Troublesome Poet is about a man who converts reluctantly to Christianity and has constant verbal battles with another king, about the new and the old gods, winning favour through taking the risk of offending him.

And now the book does have something to tell me. It is here that the connection comes: the joining of my mind to the minds of other readers, other storytellers, through hundreds of years. Whoever we are, we all have this story in common. The person who copied out these pages shared something with me – something personal, chosen. I may never know why, or much about who they were, but this book is a message, a gift from person to person, past to present, scraps of vellum written all over, read and read and read.

~~

Eventually, I can look no more, and Rósa puts *Skálholtsbók* back in its box. She takes it down to its moisture-controlled, temperature-controlled, dark, earthquake-alarmed vault with all the other books, and locks the heavy door, twice.

I set off through the rainy city, away from the University, back past the roundabout to the harbour and the main shopping area. I have another manuscript to visit, one that is more obviously impressive. *Flateyjarbók* has 225 pages, and was made from 113 calfskins, two pages cut from the centre of each skin. It is sufficiently important to be one of a select few manuscripts on public display, behind earthquake-proof glass in a dimmed inner sanctum of Reykjavík's elegant Culture House.

The route to the manuscripts takes me through an exhibition. In a video in one corner, brass bands play buoyantly, and excited schoolchildren wave flags. The Prime Ministers of both Denmark and Iceland make patriotic, joyous speeches. It is 1971, the text explains, and a national holiday has been declared to celebrate the return of two books, *Flateyjarbók* and one other, a codex of the Elder Edda. It is the start of much more: eighteen hundred manuscripts will come back to Iceland over the next twenty-five years. The broadcast continues until these first two tomes are handed over to a lengthily-robed university official.

Flateyjarbók holds – amongst many other things - the earliest existing version of the Greenland Saga – the second saga to tell of Erik's life. Most of *Flateyjarbók* was written at the end of the fourteenth century, for a wealthy man in northern Iceland, by two priestly scribes. The book stayed in the family for a few hundred years, until the first owner's sister's four-times-great grandson (who lived on the island of Flatey, in Breiðafjörður) gave it to the Bishop of Skálholt. He in turn gave it to the King of Denmark, and it remained in the Royal Collection until its return to Iceland three hundred plus years later.

Most of the volume of *Flateyjarbók* is taken up with two sagas. These sagas tell, in turn, of King Olaf Tryggvason and King Olaf the Saint, major figures in the history of Norway of Erik's period. It is as a supplement to Olaf Tryggvason's Saga – a sub-story within it – that Greenland Saga is found.

I leave the exhibition and enter a darkened room with a glass case in the centre. Inside, six books rest, gently open, on tall plain lecterns. I walk round until I find *Flateyjarbók*. A soft light shines on the open pages, where a large letter I is decorated with red and green men, attacking each other with swords. This is a much bigger, more impressive tome than *Skálholtsbók*, huge and many-paged. The writing is very stylised, and some lines of text are picked out in red. It is so neat you could imagine it was printed.

It is not open at the right page: this is the story of King Sveirri, and Greenland Saga is seventy or so pages before, buried in vellum. But I move close to the case, looking at the handwriting, seeking out words or abbreviations I recognise.

Someone else has come closer: I can see the smear their nose made on the glass.

Later, back in London and fact-checking, I stumble across a facsimile copy of *Flateyjarbók* in UCL Library. A facsimile is a near-identical copy, scale photographs of each page, although black and white in this 1930s edition. I heft the thing off the shelf, using both arms to support it, and put it down with relief on the nearest table.

There is not really enough space: when I open the volume the cover gets caught on the reading light and I have to shift it round, so it is hanging slightly off the edge, before it will open fully.

My aim, of course, is to find the pages which contain the Greenland Saga. My instinct is to do as I would with any other book: flick through, scanning for hopeful words. I notice that the columns – each page has two columns of text – are numbered. I also notice some marginalia in more modern handwriting, scribbles on the original manuscript. I find a picture of a man pointing a spear at a fish-tailed monster and wonder what it is, and wish it was in colour. I spot that most of the paragraphs start with the Icelandic Þ, tails stretching from top and bottom to the edges of the page.

The rest of the letters might as well be in code. Digging out a transcription, I work out that I am looking for a Ð at the start of the first section I'm interested in. I read the introduction – in English – and find out that the author of the marginalia and the numberer of the columns was one

Þormorður Torfasson, who used *Flateyjarbók* as a source for his 1711 History of Norway. I cannot forgive his writing on an (even then) three-hundred-year-old manuscript – let alone one belonging to the Royal Family – but I understand why he wanted page numbers. My search for a contents page was in vain.

I find the position of the Greenland Saga by accident, when another book references it, 71v or the reverse side of the seventy-first leaf. I count. Almost at the end of the page, the inside of the Ð is decorated with leaves. I look at it for a bit, then close the book again.

~~

In a way, *Flateyjarbók* represents not so much the words it holds as the fact that they were written down at all. The very existence of Icelandic literature is a source of pride for the Icelandic nation: Icelandic manuscripts are now the major sources for not just Icelandic but Scandinavian medieval history. Out of the poverty, hunger, plagues, volcanic disasters and winter darkness of medieval Iceland, came stories both true and imagined.

Flateyjarbók's presence here in the heart of Reykjavík also symbolises Iceland's independence from Denmark. Ever since 1904, when Iceland was granted Home Rule, more loudly since 1944 when she became a Republic, Icelanders have been asking for the return of these historical documents. In an almost unique international agreement, Denmark gave Iceland back her history.

One part of that history starts on the back of a page about a third of the way through *Flateyjarbók*. It is the story of a man, exiled from Iceland, who sets off to discover new land – and finds and settles it.

~~~

Though his story is written there many times, Erik is very far from me in Reykjavík. The city has no connection to him, and its own stories shout loud, drowning his voice out. The National Museum wants me to learn about modern developments in Iceland, imports and exports and television. In another part of town I find models of Reykjavík in its short industrial period, and Skúli Magnússon, that pioneering but not very successful industrialist, stares out from his pedestal.

I track down an academic. Chris Abram is a lecturer in Medieval Scandinavian Studies in London and has come to Reykjavík to write a book about the different interpretations of Old Norse mythology. But he is happy to talk about Erik. I arrange to meet him outside the Icelandic Parliament, in a square that - yesterday - was beautifully sunny. This afternoon it is pouring with rain, so we spend the first few minutes in the café draping our coats over chairs. We don't talk about Erik in the end: we talk about why people tell the stories they do.

'The best analogy for the Vinland sagas, I always think' says Chris, 'is a Western. Those are stories about colonisation, about adventure, about pushing back boundaries – and Jesse James really lived but the Western films mythologise him. The same spirit runs through the sagas.'

I learn about the misery of thirteenth-century Iceland. At that time, their independence was waning: the Norwegians were taking over, 'and the weather was dreadful,' adds Chris. 'So people started looking back, to a better past. However bloody the Saga Age was, it probably wasn't nearly as bad as the Sturlanger Age when the sagas were written down.'

'Sort of like Golden Age myths?' I ask, and he nods. 'I like that theory,' I say. I pause. 'The trouble is that I keep hearing theories that I like. I heard another one the other day – that the Vinland Sagas were about the spread of the Gospel, about its journey west as far as America. And I was also wondering whether knowing these sagas was somehow part of being Icelandic, even back then.'

'There are too many nice, satisfying theories,' I complain

'That's the great thing about theory,' agrees Chris, truthfully if not helpfully.

And we continue to try to catch the eye of the waiter who we hope is bringing our coffee.

CHAPTER 12

FOOTBALL AND TURF HOUSES

'Welcome to the real Iceland!

Two hours north of Reykjavík, there is a town by the water at the head of Breiðafjörður. In the town, there is one bar, one restaurant and one hotel, and they are all the same place. One wall of the bar is a tribute to English football: it is draped with flags from all the major clubs, Everton next to Liverpool, Arsenal next to Man U.

Even in England I have never seen so many different teams' flags together: I am amazed they haven't got up and started attacking each other. I look at the fourth wall, taken up with a projection screen where Icelandic teams are playing.

The barman speaks English with a Southern US drawl: he has already told me he spent five years in New York and New Orleans. I decide, on consideration, that football would be a good way to further the conversation. I ask him who Iceland are supporting in the current championship.

He pulls a wry face. 'Yeah, England not qualifying kinda took the shine out of it for us.'

'What, you care how England does?'

He gestures at the wall of flags.

'Yes ma'am. Welcome to the real Iceland! Yeah, Iceland

has no chance so we have to support someone else – and it's England. When you don't go through, what are we supposed to do? Support Portugal or something?'

'Not another Scandinavian country?'

'Well they usually beat us real bad, we don't support them.'

He looks gloomy. I apologise for my national team's deficiency. The gloom does not abate.

'Everyone in Iceland supports England. Welcome to Iceland!'

At about seven, the game starts. The local (male) youth roll in, about nine of them, and order pizza. They have slightly long, slightly slicked hair and low-slung trousers, and one or two wear red football shirts. They eat the pizza and watch with great concentration, in near silence. After the game they go home.

I eat true Icelandic food – a burger with egg – and drink Egil's Malt Drink. It smells like Guinness and looks like coke and tastes like beer without the bitterness.

～

Búðardalur did not make a good first impression. As we arrived along a road containing only sheds and warehouses, the driver refused to believe I wanted to leave the bus. 'Five minutes, we go in five minutes,' he reminded me, as I climbed out. I had to show him my ticket to prove that this really was my destination: he looked astonished and then, shrugging, gave me my bag.

I am here because it is the nearest place by public transport to Erik's first marital home.

~~

In the morning the hills and the sky are grey and the only sounds are the whistling of the wind and the pinging of the halyard against the flagpole outside. I listen more carefully: faintly I can hear the TV in the bar. Standing by the window, I watch as a woman gets into a car and slams the door.

Today's mission is to get to the valley where Erik began his married life, and where there is a reconstruction of his house. As part of the research process – the tourist office is shut – I have a conversation with the lady in the supermarket.

'How far is it to Eiríksstadir?' This is the reconstruction of Erik's house.

'You drive about nine kilometres…then there is a junction, then you drive about nine kilometres more.'

'Could I walk it?'

A look of absolute shock.

'No!'

'Is there any other way to get there?'

'No.' She looks a bit apologetic and I thank her, turning away. Then I turn back and ask:

'Is there anything I should do in Búðardalur while I'm here?'

I don't know what I am expecting – the beach, at least, or maybe there's a town statue. But:

'No. No, I don't think so. No.'

~~

I take a walk. Beyond the main road there are houses and a school with music playing. Poppies, yellow, cream and orange, grow by the side of the road. The beach isn't far, and it's pretty, with pebbles and blue mussel shells and a wide view. But it's cold, and damp.

An arctic tern cries *krrrrrya* overhead and I realise I have gone back in time. When I left Iceland last year, the terns were loud and aggressive in protection of their chicks: now they are quiet, ignoring me, set on chasing each other instead.

It makes sense to go back in time, for I have gone back a little in Erik's story, to the conventionally successful part of his life, his early marriage. If I can visit his house, that is. But it's not going well. In fact, as far as I can judge, there is only one way to make the journey. It will have to be kidnap.

My victims are four Icelanders: a couple, their five-year-old son Johannes and the baby. They are true locals: they have spent many months in this area, but never been to the reconstruction. Johannes is bilingual in Icelandic and English, with limitless energy but a touch of shyness. The baby sleeps.

They are not unwilling kidnappees, but it is still mildly unethical. Icelandic hospitality would not allow that I trudge along eighteen kilometres of road in thick mist: when I declared my intention of doing so, the family, very kindly, suddenly decided to visit the place themselves. I feel bad that I have inadvertently forced this trip upon them but not that bad.

We drive through the mist. We cross a river, and reach another, and turn off the main road. Climbing up the valley, we pass a lake that fills it for a stretch, smooth water by green slopes. There are a few modern farmhouses here, and a little modern church, and expanses of grassy field as far as the eye can see, which is, in the mist, not far at all.

'Look at that, Johannes!' His father points out a funny house all made of grass. Johannes looks, and so do I, and we clamber out of the car.

'These are the stones Erik and his family walked on – the actual stones.'

We look at the floor, casting our eyes over these grey, ignorable pieces of rock, overgrown with grass. We tread reverently, revelling in a shared experience, however trivial. It is gloriously romantic, the idea that these very stones were stepped on, glanced at, tripped up on by these people of long ago. Of course, there is no way to prove that this house belonged to Erik the Red or that he ever walked under its lintel. Still, carbon dating has shown at least part of the house to be from the right period. So it could be true.

Johannes is far less interested in worshipping Erik and Leif than the rest of us. He listens as the guide explains why the timber is missing from the ruined Norse building – timber was valuable and would always be taken when a building was abandoned. Then,

'What's timber?' asks Johannes.

'Wood,' explains his mother, 'You know, like when they cut down trees and shout 'Tim-ber!"

'Tim-ber!' echoes Johannes, and as we walk down the path he runs ahead, bright in his blue raincoat, cheerfully calling out: 'Tim-ber! Tim-ber!'

We wait to hear the story. 'When Erik's father died, he offered for a wife, who lived just over there.' The guide points across the straight, shallow valley. 'Erik was accepted and his father-in-law offered him this land. It is not very much land, he was not so very rich – but he had the boat which helped.'

She makes a gesture that encompasses the valley. 'Other families lived here too. And so it was that sometimes problems arose.' She explains how Erik's slaves were watching his sheep one day when they managed to accidentally cause a landslide; the landslide destroyed a neighbour's farm and the farmer killed the slaves. 'And then Erik killed the farmer and his two sons. Just over there.' A space in the valley becomes a battle-scene, Vikings hacking with axes. 'And so Erik made himself very unpopular. In the end he realised he could not live here any more, as no-one would help him. A friend gave him somewhere else to live, two islands in Breiðafjörður. He did not live here very long – perhaps ten years.'

We go in. The sudden darkness makes me pause on the threshold, waiting for my eyes to adjust. If I had come a few years ago, I would have choked on smoke from the fire in the middle of the floor. 'The smoke was so bad we had to stop using the hearth,' explains the guide. 'We were coughing and spluttering all day. We think that is why the roof is so high – somewhere for the smoke.' Health and safety again, and when I sigh over the lack of authenticity to another guide she grins at me: 'Yes, they put up with it, but they didn't live particularly long in those days.'

The ceiling is indeed high. The space is split in three along its length: to my left, the slaves' section; in the centre a space with the fire; to my right Erik and Thjodhilde's and the family's beds. The central one, Erik's, is decorated with two panels of carved wood, dragon-like.

My archaeologist's training is fighting against the detail being shown here. I am always cynical about reconstructions. They can be done badly: the line between authentic and reconstructed can be disguised from visitors; they can make claims that are too large; they can blur chronology; the worst damage or destroy the archaeological evidence they are based on. Even the best have that standard archaeological problem, that a modern mind will see the reconstructed world through modern eyes: see encumbrances in place of normality, lack of technology in place of astonishing novelty, 'weird clothes' instead of 'what everyone wears'. Even if we could travel back in time, this problem would remain – except that perhaps if we could meet the people who wore the costumes and used the tools, overhear their conversations, join in, we might gradually sink into that life, noticing the people rather than the materials of their existence.

The trouble is, I'm enjoying this. Luckily, in their defence, good reconstructions can rediscover detail that neither archaeology nor literature can produce. The guide pulls out a large, brown leather shoe with a hole worn right through the sole. Viking shoes didn't last long. 'We made these for one of our guides, and they lasted only ten weeks. And those were cow leather, so much tougher than sheep leather which they used more often. You know, there is a hill near here called 'three shoe hill' and I never knew why... until we tried these shoes and I realised you would need that many pairs to climb it.'

Even more revealing is the weaving. In one corner of the room stands a loom, upright, warp threads hanging down and weighted with big stones. The stones are a common find at Norse sites, fist-sized lumps with holes through the centre. Bjarni had plenty at his site. Now I can see how they were used. The women did the weaving, pulling a wooden bar forward and back to allow the weft thread through, taking a step with each movement. It has been calculated, I learn, that in a day's weaving she would walk thirty-six kilometres. One woman would continue for a whole piece of cloth, because varying the tension – a consequence of varying the strength of the weaver - would make the cloth's texture uneven. To weave a sail would take one woman two years, and use the wool of two thousand sheep. Not surprisingly, cloth was valuable – used as currency and traded for wood and other goods.

Johannes tries on a helmet and poses with it. The adults heft a surprisingly light sword: it is large but I imagine even I could use it, with training. We try striking fire with a flint and a twisted piece of metal. We stand outside the turf house, itself huddled against the landscape on this dull day.

Not for the first time on this journey I realise the pampered nature of my life. There is no expectation that I will walk thirty-six kilometres to make a piece of plain fabric. My shoes come from a shop and last for years or until I tire of them. Switches – one finger movement – give me warmth and light and cooking facilities.

I wonder how much difference it makes at the most basic level: to how it feels to be alive. We tire ourselves out with different activities now, but we still tire ourselves out. We worry about different dangers, not storms and animals but loss of work and car crashes – though human conflict and sickness are still high on the list of our problems. But whether life feels different comes down to an unanswerable question: were worry and tiredness, like and cold and eugh and joy the same back then? If so, was life – not 'daily life' but 'the feeling of being alive' – so very different after all?

That's not to say I want to go back and live in the Viking Age. I would miss too much, with my knowledge of how life is now. I ask my kidnappees whether they would like to live in the Viking house. The father chuckles: 'Yes, I like the spirit of these people.' The mother looks more doubtful. The weaving and the cold have put both of us off. But Johannes has no doubt: raising his arms above his head he gives a loud, clear 'yes!'

The baby sleeps on.

Erik left Haukadalur for the islands of Breiðafjörður, a little to the west, where he lived for a year or so until his quarrels escalated towards his eventual exile. It was there that I saw the Bloodstone last year, imagined Erik's exile, felt ill and was sent back home.

I missed something out, last year. I didn't make it to the island, so the sagas say, where Erik hid his boat in his last moments in Iceland, as his exile was debated in the Assembly. I need to see it, but I have a superstitious nervousness about it too. What if I'm ill again? What if the gods see me there again and once more decide to disrupt my mission?

But as soon as I arrive at Stykkishólmur I know I was right to come: my confidence is buoyed up by the fact of being here and not being ill. The gods have been defied, or at least are leaving me alone for a bit.

Puffins still make me laugh, swimming around like ducks and then flappily trying to take off. Erik's life in the farmland of Haukadalur was easy compared to Drangar; here, life is easier still. It is not just puffins that are there for the catching. As we cross the fjord – on a bird-watching cruise, ironically the only way for me to reach the island – the crew reel out a weighted net, letting it drag across the bottom of the sea behind us. Then they reel it in, full, and pour its contents onto a table.

Bristling, spiny sea-urchins land on tightly-shut clam shells, and a starfish clenches. A twelve-legged creature lies still, a pink-petalled flower, white spines circling its red centre. A green crab scuttles robotically across the table, leaping blindly off the edge, while a twisted shell grows fine red legs and sneaks off in the other direction.

An American woman takes responsibility for rescuing most of these creatures, throwing them off the side from gloved hands. Meanwhile the crew set to. They lever open clams, pulling out a lump of white flesh and discarding the rest. They hack open sea-urchins, revealing a black mess from which a bubbly orange paste is skilfully extracted.

Not without qualms, I taste. To my great surprise, they are both sweet, only slightly fishy, the clam slightly chewier.

'You know what you're eating?' the American woman enquires, pointing at the orange paste. I don't, but it turns out to be roe. 'Worth a fortune in Paris,' she adds, wrinkling her nose at the suggestion she try some. And, I think, to someone settled on these shores, but for a different reason: it's the easiest food I ever saw caught.

~~

A mermaid was once captured on an island in Breiðafjörður. Nowadays, there are just puffins and kittiwakes. But the island itself is made of square spaghetti, thick, regular basalt columns clumped vertically together with a topping of grass. All the islands here are made of basalt columns, some hexagonal, some square, formed by an even pattern of cracking in the volcanic rock. One set of columns is wiggly like corrugated iron.

The captain is pointing something else out now: an island rising to two points from the sea. 'You can see that it is a good hiding place,' she explains, 'and it may be that in those days the island was covered in trees too so he could hide his boat amongst them.'

Up close, this is a junk-heap of basalt columns piled on each other, russet and beige with scraps of grass growing where it can. Black sea-birds, shags, nest on the steep outer cliffs, craning their long necks over the edges of basalt hexagons. In the bay between the twin peaks, there is a gentle beach. It is here that Erik's boat was drawn up, while he was hidden from his foes, from here that he sailed out proud between the islands and away.

He told [his friends] that he was going to search for the land that Gunnbjorn, the son of Ulf Crow, had sighted when he was driven westwards off course and discovered the Gunnbjarnar Skerries; he added that he would come back to visit his friends if he found this country.

Eirik put out to sea past Snaefells Glacier...

CHAPTER 13

NUKA ARCTICA

There is no public ferry from Iceland to Greenland, and few other ships make the journey. But Erik went by water and so shall I. I am going by cargo ship. I have no idea at all what this will entail. My imagination is full of oilskins and sailing equipment, and super-calorie-efficient foodstuffs for a long voyage. Maybe there will even be ponies, like Miss Ethel B. Harley had on her Victorian cargo boat. My friends are suggesting I bring limes to stave off scurvy, and asking where I will sleep – inside a container? On deck? A while ago I did send a tentative email to Royal Arctic Line, asking if I needed any special equipment. A friendly reply came back:

Nuka Arctica is a modern ship with all the modern equipment, and I am sure that you will be in good hands, and that the staff will provide you with whatever you need.

My anxieties are not entirely allayed, but I have decided not to buy a boiler suit after all. In support of the reality of the scheme (which in moments of anxiety I doubt) I have the captain's phone number and the following instructions for finding the ship:

Nuka Arctica will arrive in Reykjavík June 15 around e.t.a. 0900 hours and normally she sails around 1600 hours the same day. I do not have the exact address, but *Nuka Arctica* will be easy to find in Reykjavík harbour because of its size.

So I am to look for a large ship in Reykjavík harbour at nine in the morning. Further internet research comes up with an image of a large red ship full of containers, and a GPS tracker so I can see that, right now, she is approaching Iceland from Europe. Local research establishes that there are two harbours in Reykjavík. Yet further local research establishes that locals don't know which one the cargo ships use.

The harbours are about forty minutes walk apart, without a backpack; with, it would take a painful hour.

I need a lookout point.

～～

Reykjavík is full of wonders this evening. There is a shop full of fish-skin that has been made into leather, with the same smell and softness but one surface always textured with fish-scales. I can't understand how something as gel-like as fish skin, fatty and sometimes fried crisp on a piece of salmon, can become clothing or a bag. 'How do you make it like this?'

'Just like leather. And it is much stronger than leather. For the same thickness, the fish is much stronger.' He tugs at a piece, showing me that it won't tear.

At one end of the harbour I eat fish and chips, the skin thick with munchable batter. Further along the shore, the sky is mimicking fish, mackerel scales of cloud smeared across it. Ambling further, I reach the second harbour. There are piles of fishing nets, dwarfing me, small black woven hills with occasional bright floats. Containers, the lego of giants, stack up neatly beyond them, and an enormous cruise ship, *Aida*, is supping on German tourists. The true giants' playground is secure behind a wire fence: there, an immense crane leans over the dock and the red, blue and white lego pieces are built up even higher.

~~

My lookout point is near this second harbour. At half past eight, wrapped up warm and clutching breakfast, I set off. It is nearly raining: sometimes a few drops escape from the sky and splash on my raincoat. *Aida* is disgorging tourists into buses. A couple of joggers – they wear leggings here, not cycle shorts – pass by. I am prepared for a long wait, but when I arrive at my lookout a ship is already in sight. There is no doubt that it is she – a red fuzz against the grey fuzz of mist on the water. Very faintly, I can hear a chugging, but the oystercatchers and terns are making a racket too, much closer.

I curl up as tightly as possible on the dock wall to watch. She is moving, but so slowly that to see it I have to shut my eyes, wait, remember and open them again. I take a picture and zoom in, to check the name just in case another red ship should arrive at the same time. But it is *Nuka Arctica*, growing with every moment.

She is piled up high with containers. I try to count them, to estimate her size. They are two to four high, arranged longways with five filling the length of the ship. There must be about eight across the width. That makes over a hundred containers – over a hundred lorryloads. Behind the lorries is a tower, tall and white with windows all the way up, and what I guess is a wheelroom on top. Above that, a small plume of black smoke rises from the chimney.

She passes my lookout point and I follow her until I am blocked, by the fence to the container yard, last night's giants' playground. There is a small but significant notice by the gate: Access to authorised persons only. There seem to be no people here at all: it is Sunday morning and nobody but the mad (tourists and joggers) is awake. I peer through the diamond-shaped holes in the fence, then walk round the back of the building, hoping for another entrance. But there is none, and the fence is secure.

By the gate I find a small button, mysteriously labelled. I press it. After a while there is a crackling.

'Hello?'

'Hello, do you speak English?'

'A little.'

'Um, I wonder if you can help me, I am supposed to be going to Greenland on the *Nuka Arctica* and I don't know how to get to her. Do you know how I get on board?' Only it is more entangled and less comprehensible than that, and a miracle that he understands.

'You cannot come on board now because the police are there. But in an hour you can.'

The police? I start, but have more important things to ask about. 'So I just come back and ring you again?'

'Yes.'

~~

There is still one thing I must do before I leave Iceland. Yesterday I found a market stall selling a fine selection of Icelandic fishy delicacies – including rotten shark. Small cubes of it were crowded into little sealed plastic pots beside the bags of matted dried fish.

One of these pots is in my bag now, and much as I don't want to taste it, it is getting hard to ignore. I sit on a bench and fiddle the lid open. Immediately I feel my stomach clench and have to stop myself gagging as the smell of ammonia blocks out all other aromas. I shut the lid.

A few deep breaths later, I try once more. The stuff comes with a little cocktail stick. I plan to poke at the cubes a bit before, maybe, tasting. But once the lid is open my stomach's response overwhelms my mind's. I manage one poke, feel a little rubbery resistance, before I have to shut the lid, gaspingly breathe fresh air.

I decide to postpone. I wrap the shark firmly in layers of plastic bag, and put it away again. I collect up my possessions and march, spare shoes dangling by the laces from the backpack, down once more to the harbour.

～～

Eventually, it is time to ring the bell again.

'Someone is coming to talk to you,' says the voice. I wait. A car approaches the gate, a light flashing on top of it. A uniformed woman, neatly grey-haired, steps out.

'You want to travel on *Nuka Arctica*?'

'Um, yes,'

'Do you have any documents?'

'Um, no, but I have the captain's phone number!' She looks unimpressed. Then it occurs to me that I do have one thing, so obvious I had forgotten it:

'I have a passport, of course.'

'And they said yes, you could travel with them?'

'Yes.'

'You should come in the car.' Once inside she asks again: 'They said you could travel with them?' When I affirm it, she nods. I show her my passport but she doesn't seem interested. We slide almost silently round the heaps of containers, light flashing. I don't know whether to feel privileged that I am in this part of the port, or nervous at being in a police car.

We come to the water – and there she is, towering above us. 'There is no-one there,' says my guard. 'Perhaps they've all gone into town,' I suggest merrily, the edge of nerves slipping uncontrollably into my tone. But 'no, nobody has gone into town.' She relaxes and tells me a little more. 'They are taking forty containers, and then they go, around 2pm. I will have to take you on board.'

I reload my backpacks and follow her, wobbling only slightly as we climb steps that are something between stairs and a ladder: it reminds me of walkways in adventure playgrounds. As we reach the top, a man emerges, round of face and clean shaven, wearing the same red as the ship. He shakes my hand. 'Ah, come in, come in!'

'You are expecting her?' asks my guard, and I realise she has been wondering what to do if they are not.

'Yes, yes' comes the reply, slow and considered. 'Come on

up,' and I follow, only briefly pausing to call back thanks to the policewoman. We come out of the narrow staircase into an office. Passing through, I meet the captain, smart, with clipped grey hair and beard, surprisingly unpiratical until later I spot his pipe. Backpack still threatening to unbalance me, I follow the Chief Officer, who has now shed his red outerwear, up hundreds of circling stairs. 'Yes, yes,' he begins, 'Yes, yes, we eat at twelve o'clock in the Mess, supper is at half past five, breakfast is at eight o'clock.' His tones are gentle and rhythmic. He finds me a key and lets me into my cabin, then leaves me.

I collapse on a sofa and roll out of my backpack, and look around. Compared to my imaginings, this room is palatial. I have my own shower, cupboards, a desk and a bed in addition to the sofa. There is even a hifi, on a suspended shelf above the desk. I investigate the window, with its neat blue curtains: there is a container outside it, red with white writing and metal bars, and oddly enough a paper parcel tag.

A female voice speaks from the doorway. 'It's not a very good view, I'm afraid. There was another cabin higher up but it is small, very very small, and we thought you would be more comfortable here.'

Pernelle, the stewardess, is the only woman on board apart from me. And I am not in the least dismayed by the view: when else in my life will I be able to look out on a container? Sea views you can have any time. Pernelle continues:

'I am going to eat my lunch now but you will probably want to wait until twelve, when the others eat. We eat at twelve and half past five, and breakfast is at eight.' She smiles and sets off down the corridor.

I empty my backpack on the floor, change my shoes, and brush my hair. But I am far too excited to stay in the cabin. Shutting the door behind me, so the chaos is hidden from any nautical eyes, I follow Pernelle.

~~

The Mess is a square room, decorated so as to feel faintly cottagey with patterned curtains and tablecloths on the three long tables. On a fourth a buffet, always including herring but varied in its other content, is laid out every meal. This time there is masses of fish, hard-boiled egg, sauces and a pile of raw mince with an egg in.

Seating is by rank. On the opposite side of my table are the Captain, Chief Officer, First Officer and Second Officer. On my side are the Chief Engineer, First Engineer, Second Engineer and – anomalously – me. Everyone turns up on the dot of twelve, except those who are relieving people on duty, who come early, and Pernelle and the Mess Officer who are already there. Manners are better than mine, I notice nervously, as the people around me eat their open sandwiches with knives and forks rather than scooping them inelegantly to their mouths. I imitate.

After lunch, the captain registers me on the ship's computer as a Supernumerary, which could sound important if I didn't know it meant Extra. 'And this paragraph here says that if we do not stop in Greenland – but we will – but instead go to South Africa, you will have to work out how to get home for yourself.'

I sign blithely, feeling suddenly that I am on the ocean, on a ship that could go anywhere.

'Tell me if you are going to,' I request.

The captain laughs. 'OK, we will tell you. And do you know our mealtimes? We eat at twelve, at half past five, and...' but he stops, seeing me nodding, and smiles. 'But you know that already.'

～～

I have permission to spend as much time as I like up on the bridge, the highest point on the ship. To get there are more stairs, up and up and up. On each level a different picture hangs in the stairwell. I take to navigating by these pictures, racing up and down the stairs until the right one comes into view. On Deck Eight – my deck, as I already think of it, though it is Pernelle's too and there is a sitting room for the whole crew there – the picture is of a whale's tail, splashing into the ocean. But the bridge is easy to find because there is nothing higher. The steps stop abruptly at a doorway, with a glass window. The door is locked, and I have to wait, that first time, until one of the officers appears and lets me in.

The space is full of mysterious instruments and important-looking chairs. Window stretches all around. Outside, Reykjavík is still there, the container yard with its cranes and the buildings beyond. Seawards, there is an island with a single house.

But mostly what I look at is the ship, the rows of containers ahead of us and the two red crane towers for lifting them on and off. One of the cranes is moving, folding down, forming a bridge from the tower almost to where I'm standing. Its driver steps out of his cabin, walks along the crane and secures it at the near end with a yellow bar.

The ship starts vibrating, throbbing. The radio boops. Customs officers come on board and depart again. There are four or five people on the bridge now. The sun comes out and the rotors on the roof cast spinning shadows on the containers.

Now we are making ripples, slowly shifting away from the quay. There are whirlpools behind us, and the throbbing is a slow chug now, with a deeper rumble below. The windsock on the nearer crane tower points straight at the bridge. At 1.40pm we move out past the island, and past *Aida*. There are kids fishing off the end of the harbour. We pass the city and the old port, full of tiny boats. Beyond it I can see Hallgrimskirkja, and I think about Leif, striding out in front of it, facing the New World.

~~

The first time Erik made this journey, there was just the one boat, and Leif was left at home. (At least, I assume so – the sagas mention him wherever possible and I imagine they would have told us if he had he gone too). The second time Erik crossed, there were twenty-five boats, filled with animals, women and children including Leif. Yet if each ship was about the size of Gunnar Marel's *Íslendingur*, each was about two of our containers long: we could fit the whole fleet on board, no problem.

It was a remarkably bad crossing. Of twenty-five ships that set out, only fourteen made it to Greenland. Some of the others arrived back in Iceland: some were lost forever. On one of those that arrived safely, there was a poet, a Christian from the Hebrides, who has left behind only a wail of fear:

'I beseech the immaculate Master of monks

To steer my journeys

May the lord of the lofty heavens

Hold his strong hand over me.'

Scholars since have speculated that there was an earthquake underwater, causing immense tidal waves. But that need not be the case. This is a harder crossing than that from Norway to Iceland. Twenty metre high waves are not uncommon in the North Atlantic: a more skilled sailor than Gunnar Marel could lose a boat. The fog and the changing winds could make navigation impossible and – as if the other dangers were not enough – icebergs could loom out of nowhere along the Greenland coast.

~~

And, of course, Vikings did not have lifeboats, life jackets, fire extinguishers, a gym, a laundry and meals served at twelve, five-thirty and eight. I am given a safety tour as we move away from the harbour. The First Officer – John – explains how to climb into the ejector boat, attached by one hook to the sinking ship, and strap myself in. When everyone is inside, the hook will be released and the boat will shoot back off the ship from about deck six, crashing into the water. 'That is why you must strap yourself in.' There are some others with a different mechanism. 'And there is one at the front of the ship too, in case she breaks in half and you are stuck at the other end. You have seen Titanic? Well, this is what we use instead of lowering boats over the side. But I will try not to hit any icebergs.'

We put on earplugs and climb down into the engine room. The engine churns noisily below us and around us, a giant roomful, its sound far bigger than our voices. John gestures up a ladder and I understand that it's the emergency exit.

But I am most impressed by the cargo hold. There are more containers in the ship than I had estimated – they are five deep as well as piled high above the waterline. In total there are about three hundred and fifty, each forty feet long. To get into the cargo hold, John turns six handles which seal the door closed. We step over a foot high ledge and stand in a corridor that reaches to the front of the boat. A thick pipe runs along the ceiling next to the halogen lights, and the walls are broken up regularly by vertical steel, reaching from floor to ceiling. On the right are more doors like the one we came through, behind which are the containers. Everything except the lights is painted cream.

'If you open any of these doors, make sure you close them,' John taps the side of the boat, which echoes satisfyingly. 'Out here is just the sea. If there is an accident we can flood this whole space without having to worry about the cargo – if the doors are shut.'

I resolve to shut doors behind me.

Our cargo is impressive, but it's nothing to what's been transported across this ocean before. Forget the animals that Erik and his settlers carried: they were live but not dangerous. The sailors who are most worthy of our awe are those who carried a cargo that would have happily eaten them - live polar bears.

A male polar bear can be three metres long: four would fit into one of our containers, about eight into a Viking ship. To commit an eighth of one's cargo space to one item demonstrates its value: if that item is a carnivorous animal, such a commitment begins to suggest madness. But these bears were taken from Greenland to Norway – at least a week's voyage. What is more, polar bears are designed for cold climates, well insulated and liable to overheat in climates warmer than the Arctic. To share a small space surrounded by icy water with a large, powerful and increasingly hot, hungry, angry bear must take either insanity or extreme motivation. It was the latter: each bear was a gift for a different king.

One of the bear transporters, Einar Sokkason, brought the king not only a gleaming white bear, but walrus ivory and strong walrus-hide ropes. In return, he received 'honour and respect' from the king – and something more, a long-awaited bishop for Greenland. The unfortunate bishop was not very keen to take up the post. He declared that he was not fit for such an honour, and that he would miss his friends, and that he was anxious about the unruly Norse Greenlanders. He eventually agreed, or was forced, to go, on condition Einar was made his defender. The bear had clearly made an impression.

Another bear was transported by an Icelander named Audun[4]. He invested everything he owned in buying the creature when he was wintering in Greenland, and then brought it back to Europe to present to King Svein of Denmark. Unfortunately, the first king he met when he reached Europe (bears are conspicuous and attract kings' attention easily) was Svein's arch-enemy, Harald of Norway. Even at the request of royalty, Audun refused to give up his bear, eventually – after an encounter with a corrupt steward – giving it to the right king. It made his career: Audun was not the type to stay put and prosper, as he was invited to, but even after his travels reduced him to vagrancy he was welcomed again and again to the king's table.

4 To follow up either these two tales, look up Greenland Tale and The Tale of Audun from the Westfjords.

Nuka Arctica is rocking forwards and back, gently. 'It is nice, when it is like this, like being rocked to sleep,' says the Second Officer. But I know it is going to get worse. The captain has warned me to stow everything safely tonight, with the ominous words, 'I think you will experience some bad weather.'

For now, I watch the front of the boat push the waves aside, rolling the water over, twisting it till it crashes in powder-spray and dissolves back as swirling foam. There are turbot over the stern, swooping in low arches over the water. There is music playing in the bridge, as we rock onwards, into the evening.

～

I feel sick.

Food helps, for a while. But then I have to go outside and inhale deep, sharp breaths of air, standing on the aft-deck by the empty swimming pool. I breathe, and concentrate on the horizon, and breathe, and concentrate, and breathe, and concentrate, but it is no good.

I am sick.

I am sick again.

That night, I dream that I am being held upside down by my ankles and shaken, and rolled from side to side. I stagger down the stairs for breakfast and the room is moving from side to side so much that I hold my arms out to balance. I refuse cereal, sure that the milk will slop out of the bowl. Now I see why the jugs are heavy-bottomed and the condiments in special trays, and the food clingfilmed underneath as well as on top. The world sways. And then I feel ill again, and go back to bed again, and am sick again.

~~

I wake up to sunlight on the container outside my window. I have a vague memory of people knocking on my door, telling me I won't die. I remember knowing that, but deciding I would not get out of bed for two days, happy to starve to death rather than be sick again. I remember being awed that Pernelle had been to the gym, when I could barely stand. And I remember thinking about Gunnar Marel's ship, and Erik's – 'it is not so hard to sail across the Atlantic in a Viking boat, you just do it, just do it… just do it…'

I sit up, testing. The ship is still swaying madly, but being vertical is not too bad. Perhaps the tablet I cheatingly took has started to work. I pull on my shoes, but laces are too hard and I leave them undone. I hold the wall and stand up. Then, steadying myself on it all the way, I stagger outside.

The sea is churning, boiling. The water has formed great rolling mounds, like great fat seals turning under the ship, a murky grey-green. The deck rail swings to left and right, thirty or more degrees off the horizontal. But in the spray as we crash through the water, there are pieces of rainbow, scraps and ribbons of colour, red through golden through green. Sometimes the spray is lit up with just one or two shades; occasionally the whole spectrum is there, through to violet. The twists and spirals of spray are overlaid with colour.

Nibbling at the rye bread with cold potato that Pernelle has made for me, I gradually feel better.

~~

We are travelling through the North Atlantic, about to round Cape Farewell – the southernmost point of Greenland – and take the righthand route up the Davis Strait to the North.

Erik is not the only traveller from Europe to have discovered this stretch of water. After the colonies he founded lost contact with Europe, and disappeared, knowledge of this part of the world faded too. Perhaps Columbus heard rumours, travelling to Iceland before finding America in 1492. But whether or not he knew of Greenland, he did not investigate it and the first of the new wave of European explorers to set foot there did so almost by accident, engaged on quite another quest. By the sixteenth century, this corner of ocean had become peculiarly interesting – because according to new theories it was the opening of a north-west passage that led all the way to China.

One early sailor was John Davis, who set out in charge of two vessels, *Sunshine* and *Moonshine*, in 1585. His voyages are recorded by John Janes, 'Iohn Ianes... sometime servant to the worshipfull Master William Sanderson.' They leave England, passing round the Scilly Isles, and head north. After several weeks' voyage, Janes writes:

'The 16., 17., and 18. we saw great store of Whales. The 19. of July we fell into a great whirling and brustling of a tide, setting to the Northwards, and sailing about half a league we came into a very calm Sea... here we heard a mighty great roaring of the Sea, as if it had been the breach of some shoare, the air being so foggy and full of thick mist that we could not see the one ship from the other.' Not being able to find ground, the Captain, the Master and Janes set out in a smaller boat to explore, commanding the gunners to shoot a musket off 'at every glass' so as not to lose them. 'Coming near the breach' continues Janes, 'we met many islands of ice floating, which had quickly compassed us all about, and did perceive that all the roaring that we heard, was caused only by the rowling of this ice together.' The ship's company gave them up for lost but they eventually returned to the vessel, loaded with ice which melted down to make good drinking water.

John Davis named the Davis Strait but did not discover the north-west passage. The quest went on, without success, for several hundred years, building on his and others' discoveries. Two of the searching captains were never seen again. One Henry Hudson (of Hudson Bay) was marooned by a mutinying crew in 1610. In 1845, John Franklin would have made it, except that his ships froze in the ice for a year and a half. His crew, leaving a note for the Secretary of the British Admiralty, tried to make the journey home overland but never reached safety. It was not until 1906 that Roald Amundsen of Norway – the same man who first reached the South Pole – discovered and sailed through the north-west passage. His discovery has not been much used: the passage is generally – though decreasingly as sea temperatures warm – blocked with ice.

~~

Up on the bridge, you can imagine you are flying. The wheelroom is bird-shaped, two wings with the controls in the centre. The sea swirls below. I sit by the window, half-concentrating, and stories ebb and flow around me.

'We took a ship up the Amazon once, to provide cargo to a gold-mining community. The locals come up in canoes, and try to buy things – they trade their goods for shampoo and so on. Once they brought a stuffed crocodile.'

'To eat?'

'No, stuffed the other way.' It takes me a while to clock and he carries on. 'But after a few days it began to smell. They had not used proper preservatives, you see. But it was quite funny – the man who bought it had a crocodile on a lead, following him around the deck.'

And tales of Greenland: 'You know, there are gold mines there too... and it is so cold there in winter they have to estimate how many people will die in advance and dig the graves. Yes, yes, it is too cold to dig graves, and you cannot use dynamite in a churchyard.'

'They used to say that in Viking days they just dropped seasick Vikings off at the Faroe Islands. But the Faroese do not like that much. We often have Faroese crew and we tease them...'

'And last year it was minus twenty-eight degrees when we were unloading in Sisimiut. Your coffee turned to ice. But the Greenlanders – they just carried on working, out in it for hours at a time.'

'I bought a polar bear cranium once, in a souvenir shop.'

Apparently the storm last night was small. The waves were only five metres high, not twenty as they can be in winter. In storms like that, the Captain explains, you stay put and wait till it's over.

Ice is causing far more disruption to our journey. We are in touch every six hours with the Danish Navy, checking in, and an ice patrol in South Greenland sends us fresh ice charts daily. *Nuka Arctica* is an icebreaker, one of the toughest ships there is, but still there is some ice that could puncture a hole in her steel shell. The Captain started telling me about it last night, puffing at his pipe, adding in tales of flying helicopters to hot springs in his ice patrol days. Now he explains it to me properly, opening drawers in the big plan-chest and pulling out a chart of Greenland.

'There are three kinds of ice we are dealing with here. The first is polar ice. It is ice from the Arctic and it is very strong. You see, it leaves the Arctic and maybe for five to seven years it travels and refreezes, travels again and refreezes. It comes down in the current along here.' He indicates a path down the east coast of Greenland, round the tip and – surprisingly – up the other side along our path. 'The ice can be three to five metres thick when it starts. Perhaps it is not so thick when it reaches South Greenland but it is very hard, very dense, dangerous.'

He stoops again to pull out another chart, this one of the West coast of Greenland. 'That is the first kind of ice. The second is icebergs and growlers. An iceberg is ice from a glacier, thousands of years old. Imagine how hard that can be. As hard as concrete. A growler is when a piece breaks off an iceberg. They are marked like this on the ice chart' – an iceberg a triangle, a growler the same with its top chopped off – 'and when they are shaded in, there are very many. An iceberg is dangerous but you will see it - a growler maybe not. Most of the ice is below the surface, so even in calm weather you only see the tip. If it is rough like it was this morning the swell can hide growlers completely but under water they are big, very dangerous.'

He shows me places on the map where the glaciers spill over into the sea. Greenland's ice cap sheds icebergs straight into the water: some fjords are full of them and often they reach the open sea. But the captain is continuing. 'The third sort of ice is winter ice. That is ice just from this year – in winter it comes down maybe as far as Nuuk. This we can drive through, up to a metre's thickness – though there needs to be a weakness in it. There has been less and less winter ice in recent years.'

In winter, the northernmost ports in Greenland are closed, but in spring, particularly in June, it is the fjords on the tip and on the south west coast, where I am trying to go, that have the problems. Polar ice, particularly heavy this year as the winter was cold, is clogging up the sea. I hoped initially to disembark at Narsaq, a town just west of the southern tip, near where Erik is meant to have settled down. Thanks to the ice, it is Greenland's capital, Nuuk, over four hundred kilometres further north, that will probably be our first stop in Greenland.

~~

Next morning there is ice to be seen to starboard, a clear streak of light across the horizon. Binoculars show it as a sparkling line, then lose their grip on it, sparkles dissolving into a grey blur. I focus frantically before taking them down. The blur is still there: it is fog.

The weather round here has clearly not changed since Davis' voyages. But we have a full tank of water and a sea-chart, and no need to set off between the icebergs. Somewhere beyond all the fog and ice is Greenland.

The fog comes and goes all day. I sit up on the bridge with the officers, sinking into the rhythm of sea life, watching on as they change shifts every four hours, eating at eight, twelve and five thirty.

Now, I am a sailor. I never leave a door unpropped, and I never leave a glass on a smooth surface. I am happy to wander up and down the steps on the outside of our tower, tens of metres above the water, breathing the clear air and watching the birds, but I can sit inside too, reading or writing or chatting or watching for whales.

I know what some of the equipment does, the GPS which marks our route and the radar which skims the surface of the water for ice. I watch that when the fog comes in close and there's nothing to be seen outside but smooth blue-grey.

~~

There is a constant humming alongside the engine noise, louder when I open the window in my cabin. It is the working of three hundred refrigerators, containers keeping their contents the right temperature. I ask the Second Officer, Kim, who is on duty, about the one by my window. It is Kim who has explained to me how all the equipment on the bridge works: as well as the GPS and radar, the lights that shine a thousand metres ahead, the windscreen wipers, the gyroscope and the machine for registering other boats nearby. Kim is in the last part of his officer training, which has taken five and a half years, at sea and in college alternately.

'Hmm.' He types something on a keyboard, and a plan of the boat pops up on the screen. 'What deck are you on? Eight? Then I think it is likely to be either this one... or this one. There is not much information about those.'

He points out a small blue container in the centre of the ship. 'That one is something dangerous. We have dangerous goods marked on the plan, things like dynamite and phosphorous.'

'Do you carry many dangerous goods?'

'No – well, more things are dangerous than you think. Perfume can be dangerous.'

For my containers there is weight, destination number, and temperature. They are going to Nuuk, like me. 'Oh, hold on,' adds Kim. 'This one is at minus twenty-two degrees. Very cold – deep frozen, so probably meat. And this one is at eleven point nine degrees. That means it's bananas. Bananas are always at twelve degrees. And you know there is a story about the bananas – in East Greenland they do not have them for months at a time and when the first ship arrives, the message goes swiftly round town and that day everyone is walking around eating bananas.'

~

In our tower, in the middle of the fog, in the middle of the ocean, the pulse of the days beats gently on. One evening I watch a classic Danish film about a rickety old steamship where life revolves around drink and song, and a telegraph officer grows roses in his cabin. 'That's one crew member we don't have these days,' remarks our captain, puffing on his pipe.

Above three thousand metres of water, sixty miles from the nearest land, yet with satellite phone and email access, we are isolated but not isolated, alone but not alone. There is a constant cheerful banter amongst the crew, who call home regularly, exercise, eat, relax and get on with their jobs. Most of them work six weeks, then have six weeks off, a cycle that lasts all year.

One afternoon I take a stroll down towards the icebreaker. It's quiet at the front of the ship, or seems so apart from the hum of the fridges. I go through a space under a pile of containers, up a red metal ladder, till I am standing right behind thick metal, reinforced hull. It rises red above me: I can't see over.

This is all my world now.

~~

That night, we move into a glowing whiteness. The sea is soft grey, the round bumps of waves rippled all over, like an eiderdown with a crumpled cover. Above it the mist muffles everything but the sun, a bright disc, its light stolen and spread through the cloud surrounding it.

Up on the top deck, I step out of the back door into the cloud. I can just make out our wake, and the birds still skimming it. I can feel the dampness of the mist, its chill.

But strange things are happening to the light. Behind us and slightly to our starboard side, there is a ring of brightness, visible and invisible as the cloud shifts about us. It is on the sea and in the air, brighter and duller, here and gone. Once it takes on the colours of the subtlest, softest rainbow, encircling us, then fading. It hovers on the threshold of the imaginary, then glows back stronger, a golden-rimmed circle.

We have sailed off the edge of the world.

NEW LAND

CHAPTER 14

FULL CIRCLE

'Ice!'

I can't see anything. I scan the horizon from left to right and shake my head. John passes me binoculars and points them in the right direction for me. 'Oh!' At first it's no more than a faint shininess in the sky. Then it becomes a white patch, floating above the surface. Only later do I work out its shape, somewhere between a stegosaurus and a dolphin, and see that it is not flying but resting on the water. I keep the binoculars trained on it, looking at the different shades of marks and scratchings. There is a bird sitting on it. The colour, bright blue-white, sets it apart from the rest of the scenery, making it other-worldly.

'Look over there! – to the right! – whales!' and when I look there are three or four, slicing through the water, their fins going up and over and round in silhouette. They dive, and I return to gazing at the iceberg. 'This is the first ice you've seen?' asks the captain, who has appeared on the bridge. 'We are going to go off course and be five minutes late, so you can look at this ice.'

But by the time I have finished admiring that piece, there is more.

After lunch, the sea is glassy like honey, and the horizon to starboard is blue-white. Bergs are floating about at a distance. A chunk of ice flat as a table passes us closer by – perfect for a bear to sit on. Over lunch I have been trying to decipher a Danish article about the polar bears that travel on the ice – two have arrived in Iceland already this year.

How would it feel to be an icebound bear? The great creak as the edge of the sea ice snapped off; the swift movement of the frozen slab away from home, faster than any bear could swim back; the realisation that the moment for jumping and swimming was long gone, that the only choice was to wait…

'Alex! – she's asleep or something…ALEX! WHALES!'

I start, grab the binoculars and cross the bridge to where one of the crew is standing and pointing.

'A minute ago it jumped right out like a dolphin.' But I am in time to see something sleek and grey and a puff of spray blown out of a blow-hole.

~~

'Hey, Alex – see that iceberg? To the right of it, look. A black silhouette. That's Greenland.'

I can't see anything: just cloud and sea.

'There – it's not a cloud or anything, it's Greenland.'

I look through binoculars but still can't make it out.

John laughs. 'A good thing I'm navigating and not you! No, look again – now! Now it's very very clear. You can see it even without binoculars. Mountains and ice.'

'There!' I exclaim, rather late. 'Mountains and ice!' A shadowy blue-black silhouette on the horizon, dark with light patches, focused through the binoculars into mountains and glaciers.

'Yup, that's Greenland. Mountains, mountains, mountains, ice, mountains.'

~

John Davis was not much impressed with his first sight of Greenland. 'The 20th,' Janes continues, 'as we sailed along the coast the fog broke and we discovered the land, which was the most deformed rocky and mountainous land we ever saw: the first sight whereof did show … in form of a sugarloaf … over the fog like a white list in the sky, the tops altogether covered with snow and the shore beset with ice a league off into the sea, making such irksome noise as that it seemed to be the true pattern of desolation, and after the same our Captain named it, The Land of Desolation.'

The creaking and groaning of the ice, drowned out for us by the refrigeration units, must have seemed as unearthly to the Norse voyagers who approached this coast for the first time.

Davis, with various ships, made two further voyages to these seas. Janes describes encounters with the inhabitants, just north of the Land of Desolation. First there are islands, then on one is found a shoe, leather and fur, then natives are spotted and halloo-ed. Through sign language, dance and imitating gestures, the groups temporarily became friends. Davis' ships left loaded with objects given and bartered for. 'We bought the clothes from their backs, which were all made of seals' skins and bird skins...' Skin canoes were greatly in demand: 'They took great care of one another: for when we had bought [one of] their boats, then two others would come and carry him away between them that had sold us his.'

'Their pronunciation was very hollow through the throat, and their speech such as we could not understand: only we allured them by friendly imbracings and signes of courtesie,' explains Janes, following up with a helpful list of vocabulary for any following voyagers. These forty words were mostly practical terms such as 'tucktodo – fog' 'kesinyoh – eat some' and 'maatuke – fish' but include, presumably for those with other, just as practical needs, 'canyglow – kiss me.'

I am not quite at such a disadvantage, but my language skills are not ideal for this trip. Again, I find myself cramming a language at the very last minute. I have a choice, because today's Greenland is bilingual. Greenlandic, some relative of the words in Janes's notes – though not a very exact one, whether through change or his inaccuracies – is still spoken. But there is a European language too: Danish.

Denmark and Greenland have a relationship that goes back a long way. A significant family of visitors arrived from Denmark in 1721. Hans Egede was a missionary with a vocation to convert the Greenlanders, who he assumed would be the Norse colonists known to him through the Icelandic sagas. He, his wife Gertrud Rasch, and his four children, with others in support, set off with provisions to found a missionary outpost. On arrival they found no Norse, but only Eskimo – Thule Inuit as they are now known. The mystery of the Norse disappearance was to puzzle scholars for years, but Egede, initially, had bigger problems. Not only did he have to survive in great isolation, and explain an entirely foreign religion, but he was faced with the challenge of doing so in a language that had nothing in common with his own. The group's efforts brought both the Bible and the Danish language to Greenland.

Denmark eventually established colonial rule and amid the complexities of that, Greenlandic had a narrow escape from extinction. But now it is not even endangered. Both Greenlandic and Danish are taught in school, and both are used in government and business. Danish is another Scandinavian language, a bit like Icelandic or Norwegian. If I tried to learn it, my English and German would help me. But – partly out of perversity, partly because it seems more appropriate to learn the native, and not the colonising language – I have decided to learn some Greenlandic.

Unfortunately, it is proving ridiculously hard. Partly, this is because Greenlandic is so little like any language I know. Numbers are one of the best ways to recognise related languages: words for one, two and three tend to be very similar. Here they are in Greenlandic: *ataaseq, marluk, pingasut*. They continue as incomprehensibly up to twelve, where Danish numbers, a little more familiar, have been adopted.

I have read up a bit about the grammar, but what I have learned is not encouraging. Presumably because of the way the language was written down when the Europeans arrived, whole sentences in Greenlandic can be written as one or two words. For example, '*Inimik attartungasaateqarpise?*' apparently means 'Do you have any rooms?' The long word – a combination of parts, each with meaning – is to be read backwards, so 'do you have' is somewhere at the end and 'rooms' at the start.

Knowing all this, I am slightly better off than the Egedes or Davis and Janes, but not much. Pronunciation is a complete unknown: place names are just a scramble of letters. Greenland is called Kalaallit Nunaat. My itinerary in order is Nuuk – the capital – then a boat journey south to Qaqortoq, Narsaq, Igaliko, Qassiarsuk and Narsarsuaq. Confusingly, Nuuk and Qaqortoq have Danish names too – Godthåb and Julianehåb respectively. Narsaq seems to have only an alternative spelling

– Narssaq. *Nuuk* means rocky headland; *narsaq* means flat place; *narsarsuaq* means big flat place. Greenlandic place names repeat, so since there are many rocky headlands there are many Nuuks, but only one is the capital.

Hopefully, I memorise two words. *Qujanaq* is thank you. *Qujanarsuaq* is thank you very much.

~~

For a while Greenland is bathed in a strip of light; then the fog returns and she vanishes. Occasionally, over the next hour, she reappears, and I stare through binoculars at curious dark cliffs and ice reaching down to the water.

We are beginning the approach to Nuuk: slightly more complex navigation, slightly more activity amongst the Deck Officers. More charts are pulled out, and the radar shows land that I can just spot outside, low dark mounds in front of the Greenland coast. A crooked, wedge-shaped mountain dominates the skyline, a lopsided triangle with its top cruelly hacked off, bleeding snow down the cracks in its sides. It is part of an impenetrable-looking coastline that seems to stretch on forever.

Colour is filtering into the landscape. The glaciers are creamy in the sunlight and the icebergs in the water blue-tinged. There are spikes on some like the points on waves. The mounds are resolving themselves into islands, browns and yellows pushing through the blue. 'Have you seen the city?' someone asks me, so I look and see grey shapes on a low slope.

The islands grow, and waves splash on brown, weathered rock. Nuuk gradually becomes three-dimensional, red patches and tower blocks visible through the binoculars. Now we are surrounded by mountains and islands. Nuuk comes into colour, red, yellow green and blue houses and five big tower blocks, coloured on one side and grey on the other. There is another cluster off to the right – 'yes, this new suburb has been built in only two, three years,' says the Chief Officer, pointing it out.

~~

A small motorboat passes in front of an island, and for a moment I grasp the scale: this is no islet but a mountain on the water that it would take a good day to climb. And it is one of many such enormous islands, worn smooth, lifeless, that rise through the water in front of the jagged coast, dark rock by dark water, empty. There is nothing alive there, only pylons occasionally breaking up the stony surface. We move past the islands, and as we come closer to Nuuk I can see grass by the houses, but nothing else is growing: there are no trees and there is no wild vegetation. I thought Iceland was barren, but her emptiness was filled with shrubs and moss. This is a flooded moonscape.

Yet – there are humans here. As we approach the port, men in Royal Arctic Line red gather at the quayside. One rides a bike across the container yard. Others move little beepy trucks, filling containers with stacked pallets. Rope is thrown and caught, and the engine's pulse slows and stops.

I realise I do not want to leave. It is not only fear of the empty landscape outside: this boat is my home now, their customs my customs, their routines my routines. The crew have supported me through seasickness and storms, shown me whales and changed the ship's course so I can look at an iceberg. Putting off leaving them behind, I stay for dinner.

A blond man with a handlebar moustache and a child comes aboard. He is chatting to the captain, and sits casually in the Chief Engineer's seat at the table. Everyone looks a bit edgy, but the visitor talks blithely on. The Chief Engineer comes in and coughs. The visitor realises his mistake and moves one seat to his left. Everyone looks a bit stressed, and worries about what the First Engineer will do. The captain saves the situation, fetching another chair so the visitor can sit without disturbing the order of seafaring life. *Landlubbers*, I think, forgetting for a moment that I am one myself.

Eventually, I put on my boots, load up my backpacks, and say my goodbyes. In the captain's office, the Chief Officer and Second Officer Kim are about to step outside, kitted out in their bright red boiler suits. I haven't seen Kim in his before and somehow the sight makes me laugh. He looks at me, got up like a turtle with backpacks front and back, and laughs too.

Clambering down from the wobbly steps, I narrowly escape being run over by a truck suspending a container in its jaws. Somehow I find the way out of the yard, onto a limp grey road. I march up it, ignoring the tears on my cheeks. I march right past the Seaman's Home, where I am meant to fetch a key. I stride all round it, looking for the way in, determinedly holding my head up and breathing deep. I wipe my cheeks and smile about the key, and refuse a taxi. I pace up the road till I find a suitable rocky outcrop, and then I sit down, propping up my pack, and burying my face in my arms.

'Sailors come, sailors go – that is the way of it,' were the First Officer's words as I sighed over having to leave. But I am not a sailor: I don't want to come and go. And I don't want to stay here either, where nothing grows and I can't speak to people and the sea is full of ice and the mountains are huge and ominous. I want to sail on forever. And I want to go home.

～～

Next morning, the sailors have gone, and I am marooned. Intellectually I know where I am: in the capital of Greenland, on its west coast, having sailed all round its southern tip and up the other side. My explorations have already started but the city is increasingly catching me out. It is not, always, that things are so very different: it is more that I never know when they will be and when they will not.

That first evening I set off across town. A dandelion was the tallest plant I could spot, and it was shorter than dandelions should be. I passed a field of white crosses, and followed two hoodies down the street. One hoody was orange, gold trainers pacing below, the other black, paired with jeans whose pockets reached to knee height.

I found my building: the tourist office has arranged for my accommodation in a B&B in Block #. A pile of junk sat outside one doorway, a pushchair outside another. I climbed the wooden stairs, admiring the graffiti. The space smelt of wood, and echoed. I rang a doorbell.

A voice: 'Wait, wait, a moment, a moment!' The door opened and I was rushed inside, nearly knocking over a tall vase by the door, much to my and my new landlady's distress. 'You like coffee? Something to drink? Please, sit down!'

In a flurry of hospitality tea and chocolate cake appeared, and I found myself in the corner of a sofa in a room full of pink candles, photographs, fabric flowers and ornaments. My landlady, I learned, spoke no English. 'I not do English in school. I speak Danish and Greenlandic – perfekt! – but no English.' She had invited over a relative to translate. My landlady was nothing but European looking, while her relative

– a sister-in-law I think – had the long dark hair and slightly rounder eyes that I supposed must suggest Inuit origins.

It took about half an hour to establish that I do not smoke, that I would always lock the door in case of burglars, that there were not many burglars, no, it was just in case, that my landlady was from Sisimiut in the North, that she had never seen a polar bear except in a zoo, that I should water the plants when she went away, just for a little while, that upstairs were some crazy young people, that downstairs they drank far too much, many people in Greenland drink far too much, that North Greenlanders were better than South.

Then the relative departed and we settled down to watch the Danish weather forecast – which included the information that it was raining in London, but nothing about Greenland – and a Danish programme about teenage pregnancy. The presenter's hair was so blonde it was almost green.

～～

I have been wandering about the town ever since. This is the list of my findings:

Day One

Smooth rocks, striped in wavy patterns, and a giant post box filled with letters to Father Christmas.

A house where washing and fish are hanging out to dry.

Children and teenagers messing around on the beach, late in the evening.

A red wooden cathedral.

A parking lot, surfaced with grey sand and litter.

Wooden walkways, paint falling off the sides, leading to not-quite-where-I-want-to-go.

Joyriders.

Day Two

UHT milk, almost making me splutter rudely as it surprises me at breakfast.

A sleek modern office.

A scheme to paint transport containers with contemporary Greenlandic art.

The supermarket: European brands, food and language but giant packs of meat.

Greenlandic shrimp, fresh from the freezer, sweet when defrosted under the tap.

Kids painting pictures on the builders' hoardings.

A rocky mound by my apartment block where I watch my shadow, sharp in the bright evening light.

A blacker shadow, a raven, flapping across the sky.

Deep ditches by the side of every road.

Unfamiliar faces: a woman who looks classically Danish in one light and not, quite, in another – but the not quite side is hard to place: an angle of the cheekbone, or darker skin or hair, or larger eyes.

An art gallery and cinema, built to sweeping modern lines.

The view, always the view, of dark snow-patched mountains and weathered islands in the blue sea.

Kids on bikes.

A coffee-bar serving burritos and lattes and fruit smoothies.

Four young men and a toothless woman, drinking beer on the grass: 'Whoa, a looooong way from home.' Her grey and white streaked hair falls dead straight from her oval, brown face. 'What you doing here? Tourist?'

A tourist shop selling sealskin boots and twisted carvings in white horn.

~~

Nuuk is defying me. I expect it to be cold: I am in Greenland, which holds one of the largest ice masses in the world. Yet the light is dazzling, and in the sun I can burn. I expect to find different customs – Greenlandic food, clothing, kayaks – but there are European supermarkets and cars. Yet something of that difference pokes through – a woman pushing a pram with a kayak paddle balanced across it, a trio of women in their national costume, their sealskin boots reaching up to furry trousers decorated with strips of coloured ribbon, and their bright tops beaded.

On the third day, accidentally, I escape the town centre. I am looking for history, a way to understand this place. I believe I am going to some old Inuit ruins. 'That way – there – there is a flagpole, you can't miss it,' says my lift.

I find another field of crosses. As I approach, they are bleak, calling up ideas of war, fields of unknown soldiers. Closer, each one has its plaque and the graves are covered with multicoloured fabric flowers. Behind the graveyard is the sea, deep dark blue, and for the first time in Greenland I hear a twitter of birds.

Scanning the ground for ruins, I find something better: life, flowers. There are great patches of a low-growing dark-leaved plant, leaves tiny and fat. Its pink flowers dare to defy the climate. There is alpine silene, little dense grey mounds of it. Lichens cover the rock surface, not the great frothy mounds I saw in Iceland but thin black or grey coats, covering the rock so its true colour is often hidden. The plants crunch, crisp and dry underfoot. Where they give out there are patches of pebbles, harder to walk on. It strikes me that this is how the Alps would look, if you flooded them above the treeline. It strikes me that this is another contradiction, living things in this barren place.

There is a school group playing on the slope, in brightly

coloured clothes, making the noise of a playground. They have written words in the stones, drawn hearts with them. I ask a teacher where I am: it is not where I aimed to be. I explore further anyway.

~~

I catch a bus. Actually, I fall flat on my face running for it, sliding on a gravely surface, and the driver waits for me. I clamber on and smile at him gratefully.

'This is a school bus.'

'Oh. Then I can't come on?'

'You are very welcome.'

The kids are small and interested and ask their teacher how to ask questions. 'Where you from?' pipes up one girl. I answer 'England' and they are silenced for a space. Then:

'Liver-pool!'

'Manche-stah!'

I nod, and the Manchester supporter, black and orange haired, gives a victory punch before I realise he's misunderstood me. 'No, London,' I admit. They look disappointed. I ask through their teacher what they like best about Nuuk. The Manchester supporter answers at great length, with many gestures and expressions. 'It is hot,' translates his teacher.

Eventually I find my ruins, between the pebbly beach, an

old red wooden building and a construction site. They consist of low wide walls, turf or covered in turf, in a grassy field. The walls make up square rooms, about my length along each of the sides. Most have a ledge across one end, which I deduce is for sleeping on. Opposite it there is a winding entrance passage, four to eight paces long. When the buildings were standing, these were tunnels, a way to let people come in without a draught or masses of cold air. Now, though, everything is open to the elements. A wind is blowing from the water, and I shelter for a while, watching the crows and listening to their cry: *crwarrk crwaark crwaark.*

~~

When I was studying archaeology, we had a seminar on 'What is a city?' Sitting in the centre of one of the largest cities in the world, we debated it – eventually rejecting the term as too rigid, too Eurocentric, destructive to a proper analysis. But before we abolished the idea entirely, we agreed that, if cities did exist, then size was important. Probably you needed at least a million people... well at least half a million then.

Nuuk has a population of sixteen thousand and you can walk across it in an hour or so. Based on our size criterion, it should not be a city. But I feel instinctively that it is. I try to work out why. There is the obvious: a national parliament. But also there are all the areas you need to make a city. There is the twee tourist part, all wooden houses (imported), there is the housing development (where I live), there is the shopping zone with supermarkets and clothes shops. There are people selling goods on the pavement. There is a trendy gallery showing Greenlandic art, and there's a café for the latte crowd. There is a University, and a community art project. There are offices belonging to one of those big companies whose name you recognise, though you couldn't say if they were accountants, management consultants or lawyers. There are old ruins that nobody is really curious about, and there are sculptures about legends nobody really knows. Old sits next to new, rich sits next to poor, beautiful contrasts with ugly, modern surrounds traditional.

Something is always changing, buildings going up and coming down, people, people, people; crowds; drifting children everywhere. Nobody planned that it should come out exactly this way, with those streets there and that part a bit posher. It just happened. Nuuk is not perfect: on the contrary the city is very conscious of its problems. Child abuse, alcoholism, low quality building, development plans that don't quite work out right, are on the lips of all the residents I speak to. There are communities that don't quite mix, immigrants from different periods, as well as ones that do. And these are all problems too big for one person to solve. But they are not all of Nuuk: there are things to be proud of too, successes as unpredictable as failures.

I think that what makes a city is this feeling that it is a living thing, out of control in ways both good and bad. It is an alive place, a vibrant place. After three days of mental onslaught, I find that that appeals to me. To my great surprise, I have come to like Nuuk.

~~

In the chaos of first impressions I have almost forgotten to look for Erik. But it is easy enough to describe Nuuk in Erik's time: there was nothing here. There was never anything Norse here and the headland must have looked much as it would today, if you scraped off the city. Rocks, a few plants, crooked mountains, islands and ocean. Further into the fjord, Norse farms made up the Western Settlement, one of the two areas of land the Norse colonised. According to the sagas, one of Erik's children later moved there: not Leif but a brother. Erik was based far further south, at the Eastern Settlement which I will visit in a few days time. In Erik's first foray, he may not even have come here.

Not only Nuuk was empty when Erik arrived. All of Greenland was unpopulated except for one corner, far to the north of where the Norse would settle. But it was a recent emptiness. Erik and his crew were not the first human beings in Greenland.

The earliest evidence for people in Greenland comes from 2400BC. Two sets of archaeological traces – two 'cultures' in archaeology-speak – turn up on different parts of the island's coastline. The culture in the North lasts four hundred years. The one in the South lasts seventeen hundred. As it fades, a new set of traces emerges in the North and persists there for three hundred years. Meanwhile, something rises again in the South.

All these traces were left by groups who came from what is now Canada: archaeologists discuss arrowheads – or lack of them – and evidence of harpoons. And after the year zero, there are no traces of human life in Greenland for over seven hundred years.

In about AD 750, something appears in the far north-west, known as the 'Late Dorset' culture. It was still going when Erik founded his Norse settlements – but so much further south it's unlikely the groups met. A hundred years after the Norse, however, another group arrived in the south. The Thule people came across the water from the West, and their descendants make up a large part of Greenland's population today. In the early days, this cultural group had dog-sleds, kayaks and umiaqs – special women's boats – and they built graves and winter houses, unlike any previous groups from the American continent. Geographically, the Thule culture has been the most successful ever in Greenland, and its traces can be found all around the Greenlandic coast.

After four hundred years, the Norse vanished, in mysterious circumstances. But later groups came from Europe. There were the whalers, from Northern Europe, who did not often settle, and then finally Danes, in the eighteenth century, who did. Missionaries first, then traders and governors settled in groups around the Greenlandic coast.

~~~

Those eighteenth century European-Inuit encounters were meetings of aliens: not alien species but alien ways of life. Each changed the other. The women of Thule started to use ribbon and beadwork on their clothes, so that the fur boots, short trousers, coats and hoods acquired a touch of bright colour. The Danish traders and officials commissioned patchworks of birdskin, used by the Thule for clothing, to hang above their fireplaces. I see them in museums, puzzling feathered rectangles that look like fur but have more patterns and deeper softness, the skins of hundreds of birds.

A whole art-form arose with a mixed-up history as Inuit *tulipak*, evil spirits, were carved multi-headed and twisted into walrus tusks for the European mantelpiece. Christianity crossed the other way, the residents of Nuuk eventually requesting – and acquiring – a proper place of worship, Nuuk's wooden cathedral.

It wasn't all happy sharing. Thule Inuit were kidnapped and taken to Europe where they were displayed as specimens. Alcohol was brought by whalers to a community that had not known it. Smallpox killed thousands, both European and Inuit. Tuberculosis was rife. Money arrived, and guns. Hunting methods shifted; resources were over-used. In 1774, Denmark declared a state monopoly on trade with Greenland: it was effectively closed off to the rest of the world.

In the 1950s there was a change of policy in Denmark. Greenland was opened up, and was to be brought into the twentieth century, to become a province rather than a colony. Money was poured in. The Greenlanders were to live in cities and settlements, to speak Danish, to have electricity, sewers and running water, to have jobs. Apartments were built, and boats carried hunting communities to the new towns. Jobs were organised, and entertainment and education. The 1950s left a redistributed population and Danish habits, but gradually Danish newspapers filled with statistics about Greenland's problems. Hunters, used to being their own masters, had been forced into working nine to five days in factories – if they had jobs. From being important members of a small community they became just like everyone else. Communities crumbled. Alcohol flowed.

Soon, Greenlanders defended their language and fought for greater autonomy. The revival of the language was a huge success: it is now controversial for Greenlanders not to speak Greenlandic. Progress was made towards independence, though more slowly: at the time of visiting, Greenland had Home Rule Government. In everything except defence and foreign policy, decisions about Greenland were made in Greenland's own parliament. Since then her independence has progressed further still. And some of Greenland's Thule past is returning, renewed: kayak clubs as the old hunting vessels become sporting vessels; the language loud, different and strong.

<center>~~~</center>

Some of the earlier Danes were curious about another cultural clash. What happened when the Thule met the Norse? What did they think of one another? In the late nineteenth century, Danish governor Heinrich J Rink, and his wife, Signe Møller, sought out and translated Thule legends in general, but asking particularly for stories of encounters between Thule and Norse.

They knew the Icelandic sagas, but the sagas don't have

much to say about Thule-Norse encounters in Greenland. In their American adventures, the Norse met 'Skraelings' and traded with them and fought them. The American Skraelings are described in Erik's Saga as 'small and evil-looking...[with] large eyes and broad cheekbones.' They have a great wish for red cloth, a fear of charging bulls and a strange weapon, a large sphere the size of a sheep's stomach that they catapult into the Norse camp. Behaviour on both sides of the encounter is bad, with unprovoked attacks and much murder, and the Norse are eventually driven away.

In Greenland, Skraelings – this time local – are referred to in a much later document, the testimony of Ívarr Bárðarson, a fourteenth-century employee of the Danish church. Ívarr declared that it must have been Skraelings who attacked and destroyed a settlement that looked recently abandoned when he visited. Later research has not supported his allegations – but the fact that he held this opinion suggests that relations were not perfect.

Rink and Møller's collection of Thule stories is just as awkward a source as the sagas: it is oral history recorded centuries after the event. As Rink and Møller observe, the same tales are told about many places, in the Americas as well as in Greenland, with only small differences. Still, there are some good stories. I like the one about the kayaker, out hunting one day, who sees a Norse tent and hears the murmuring of voices within. He goes to have a look, and beats on the side of the tent. Silence falls. He waits, then strikes the tent again. After much waiting, and puzzlement, he peers inside – and finds the Norse all dead from fear.

And then there's the one about the Inuit girl fetching water, who sees red in the reflection. Turning, she finds herself surrounded by Norse, and flees back into the house.

But fear isn't the only response that's recorded: sometimes, friendships are built, like the odd one in this story.

The first meeting of the Kalaadlit (Thule) with the Ancient Kavdlunait (Norse) in Greenland (Abridged from Rink and Møller's 1875 book, Tales and Traditions of the Eskimo)

In former times, when the coast was less peopled than now, a Kalaadlit boat's crew landed at Nuuk. They found no people and traversed further up the fjord. Half-way up they came upon a large house, but on getting close to it they did not know what to make of the people, since they were not Kalaadlit. They had quite unexpectedly come across the first Kavdlunait settlers. These likewise for the first time saw the natives of the country, and treated them kindly and civilly, but the Kalaadlit nevertheless feared them, and made for their boats. On getting further up the fjord, they found many more Kavdlunait stationed. However, they did not put in anywhere, but hastened away as fast as possible. When the boat and its crew returned from their summer trip in the fjord, they told their countrymen all around of the encounter with the foreigners, and many of them now travelled up to see them. Later on in the summer even more arrived, and the foreigners began to learn their language.

At Kapisilik a pair, one from each group, became close friends, constantly together and competing at different feats of dexterity. Their countrymen enjoyed watching the contests. As both were first-rate archers their arrows always fell side by side. One day the Kavdlunak said: 'Come, let us climb that mountain, and stretch a skin as a target on that island yonder. He who fails to hit the target shall be thrown from the cliff.' The Kalalek protested: 'We are friends, neither of us should perish!' But eventually he was forced to agree. They climbed the mountain together, accompanied by a crowd of spectators. The Kavdlunak aimed, and missed entirely. The Kalalek had his turn and pierced the skin in the centre. According to his own desire, the Kavdlunak was hurled down the precipice and his countrymen thought it only served him right for having so recklessly pledged his life. From that day until the present this mountain has been called Pisigsarfik – the shooting place.

~~

Hans Egede had a lot to say about the Greenlanders he encountered. In his book about Greenland, he described their customs: how when you go into a house you had to remove all your clothes so they could be dried for you above the fire, how you could not eat at once on arriving lest you look starved or greedy. He described their winter houses, low huts of stones and turf lined with skins, windows made of 'the bowels of seals dressed and sewed together, or of the maws of halibut... white and transparent.' Several families, he related, shared one house, each with their own room and hearth, above which burnt a great half-moon-shaped lamp, filled with train oil – whale oil. Over this was cooked the food.

'For those who are not used to this way of firing, the smell is very disagreeable, as well as by the number of burning lamps, each fed with train oil, as on account of divers sorts of raw meat, fishes, and fat, which they heap up in their habitations, but especially their urine tubs smell most insufferably, and strike one, that is not accustomed to it, to the very heart.' Washing hair in urine was another much disparaged habit.

Testament of Greenlanders' opinions of the Danes is harder to find, but Egede occasionally mentioned it, as 'when they see our drunken sailors quarrelling and fighting together, they say we are inhuman; that those fighters do not look upon one another to be of the same kind. Likewise, if an officer beats any of the men, they say such a fellow treats his fellow creatures like dogs.'

~~

The National Museum's Museumsinspectør – curator – Georg Nyegaard is already talking as he leads me through a library and up a narrow set of stairs. He fumbles with a key and then throws open a door to a room full of shelves stacked with boxes, dimly revealed under yellow light.

'There is one site that is especially interesting, called the Farm under the Sands. The remarkable thing about it is that the preservation is so good. And we have much of the material here.'

I have read about this site, which is part of the story of the Norse disappearance from Greenland. The ruins of a farm in the Western Settlement, inland from Nuuk, were frozen in the permafrost so that archaeologists found them almost intact. Even animals and insects were preserved, the insect remains showing how the farm was abandoned; different species thriving or failing as the uninhabited parts of the house cooled down. I did not know the finds were here.

'Is there anything from Erik's period?'

'Yes, or approximately: it goes back to the eleventh century. But there are indications that they were not there continuously. They left and came back.' He unwraps a bundle of bubblewrap in the corner of the room. 'This was for the animals to drink from.' It is a large soapstone trough, dark and smooth. 'And we found stools too, made from whale vertebrae.' Before I can respond to this he goes on. 'And we found an entire loom –

the upright sort.' He pulls out a piece of wood and I peer at it curiously.

'An entire loom? Why did they leave that?'

'We don't know.' He has pulled a box off a shelf, and opened it, lifting out a curved piece of wood. 'A shoe last, correct to one person's foot,' he explains. We look at carved crosses, which were placed around the room, it seems before the group left, and a carved wooden ornament: 'We are not sure what this is.'

Georg rummages further and produces a bowl of darkened wood. There is another cross, and a wooden scoop. There is a box lid with runes on the inside. Dark wood again, carved with crosses and abstract shapes a bit like fleur de lys. 'Runes are often found on what were personal possessions, labels showing who owned them. There were two items like this here. We know the names of two people, Bjork and Bardar.'

But I want to know why the people left. 'We don't know. But we did not find any traces of panic, and not one human bone in the entire site.'

He looks up from his search amongst the boxes, remembering the excavation. 'Preservation was so good… even the smell of what had gone on was there. In the cowshed you could smell cow, in the sheep barn you could smell sheep. Every week tourists came to visit by helicopter, the only way to get there, and they were very impressed by the smell – to smell history, that is unique.'

'We excavated almost all of the site but the last part the river eroded away before we reached it. That was how the site was discovered in the first place.'

'Was it the river that covered the site in sand too?'

'It seems that way.'

He shows me a strip of wood with a deep, narrow groove across one end. 'Now this is the most common find on all Norse sites with good preservation. It is part of a barrel, a stave from the side.' He shows me how a ring of staves would stand round a circular base and be bound together. 'They were bound with baleen or metal, and we found a lot of baleen on this site. Usually you do not find baleen in paces where you find bone. Bone needs non-acidic conditions, baleen acidic. But here we had both.'

'Baleen is part of a whale, isn't it?' I hold my fingers crossed, and am pleased when I'm right.

'Yes, the Greenland whale. This sort of whale has no teeth, it sort of filters the water for food, and baleen is what the filter is made of. But we do not know how they got the whale. Perhaps they killed it – it's a slow whale.' He shrugs. 'It's possible. But it might also be that they were often stranded – the population of whales was much larger then.'

The information pours over me, fascinating details that I try to relate back to Erik. He shows me a comb, small plates of reindeer antler held together with a greeny piece of bone. 'This comb is connected with lice. We had an entomologist on the excavation, and we found a lot of small louse eggs.'

Now that's a connection to have to a Viking explorer – combing for nits. I scratch my head as Georg mentions another. 'We also found quite a lot of bones of small mice – it is interesting how this small animal has followed man all the way to the remotest parts of Greenland. Even their fur was preserved.' Georg describes mice huddling by the last embers of the last, fading fire in the Western Settlement. 'Whatever happened to the Norse, it was a huge tragedy for the mice. They just died out.'

Then he tells me about Norse fabrics, some woven from the fur of the white Arctic hare, and a whole room just for weaving. We look at a basket lid. 'Willow, as far as I remember – yes, not completely identified yet but probably willow.'

'Willow grows here?'

'Dwarf willow, yes.' And he shows me where bases of barrels have been repaired. 'They were very busy during the winter, and they had a lot of time.'

There is another comb, this one single-sided with a curved back. 'Antler is a very good material for combs – it doesn't break as easily as bone.' And a small, dark knife. 'It is very seldom you find metal – they reused it. You know, the Norsemen were not self-sufficient, they needed to import. If they had to make a new boat they would import timber. And metal they also imported. Perhaps salt too, perhaps wax for church. There are big stone mortars that suggest they imported grain too – though we have never found grain or carbonised grain. We don't really know what they were using the mortars for.'

Despite his hurry to show me things, every time Georg unwraps an object he replaces it carefully, putting the box back where it came from, so the room is organised throughout. Now he walks behind another shelf, thinking.

'In a few instances, we also have something from the Inuit – the Thule. At this site we found a small comb.' He pulls out a box and shows me.

'How do you know it's Inuit?'

'The shape – it is completely different.' Its teeth are only on one side and its length is parallel, not perpendicular to them. 'On this site we found a comb, on another a piece of a bird dart – it seems that when you excavate a Norse site there is always something.'

He puts away the box. 'There were three different peoples in Greenland in the thirteenth century, you know. Three. Dorset, Thule and Norse.'

I nod. 'It seems to me that the whole history of Greenland is comings and goings, comings and goings. The Norse weren't unusual, just another group.'

'Yes, there were many immigrations,' Georg agrees. 'But then this group was the first from the other side. And the Norse saw that people had been there before. They came to an empty land, but they were arriving at a place where people had lived, people from the other direction. This is an important moment, a first for human history. It is the first time the human race had gone full circle of the Earth.'

∿

They found [in Greenland] human habitations, both in the Eastern and Western parts of the country, and fragments of skin-boats and stone implements; from which it can be concluded that the people who had been there before were of the same kind as those who inhabit Vinland, and whom the Greenlanders call Skraelings.

Ari the Learned, c.1127 (translated by Magnusson and Pálsson)

∿

Once there were two men who desired to travel round the world, that they might tell others what was the manner of it.

This was in the days when men were still many on the earth, and there were people in all the lands. Now we grow fewer and fewer. Evil and sickness have come upon men. See how I, who tell this story, drag my life along, unable to stand upon my feet.

The two men who were setting out had each taken newly a wife and had as yet no children. They made themselves cups of musk-ox horn, each making a cup for himself from one side of the same beast's head. And they set out, each going away from the other, that they might go by different ways and meet again some day. They travelled with sledges, and chose land to stay and live upon each summer.

It took them a long time to get round the world; they had children, and they grew old, and then their children also grew old, until at last the parents were so old that they could not walk, but the children led them.

And at last one day, they met – and of their drinking horns there was but the handle left, so many times had they drunk water by the way, scraping the horn against the ground as they filled them.

'The world is great indeed,' they said when they met.

They had been young at their starting, and now they were old men, led by their children.

Truly the world is great. The two friends who set off to travel round the world – from *Eskimo Folk Tales*, collected by K Rasmussen and W Worster, 1921.

～

I am walking on a wide road. A small girl in pink, dark hair swinging to her waist, is drawing a hopscotch grid across the middle of it. I pause. I am on the edge of walking onwards – I am walking in the road myself, after all, and children play all over the place in Nuuk. But cars do come this way. I have seen them joyriding, later in the day. There are other places to hopscotch. I try to talk to the girl, pointing at the parked vehicles.

She listens to me politely, and uncomprehendingly, then carries on. As I talk to her, a car steers around us. She is at least aware of them, looking up when they come. I nearly walk away a second time, but then she kneels down, crawling on the surface. She is almost invisible with smallness. I climb the steps to the nearest house, and talk to her brother, her mother, her father – finally an English speaker. I explain the obvious, that a car might come. 'She knows,' he replies, puzzled by my worry. 'They have played there before.' The kids gather round now, aware of some disturbance, some kind of trouble. I feel increasingly paranoid. 'Okay.' I smile, hoping to win back some credit. 'I just wanted to make sure.' An attempt to justify myself: 'Where I come from it would be very dangerous.'

They nod and watch me go, a stranger wandering through the streets, up the wooden walkways, away.

CHAPTER 15

LAND OF HIDDEN RICHES

The sea crumples around the islands, dark turquoise to their blacks and browns. Behind us, Nuuk is shrinking away, dwarfed by the landscape. The mountains are still rugged, stark: layers of cloud streak across some while snow makes a patchwork on others.

There are no icebergs today. On the sunny side of the boat, people are lying in deckchairs absorbing the warmth, some aiming for a suntan with their trousers rolled up to the knees. Two boys in blue hats chase each other up the side of the boat, laughing.

We come out from among the islands, and the coast becomes an endless panorama, a wild, continuous sculpture in black and white. A pair of mountains frames a fjord ahead, one steep like the nose of a shark, spiking through the water. They are a gateway to a mist-shrouded land.

For a moment, I am in the middle of an Alpine lake, bright light on blue water encircled by rock. Then the scale shifts, and this is the ocean, hundreds of kilometres of coast.

I go inside, to fetch sunglasses and suncream. This is a passenger ferry and feels very holidayish, the café full of cheery faces and the corridors hung with maps and Greenlandic art. The couchette berth I'm sharing has a porthole.

We are sailing south towards what Erik founded as the Eastern Settlement, where he and his family lived out most of their days. A town called Qaqortoq is my destination, on the outer edge of a fjord. The journey there will take a day and a half. Qaqortoq is about the fourth stop, and between stops there is nothing but wilderness.

It's coastline that has seen almost no human impact. In Erik's day, this journey was undertaken as part of a hunting trip, the *Nordrsetur*. Men from the Eastern Settlement would voyage up to the Western, and then go as far or further again to where seals and walrus and bear inhabited the beaches around Disko Island.

Walruses are animals that you wouldn't believe in if they turned up in a work of fiction. They're enormous creatures, males growing up to three metres long, and weighing up to fifteen hundred kilos, females rather shorter and half that weight – but still more than ten times as heavy as me.

They are such powerful swimmers that they can break through pack ice twenty centimetres thick. They can dive over a hundred metres in pursuit of the clams and cockles that live on the ocean floor and are their main food. At that depth, where there is very little light, they find food by feeling for it with their several hundred whiskers. They do all this in conditions of freezing cold – they may have as much as ten centimetres of blubber providing insulation just under their skin. Walruses are insulated enough that they are quite happy to sit on icebergs between dives.

Walruses feed intensively and then go for long periods – up to two weeks – without eating at all. During these periods they haul themselves out of the water at particular places – echouries – thousands of them together and, according to Molineux Shuldham, a 1775 observer, 'amuſe themſelves for a conſiderable time, till they acquire a boldneſs, being at their first landing ſo exceedingly timid as to make it impoſſible for any perſon to approach them'.

Shuldham describes eighteenth-century – and in retrospect deeply unsustainable – hunting techniques. At night, when the wind was right, blowing away from the echourie, the hunters would sneak up on their prey and attempt to make a cut through the centre of the pack, dividing the group so some were driven away from the water and killed, fourteen hundred or more in one session. It was dangerous, but lucrative. Walrus tusks are ivory, and the skins could be used for rope, at home or abroad. The fat could be boiled down for oil: one walrus produces over a barrel.

Hunting techniques in Erik's day must have been different, not least because they had smaller boats and no guns. The summertime *Nordrsetr* hunt pursued not just walruses, but polar bears and seals, but the capacity of their boats would have limited the amount of cargo they could bring home. Probably only skins and ivory were brought back, perhaps some fat: the meat was abandoned.

But the great challenge of the *Nordrsetur* was worth it for the goods. So long as the Greenlanders had ivory to sell, they were assured visits from European trading ships, so they could buy metal and other products not known locally. The *Nordrsetur* may also have been a rite of passage for men, proof of toughness. Populations of outlaws in the most northern places may have played a part too – people with less to lose were more likely to take risks.

So I am trying to imagine myself on a Viking ship full of walrus tusks and furs, coming successfully home from a hunt. As we go south, we start to pass icebergs. The first one is bright white, the shape of a church. The second is a bear lying on its side, glowing blue. The third has a chipped-off feel, a chunk of freshly cleaved chalk.

~~

This boat is mainly a pleasure boat, but I have stumbled across one group that is here on business.

'Oh, we're looking for rubies,' the guy in the cowboy hat tells me nonchalantly, as if this were a perfectly everyday way to spend time. I blink. Rubies? But their conversation is continuing, flicking from topic to topic, what to eat for lunch, whether there will be many icebergs on the voyage. It is a while before I can get a word in edgewise again.

'So how do you find rubies?'

'Oh, they're horribly awkward rocks. They form anywhere there's an igneous or a metamorphic context,' he answers. One of his colleagues, a woman in very sensible outdoor gear, black hair curled tightly on her head, chips in.

'You could make a ruby by having a bonfire on some basalt.'

'So if they're so easy to make why don't you just do that?' These guys have come from Canada and Denmark on their quest: it seems a long way for something you can make at home.

'Because they come out too even,' she explains.

'Imperfections are in fashion,' says Cowboy Hat. He's tall and tanned, pulling the hat on and off his head and turning it in his hands.

'Can't you just make them badly?' I imagine myself finding a basalt outcrop and lighting a fire – I doubt my rubies would be very even. Cowboy Hat laughs,

'Imperfections are in fashion because they show it's real. Basically they're valuable because they're rare, people want to imagine some sexy guy off prospecting, striding over the mountains...' He grins, 'But it's people like us.'

The group laughs and another woman chips in: 'I don't know, I think we're a pretty sexy team.' There's more laughter.

There are five or six of them, and others keep emerging, claiming jet lag as an excuse for napping. This woman has the look of someone in charge, and it turns out she is: while many of the team are students on a summer break, she works for the company year round. She fills me in on the basics of ruby-hunting: a three month field season, in this case twenty kilometres from the nearest settlement. The rest of the year is spent processing the information gathered.

'I was in Baffin last year,' answers Cowboy Hat, when I ask him why he's blasé about the icebergs that keep drifting past the cabin windows. 'I sat on an iceberg.'

'What were you doing on Baffin?'

'Looking for sapphires.'

I double-take again. 'Did you find any?'

'Yes! Nothing for five weeks, then – kazaam – jackpot!'

I imagine a line of geologists spread across a field, slowly walking forward, scanning the ground until someone sees a flash of blue. I know there is something wrong about this image. Tentatively, I probe it.

'So are rubies and sapphires found in the same sorts of places?' I know nothing about Baffin Island, across the water from us and somewhat further north, certainly not what types of rock are there. I wonder if it's a stupid question and am relieved when it's not.

'They're basically the same. But a ruby has chromium in.

The only difference between a ruby and a pink sapphire is the amount of chromium.'

'And a sapphire has iron in,'

'That's why they don't sparkle.'

'Rubies can sparkle.'

'Rubies can fluoresce!'

'Can rubies fluoresce?'

'But what I still don't understand,' I persist, interrupting again, 'is how you know that the rubies are in this part of Greenland, not somewhere more – more convenient!'

They try to explain. It is something to do with an intrusion, with particular types of rock meeting under pressure. The dark-haired woman puts in another explanation:

'It's a bit like baking cookies. I used to work in a museum and I'd explain to the kids that rocks were just like cookies.'

'What kind of cookies do you eat?' one of the boys interrupts. She ignores him.

'You mix all the ingredients, then you heat them and they turn into something else. You might make one sort with choc chips and one with raisins but in the end they're all cookies.'

A scoff: 'You should try to explain ion migration that way!'

The interrupter receives a withering look. But I am intrigued. 'What's ion migration?' The answer has something to do with ions moving around rocks – why, I never grasp. There is a cake parallel though:

'Chocolate chips sink in cakes.'

'Do they?' The scoffer knows less about baking than geology.

'Yes, if you don't flour them first.'

'I never flour my choc chips. But I guess I make my cookie dough really thick.'

'Yeah, it's mainly cakes that you have to do it for...'

~~

The water has turned pea-green, and is full of icebergs. Two of the geologists are arguing about whether a shape in the distance is ice or a boat. 'Most boats are red round here,' I interject, in support of ice. The object is barely visible, flat on the water, picking up its colours.

Closer, it's definitely ice, a huge sheet of it, bright white and metres thick.

'You could probably park a lorry on it,' says the guy whose hair is a blond mane. 'Nah, it's way bigger,' asserts his companion. 'You could build something on it.' He pauses. 'For a while, anyway.'

It's shedding pieces, which trail behind.

'Ow, cute, like a mother with its babies, ducklings,'

'Or like it's crapping,'

'No, that's not nearly so cute.'

They squabble amicably on. We pass mountains that rise

egg-shaped from the water, and, always to port, a continuous backdrop to this voyage, cliff and glacier and uneven, spiky mountaintops.

~~

It feels warm, but when I suck the end of my pen it's like ice on my tongue.

'Did you see any walrus on Baffin?' I ask the cowboy-hatted geologist, now sprawled in a deckchair with a novel. He looks up.

'No. I was really disappointed. I didn't see any nor did I get to eat any.'

'They eat it up there?'

'I heard they bury it for four months till it ferments and then they eat it. That's how they used to get totally hammered.'

'Who?'

'The local Inuit.'

Does everyone in the North eat rotten fishy meat? Or has someone been having him on? I try to find out when I get back, but even the internet carries no tales of rotten walrus consumption – that I can find.

~~

The islands round here are softer-profiled, the texture of the rock mimicking tightly-packed vegetation. A line of white birds crosses between two ahead. I sidle up to another geologist, leaning on a rail at the front of the boat.

'I still don't get how you are going to find the rubies. Are you just going to look?'

He turns towards me. 'Oh, it's a lot better than that,' he replies. 'We have a plan. We won't look in the same place twice. We have a grid system.'

A grid is a start...

'We use the grid, and some geophysics, and geochemistry, to decide where to drill.'

Things are falling into place now. A drill. I didn't think you could just trip up on rubies. 'Yes, it's a six hundred metre drill. Is that snow on shore there?'

I peer. We have moved into a fjord and a chilly wind has started up: the glacier-encrusted mountains are ahead now. 'They're houses, not snow!'

'No, that's snow.'

'It's red and green!'

'Oh, oh yes.' The cluster of houses comes closer as we pass more islands. At the landing stage there's a small crowd, kids sitting on a stack of pallets, families meeting the boat. I watch the geologists disembark, gathering with piles of luggage. Later one of them writes to me, describing terrain so rough they have to helicopter from the camp to work, and mosquitoes so dense that a head net is daily wear. But I think they found some rubies.

~~

After the settlement (Qeqertarsuatsiaat), we go deeper into the fjord, close between islands. We are surrounded on all sides by green and brown hillside. I lose my sense of direction until the wall of snow and grey becomes visible again to port.

We pass one island closer by. A deep weathered crack divides it in two. Recent splits are sandy beige, the surfaces gradually blackening with lichen and long exposure, the crannies growing green with moss. Below the tideline, brown seaweed clings to the rocks.

~~

The ocean is the colour of a tropical cocktail, milky turquoise in the evening light, glossy smooth. The sun is low, to starboard, behind the silhouettes of two icebergs shaped like meringues or whipped cream. A third, spiky but round at each end, looks like a two-headed floating hedgehog. On the other side of the boat, the bergs are softly illuminated, so every sharpness or hollow stands out. One is jagged, chipped, concave, an ice-encrusted broken bowl. The sky is pink-tinged, grey clouds streaking across pale blue.

~~

When I wake up we are surrounded by islands, and the sea between them is full of clouds. In the night we have passed mountains as jagged as sharks' teeth, and now, behind us, they zigzag across the horizon. Nearer, a glacier makes a flat top over the mainland.

The islands are round bumps in the water, icebergs floating all round them. One great sheet has birds perched on it, and a waterfall trickling off the side where it is melting. Another comes close, so that I can admire its chiselled, smooth-yet-rough surface.

Icebergs are even more like clouds than I realised. Each has its own distinct and astonishing shape, and the more you look, the more you can see in them: fantasy animals, twisted shapes. But if you see too many they revert to solid ice, chunks of white in the scenery, something the eye passes over without seeing. They are all different, and all the same; unique, and monotonous.

Water has the same property, but more subtly. Before making this journey, I did not imagine how many forms the sea could take. I have seen it rough and wild, churning and foaming. I have seen it slow and thick as honey, and I have seen it cut through by swift ripples. Today it is so still that the only creases in its surface are the ones we make as we pass through it, and the only froth is in our wake.

This day is made of water in every form. The sea's glassy surface keeps its depths secret, but is painted with cloud, bright white against bright blue. The painting is broken up by ice, jaggedly reflecting light. Then a tiny breeze wrinkles the water, so it goes from glassy smooth to crinkled and the reflections break into hundreds and thousands of pieces, until they are nothing but blueness.

～

We have turned into a fjord, and lost sight of the inland ice. An announcement comes over the tannoy in Danish and some of the kids, hearing it, sprint for the front of the boat. I follow them, curiously. A group of twenty or so passengers is there, looking and gesturing. The kids are on the cabin roof, pointing. A photographer is lifting his long-lensed camera over the crowd.

I have absolutely no idea what they are staring at. There is an unusually large iceberg there, but surely that didn't merit a tannoy announcement. Qaqortoq, our destination? If so, it's still too small for the naked eye.

No, there is only one sight it can be – and it is, it is! A pair of black fins slide under the water. Then nothing. Then a puff of spray, an upside-down teardrop of it, and a pause; another, further west, and a pause; another, another, another, as something large swims away out to sea, hidden from view except for this trace that its damp breath makes on the clear air.

~

And then we do see Qaqortoq. Motorboats first: one, then more. Then coloured houses come into focus, spread up the surprisingly green hillside. They are yellow, green, red and blue at first, more colours distinguishing themselves as we move closer, pinks and whites. There is one green house with a red roof. There is a marina packed with little boats. As we come closer to the harbour, passengers are waving at groups on shore, who are waving back. I join the crowd getting off the boat, and tortoise it up a short street to the tourist office.

'Your room key has gone to Sisimiut,' says the woman there, apologetically. I wait around a bit while they organise something else, eating ice cream in the town square where rickety-looking whales spout water from a wrought iron fountain. Sisimiut is not a helpful place for a room key, being about twice as far as Nuuk. But perhaps it wasn't that great a room.

The tourist office gift shop sells sealskin everything and cuddly polar bears. The lady, whose hair wrap gives her olive skin and wide eyes an African look – or at least a London current-fashion African look – offers me a bowl; in it are pieces of something dark red and slightly shiny, about the size and shape of chewing gum strips. I take one and put it in my mouth. It's chewy and disintegrates gently, such flavour as it has slightly rounded, as I would imagine very old wood to taste but without the splinters. We find a room at the hostel and I pick up my bag.

'What was that I was eating?' I ask, as an afterthought.

'That? Oh, dried reindeer with pepper.'

'It comes in other flavours then?'

'Of course.'

CHAPTER 16

SURVIVAL, SUPERMARKETS, EXTINCTION

Until last week, the ice here was covering the water, so densely packed that even small boats could not sail. *Nuka Arctica*'s helicopter survey did not lie. But now it is all gone and the town – Qaqortoq is the largest in this region – is warming up. 'There's still a bit of ice!' I protest, meaning the giant iceberg sitting in the harbour.

'Oh yes, but icebergs don't count.'

~~

As I climb the absurdly steep hill to the hostel, and rebuke myself for scorning a taxi, it dawns on me that something is different. The slopes are full of dandelion clocks, and grasses – even in a quick glance I spot two different seedheads. And there are trees! One is almost as tall as the bungalow it stands next to. There even seems to be a garden centre, or somewhere selling plants in little pots outside a yellow cottage.

The water is fertile too: in the café in the square you can eat locally-caught catfish. I sit and flap my guidebook at the swarms of mosquitoes. Two guys are drinking coffee at another table, and they turn to talk to me. They are strangers too. They are from Norway.

'We are here for three weeks. We are putting up satellite dishes. For internet.'

'But they already have internet.'

'But this will be better. Faster.'

They spend their days in different places, transported by helicopter, climbing poles, fitting satellite dishes, connecting Greenland to the rest of the world.

'Where in Norway are you from?'

'Jaeren. In the south.'

'Mm, I know Jaeren.' Suddenly they become more interesting. They are both bearded but the speaker is slightly younger, broad-shouldered, blond with a long ponytail. He laughs when I tell him about my quest. 'You know, I am from Norway and I don't even know where Erik the Red came from.' I roll my eyes. 'From Jaeren.'

'Oh! But I am from Jaeren.'

'Mmhmm. Exactly.'

~~

You can climb right up the slopes behind Qaqortoq, and look into the next fjord. That evening, I sit high on a weathered lump of grey rock, looking down at the still, dark water and the white specks of icebergs. A huge island, an isolated strip of mountainside, stretches along the fjord, reddening in the sunset. Beyond the island are more mounds of land, behind them a snowy panorama lit up by a streak of light in the sky.

Softly and far off, something explodes: I think it is an iceberg. There is a gentle slosh of water, and distant birdsong, high and sweet, *pweet-o-wee-o, pwee-o, pwee-o, pwee-o*, occasionally rising in hysteria to a fast, trilling, *poreeoporeeo, preepoporeepo eepo*.

The island gets redder and redder, and the sky fills with rich purpley grey. Light catches the rocks where I'm sitting: I don't feel cold though my pen, again, is like ice on my lips.

It is time to turn for home, but instead I find myself walking up and along the slope. There is a line of cairns marking a very vague route: I decide to walk to the next. I want to see round the corner of the island, find out what lies behind it. The light is getting more and more glowing. I am high in the world, alone with the sunset and the wildness and the hugeness of the landscape. Another cairn. This is foolish but glorious. There is no path, and I am stepping from rock to rock, crunching on frilly-edged black lichen and on juniper. The birdsong is louder, the light brighter. Above the mountains, pink clouds float on the darker corners of the sky. Against the sunset, a square cairn is silhouetted above me. Just one more.

The rocks get bigger and further apart, the juniper deeper. I step into a gully, and realise that the other side is steep, two or three times my height. The cairn stands frustratingly above it. There is nothing for it but to pick a route downwards. I turn, and catch pink on the distant snow, mountains glowing. Then the sunset explodes, pink clouds turning purple, dark against shades of gold and orange.

The light is fading now. Very carefully, and as fast as possible, I walk back to the path. As I reach the first houses, the glow of the sunset is reflected in the harbour and in the town's lake. I sit on some wooden steps and watch the lights come on across Qaqortoq, a few at a time, spots of streetlights and windows. Walking back through town I pass roving teenagers, music spilling from speakers.

When I get back to the hostel, the chocolate in my bag is frozen solid.

～

One day I stretch out on a rock in the middle of town to eat my sandwich and am joined by a dog whose white fur curls like a lamb's wool. He objects to me and barks, loudly. A lady appears, long blonde hair loosely plaited, and explains he does not like strangers. Then:

Traveller: Is he from round here?

Lady: No, in fact we imported him from Denmark.

Traveller, in astounded tones: How?

Lady: My mother was coming to visit and there were no economy seats so she came business class. He sat in his box on the arm of her seat, happily all the way. He was just a baby then of course.

Traveller, still astounded: Is that common, to import dogs from Denmark?

Lady: Actually, legally it is the only way to get a dog. It is illegal – well, every female dog south of the Arctic Circle must be sterilised. It is because they are worried – the dogs north of the Arctic Circle are working dogs, sledge dogs, and they must not lose the purity of the breed. So – maybe farmers have an exemption to breed sheep-dogs. But that is the law. In reality you get all sorts of crossovers. But it is quite normal to import dogs.

So far, I have discovered that Greenlanders import food, houses, cars, clothes, cleaning products and – now – dogs. And I am sure that is not all of it. It is not that other countries don't import anything: on the contrary. But Greenland is so far, and the ratio of imported to home-grown is so high that you have to wonder what would happen if, one year, the boats and planes stopped coming.

~~

Ever since arriving in Greenland, I have felt slightly wrong about my Viking quest: superficial, touristy. It is a bit like looking for the ruins of British history in France: not impossible, but missing the point. And the more I see hints of it, the more I am curious about the Thule past. One place where I can spot it – almost - is the carvings, in bone and tusk and soapstone, displayed in the museums and sold to tourists.

These are detailed, twisted shapes, monsters with many eyes and teeth, or bird feet and beaks, hand-sized or finger-sized, fitted to the shape of their parent material. Carving ornaments is not particularly a Thule tradition – this art form came out of the meeting of Danish and Thule. But many of the carvings draw on Thule mythology.

Particularly, they draw on the tradition of the *Tupilak*. This vengeful Greenlandic ancestor spirit was traditionally called on by a shaman. The story is that the shaman would enchant a pile of bones, often together with the skull of a child. The resulting weird creature would be sent out to sea before being called back to kill an enemy. But if the enemy had greater powers than the *tupilak*'s parent it could be sent back to murder its creator. Either way, mission fulfilled, the *tupilak* would dissolve.

Not all spirits in Greenlandic mythology are murderous, nor were shamen seen particularly as evil. But it seems that it is these malicious spirits that are most often represented.

I take a particular liking to a many-eyed, beaked, duck-footed monster on display. Each line of fur is carefully placed, and the webbing on the left foot stretches wide between the bones. It is by Aron Kleist, born in 1923 and – with his daughter Cecilie – one of Greenland's most famed artists. Aron was a hunter for many years, before tuberculosis disabled him. He then took up carving using a multitude of tools but mainly a dentist's drill to make those very fine lines.

~~

'Ahh, Alexandra, and I thought you were learning something!'

In the breakfast room at the hostel is a whiteboard, normally used for messages. This morning, it is covered with Greenlandic words, and my landlady is conducting a lesson. Unfortunately, she is doing so in Danish. I have listened attentively for a while and fooled her into thinking I understand (I do – about a word in ten). But now I have asked a question that shows that, after all, I have been missing the point. We start at the beginning again. Everyone else goes back to eating their breakfast.

In fact, Heidi has already given me one Greenlandic lesson. Having got nowhere with my ill-pronounced words in Nuuk, I demanded that she teach me how to say q, a sound that emerges from somewhere round the tonsils and is a crucial part of *qujanaq*, thank you. It's a challenging. You make a U-shape with the back of your tongue, holding it as far back in your mouth as possible. Then you relax the front. Then you try to make a sound somewhere between an H and a K, and the edgy, throttled noise that emerges is somewhere near correct. 'Well done!' says Heidi, as I manage, on my second attempt, not to splutter or swallow my tongue. 'Very near – just keep practising.'

Today, I have realised that it's about rhythm and emphasis as well as strange sounds – although knowing that j is like y and how to say q does help. *Qujanaq* is emphasised *Qu*janaq. There are four new words on the board: Aj*u*ngilaq, *Aj*or*poq*, Ta*kuss*, Si*la*.

'Good, bad, see you, weather. The important words. *Ajungilaq* you can use to say okay, that is okay, food is okay, weather is okay... or if it is not, say if your leg is broken you point to it and say *ajorpoq*.' She demonstrates. 'You can do a lot with these few words. And I think it is helpful to learn them.' She looks at me rebukingly. 'Not everyone speaks English.'

I have another question. 'How do I say *one of those please?*' I think this is the most useful phrase in any language, especially coupled with thank you. I want to be able to point at things and ask.

'*Una*' she replies, emphasising the first syllable. And there is not really a word for please. 'It is body language. Smile! The politeness or rudeness comes from your body language.'

But I am closer to the Norse here than I was in Nuuk. A pair of letters, the last known contact between Norse Greenland and Europe, confirm that a wedding took place in this area on 16 September 1408, between two stranded Icelanders. According to the letters, the congregation was full when the banns were read out, three Sundays in succession, and the church where it took place was called Hvalsey. Hvalsey is just around the corner from the island I admired last night, an easy boat ride from Qaqortoq.

Stepping ashore, a dry, dusty, herby scent says sheep to my nose. And the grass is clipped, full of white, tiny, starlike flowers. The birdsong I heard last night is louder, *poree-poree-poree-poree* and there is another sound, between a tap and a cheep. It seems to come from a snow bunting, a sparrow-shaped, black and white bird. Several are perched on rocks, little bothered by us.

We (myself, a travelling photographer and our captain) follow a sheep-path up to the ruined church, whose stones match the landscape. As we come close three shaggy-coated sheep erupt from inside, *maa*-ing frantically. The photographer pursues them. I step, alone, into the church.

I disturb another sheep, an elderly ram who gallops unevenly off, leaving a strong scent behind him. The sheep have been using this as a shelter, and as a result the grass is greener. The walls are of cut stone, the doors neat, the window in the east arched and full of sky.

I stand still, breathing in the calm. The views through the two doors are of sea and meadow, brightly lit on a day when the sun is dazzling. I think for a moment about that wedding: two Icelanders, a church filled. I pause.

It is something about the placing of the windows, high in the walls, and the care taken over the masonry. Inside this building, six hundred years old, I know where East is, and I know which way the congregation faced. I don't know if they sat or stood, or how the place was decorated, but I know the gist of some of the prayers they said. There is a shared tradition between this building and the church I stood and sat and sang in at Christmas and Harvest throughout my childhood.

Outside again, I pick up some sheep's wool and try to find the ruins marked 'eleventh century' on my map. But they are just a pile of rounded rocks, roughly building shaped, full of bushes, birds calling to each other across them. It is enough that somebody settled here, maybe in Erik's time or not long after. I am drawn back to the church.

～

The disappearance of the Norse in Greenland came as a shock to those back home. Egede knew that the whalers and explorers who came before him had not encountered any Norse Greenlanders, but he hoped that, with thorough searching, they would be found. But all there was to see was empty stone buildings.

Theories abounded. Dominant for many years was that of Eskimo violence: perhaps the Eskimo had killed off the Norse, raiding and slaughtering at their settlements. But there was no evidence for this beyond odd remarks about Skraelings in ancient texts, and Thule mythology didn't give a picture of bad relations. Perhaps, then, there had been an epidemic disease. Perhaps a cooling of the climate had frozen the population out. Perhaps...

In the 1920s, the debate was reignited when investigations of some graves in the Eastern Settlement produced bodies wrapped in extremely well-preserved clothes. These were woven woollen garments, including hoods with long peaks falling well below the shoulders. Nørlund, the leading archaeologist, dated these costumes to the fourteenth and fifteenth century: carbon dating has since confirmed that they are not later than 1450.

The clothes were made in Greenland but according to European fashions, showing that even so late in the colonies' history, that connection mattered. This deduction led to theories that the Norse froze to death through choosing European woollens over warmer furs, a cold refusal to adapt to their climate.

Another theory was starvation. The Norse might have worn down their landscape with over-pasturing of sheep, not understanding the delicacy of the soil. Their hay, according to one 1930s theory, might all have been eaten by a plague of caterpillars. A mini Ice Age might have made agriculture unfeasible.

A third group of theories involve abduction and abandonment. One Thule Inuit story tells of a time when the Thule and the Norse were friendly, and the Norse were worried about raiders. One day they asked the Thule to take away their children, just in case. The Thule did so – and when they returned a while later, the village was empty, boats just vanishing. A European explanation of this story was that fifteenth-century pirates kidnapped the Norse settlers and enslaved them: English, Basque and Moorish ships have been accused. The problem with this theory is that the dates don't quite match – they are fifty years too soon.

Another set of explanations blame Europe. As the weather got colder, the voyage to Greenland got harder, with longer winters and more ice blocking the route in the spring. The Black Death had taken hold back home: survival was a struggle there even without extras like voyages to Greenland. The main Greenlandic export was walrus-tusks, a luxury item less popular in times of crisis – and as the Crusades reached further East, superior elephant ivory became easier to procure anyway. Large gaps are recorded between official voyages to Greenland. Notably, nobody was sent to replace the last bishop, who died in the 1370s. Letters took years to arrive. The lack of contact could have led to a decline in lifestyle and to more emigration when the opportunity arose.

Today's theories combine many factors. Agriculture was risky, and the Norse never learnt Inuit hunting techniques that might have got them through difficult times of year. Leadership, cold, caterpillars, a free ride to America, piracy, employment on a cod-ship, are all allowed a possible role. Scholarship abounds. To summarise, the disappearance of the Norse was originally a mystery because nobody could work out what had happened: now it is a mystery because everyone has a different idea. But these ideas, together, might paint a picture somewhere near the truth.

~

'I don't think it was climate change that drove the Norse out.'

Kenneth Høegh, of the Agricultural Research Institute, grew broccoli here last year, and the stories in the papers were all about global warming benefiting South Greenland. For some, it's the reverse of the Vikings' disappearance: if the cold weather drove them out, this new weather should make for a life of ease and plenty – make Greenland greener. But Kenneth is not happy about the warmer temperatures.

'We are having a drought! We average seventy-five millimetres of rain in June but this year we have had five. All the tourists say how it's such a wonderful sunny place but I am worried.' He frowns. 'If it does not rain all through July, many farmers will have to buy in extra fodder for the winter. And grain prices are high.'

Apparently it is not as simple as warmer-better. The climate in this area switches between sub-Arctic (sunny, cold and dry) and Atlantic (cool and wet) depending on the wind direction. One is better for tourism, the other for crops. Drought is one of the main challenges of farming here – that and economics.

'We're working on beef – beef and milk. They used to have cows here, from the 1780s. But they disappeared in the 1970s. Today we have around forty, and we're trying to make it commercial – maybe a mini dairy, but there are some difficulties. Or we might sell direct to the customer. You can buy fresh milk in the shops here, flown in, forty krone a litre… we could undercut that.'

Four pounds. Ouch: about six times home prices, not to mention the environmental consequences. Though the thought of fresh milk is making me salivate.

'Why did the cows vanish in the first place?'

'Oh, the Danish government were giving out free, or subsidised, powdered milk.'

355

Kenneth Høegh's problems are not the ones I expected: the cold winters, thin soil and erosion. When I ask about those problems he shrugs them off. 'You should not graze the land all through the winter. And it is possible the Norse did that. But we don't.' Something dawns on me.

'You don't think it's that hard to live off the land here, do you?'

He looks at me in surprise. 'No. No, not really.' He pauses. 'If I were to live here only on what I could produce, it would be seal and milk. Milk from goats, sheep, cows – there is plenty of vegetation. And the sea. You can even put seal fat on your hay if there is not enough – I read about it the other day. I don't know if they did it here, of course.'

I suggest that strategy for this year's crops, rather than importing grain. He laughs. 'The economics of that doesn't work these days, I'm afraid.'

～

A river runs through the town. Three kids in wetsuits are surfing down it, with mixed success, on giant pieces of polystyrene packaging.

～

In the museum are three kayaks, displayed one above the other, each with a pile of accessories on top. The accessories puzzle me: inflated bags and string threaded with rectangles of wood alongside what must be a harpoon and line. The kayaks themselves are objects of beauty. Dry skin is stretched taut over wooden frames, evenly pale along the length of the boats with a circular hole at the top to let each kayaker sit inside.

Propped in the corner there's an even stranger object, inflated and nearly triangular, about a metre long. 'It's a bag,' says the museum attendant, cheerfully translating the label for me. 'It's made of three sealskins. From the old days.'

'How long ago were the old days?' I ask. She's younger than me and clearly doesn't remember them.

'About a hundred, a hundred and fifty years ago they started to build houses like this building.' Before that, there would have been houses like the ruins I saw in Nuuk in winter, and skin tents in summer. 'In the nineteenth century.'

Two boys are looking around too, in their teens or early twenties. One makes a remark, gesturing at a kayak, before leaving. The attendant translates. 'He says that that kayak belonged to his grandmother's father.'

She continues:

'Young people like me, we do not remember any of this. We have not used any of these things.' Her gesture takes in the kayaks, the anoraks made of animal stomach, the whale

357

oil lamps. 'Greenland has changed so much even in fifty years. We have everything now – internet, TV, and we just go to the supermarket. It is a totally modern society.'

I ask about how people survived before the 1950s, in this area. It isn't the stereotype of Greenland, sledge dogs on the ice: they don't have that this far south. 'I know supply ships came here for a long time, but they weren't once a week.'

'No, maybe once a year,' she agrees. 'There was sheep farming, and they grew what they could, potatoes and another vegetable, kvan, and rhubarb for some vitamins – and fish, and seal. But then it all changed.'

'It must have been quite a shock for those people. How do they cope?'

She thinks for a moment. 'Well, my grandmother is eighty-two, she has TV, she uses the internet, she uses her mobile... well, she does not text, but... I think she is happy with it all!'

I ask about the objects sitting on the kayak. She fetches someone else, a man born a few decades earlier who might remember.

The explanation is in Greenlandic and I watch the attendant's expression change to astonishment, to disbelief and to astonishment again as the man puffs and gestures, miming blowing into something, repeating the mime as she fails to understand. By the end I am bubbling over with curiosity. She struggles to translate:

'They are for putting in the seals, like – oh, I don't know – I don't know the word – when you have a bottle of wine.' She mimes a corkscrew.

'A cork?'

'Yes! You harpoon the seal and then you blow into it through the hole.'

'Just straight into the seal?'

'Yes, wherever you have harpooned it. And it inflates and then – pop! – you put in one of these. And the seal floats behind the kayak.'

So a kayaker could bring home several seals, floating behind the boat.

'They knew what they were doing.' Both the attendant and I are impressed.

~~

Down by the harbour, there is a shed. In front of the shed are two tables. On the first table is a mound of green, leafy stalks, a bit like celery or rhubarb. On the second are, from left to right: seal ribs, dried, bony ridges of brown meat; bags full of shreds of other dried seal meat; and see-through bags full of very pale pink, smooth squares of blubber, like the fat you find under pork crackling but several centimetres thick.

In front of the table, a heavily moustached, dark-skinned man in overalls is packing more blubber. Slowly, carefully, he turns a bag inside out and puts his hand in. Thus gloved, he stoops to the bucket full of blubber at his feet, picking up two or three squares. They have the floppy quality of raw salmon steaks. Around them, he turns the bag the right way out, and scoops over some liquid from the bucket. The whole thing is put in another bag. Both are tied.

I go inside the shed, to where the tables are metal and shiny. Fish are spread, silvery, on one. On the other is a fresh seal, spread out in all its component parts. I can tell it is the remains of one seal in particular because its head is there, at the far end, eyeballs and sealy nose still in place, the rest red, bloody. I expect someone will buy it: I think the liver has already gone. The rest of the meat is dark, almost black.

The thing is, I have to try some of this meat. Evidence from Norse sites includes a lot of seal bones: it is pretty certain that they were eaten. And the species that are hunted here are not endangered: I checked. I have no excuse. I approach one of the men standing around outside, and gesture at the dry meat, and the green stuff.

'Is that seal?'

He doesn't really speak English but he gets my drift. 'Seal, yes, very big seal.'

'And I just eat it?' He looks puzzled. I mime putting it to my mouth. He nods violently, and mimes more enthusiastically, pointing to the dry brown stuff and then to his open mouth. 'Yes, yes.' He moves to the pile of leaves and stalks and mimes again. 'Eat, eat.' He beams at me, points at the blubber and does the same.

The idea of biting into a piece of blubber is not appealing in any way. But my friend, who had walked away a little, has returned with two green stalks. He hands me one, and bites into the other himself. 'Eat, eat.'

'Oh! Um, *qujanaq*,' I say, and bite as well. It crunches. It is very like celery: less stringy and more aniseedy, watery and slightly sweet. On a later occasion I try a piece that is bitter, but today's I like. '*Ajungilaq!*'

He looks puzzled, and thinks for a while before understanding me. 'Ah, *ajungilaq!*'

~~

I crunch it for a while, and then watch him buy a bag of dried seal and one of blubber. Again he mimes: eat, eat. He takes the bags away and sits down on the bench against the wall of the shed. It seems to be where the men sit.

I approach the stallholder, still packing blubber, smile at him hopefully and point at the dried meat. 'Um, *una*? Er, very small, tiny.' My hands are explaining the size of piece I want.

To my amazement he understands, and I leave with a shred of meat.

Down by the water is a step, perfect for examining mysterious foodstuffs. This piece is dark brown, almost black, fibrous. The fibres are thick and aligned, but twisted. I tear a clump off and the tear is red. In my mouth, it is chewy, sea-smelling, otherwise much like the reindeer was, woody and thick.

As I sit chewing a boat draws up. A thin, dark-haired lady climbs out and looks amused to see a tourist chewing seal. '*Smag god?*' she asks. '*Ja!*' I answer boldly, gambling that I understand her. When the lady finds I'm from London she is even more amazed. 'And you like it?' I nod. 'I'm just getting up the courage to try seal blubber,' I explain.

'Why not? It will not kill you!' She's right, but I am going to sit here a moment longer. The thought of it is still making my stomach anxious.

She walks off, only to return two minutes later. 'You want to try seal blubber?' She has a bag, and one piece in it. Now there is no choice. 'I'll just get a knife.'

She emerges from the cabin with a proper local woman's knife, curved blade and wide handle supporting its centre. She pulls the fat out of the bag. Up close it really is that: a lump of wobble. With the knife she scrapes off the thinnest of slivers, handing it to me on the tips of her fingers. I sniff it cautiously.

It smells foully fishy, but under her gaze I cannot back out. Reluctantly I put it on my tongue. It tastes of – nothing. Nothing at all. Perhaps there is a fishy edge to the nothing, but the main sensation is of texture: it is like eating oil.

'And you eat this for a snack?' I ask, still not understanding.

'No, no!' She is vastly entertained. 'No, we eat it with dried meat, or fish, or this,' nodding at my seal.

Suddenly I get it. This is Arctic margarine.

~~

I am watching myself naturalising. Over the last few days I have eaten musk ox (very good, like beef but subtler), guillemot (fishy, tough meat but not bad); ammassat (tiny dried fish, smaller than sardines, eaten whole after peeling off the fins), seal, seal blubber and that green aniseedy stuff, finally identified as kvan, angelica. Before this week, seals and guillemots were just wildlife, and angelica came crystallised in small, emerald cubes for decorating cakes.

It is more than just food. Standing in that hut, looking at the seal's head, I felt no particular revulsion. It didn't seem grotesque. It was just a seal head, with meat from the animal around it. I took a tour of the local tannery, and the piles of furs stored in vats of saline had no power to upset me either.

In the tourist office gift shop, there are cuddly seals, great squishy things perfect for bestowing upon five year olds. One sits cheerfully on top of a pile of sealskins with another skin draped over its back. In England, you might just possibly do that with a sheepskin – but with seals? The sight would have a lot of people in tears. Here, nobody looks twice. And I can't work out what I feel.

If you fed cows on seal-blubber-soaked feed, I wonder, *would the milk taste of fish?*

CHAPTER 17

A BOUNCY VIKING SHIP AND
A WALRUS-TUSK CHESS-PIECE

In the sagas, Erik explored these fjords thoroughly over his three years of exile.

He spent the first winter on Eiriks Island, which lies near the middle of the Eastern Settlement. In the spring he went to Eiriksfjord, where he decided to make his home. That summer he explored the wilderness to the west and gave names to many landmarks there. He spent the second winter on Eiriks Holms, off Hvarfs Peak. The third summer he sailed all the way north to Snaefell and into Hrafnsfjord, where he reckoned he was further inland than the heart of Eiriksfjord. Then he turned back and spent the third winter on Eiriks Island, off the mouth of Eiriksfjord.

Qaqortoq is at the very outermost edge of the area that is described here, the fjord complex where Erik founded the Eastern Settlement. Close to the open sea, it is more about seals than sheep, more about Thule than Norse. I have been pausing, on the brink of plunging into the fjords. And even now, as I am about to set out across the water again, my plan is to meander, not to race. Today, I will go to the mouth of Erik's fjord. Then, bit by bit, I will travel inland, exploring each place, town or wilderness, peering out into other fjords. I will stop when the opportunity offers, at Narsaq, Igaliko and finally Qassiarsuk, the modern-day identification of Brattahlid, Erik's homestead.

Before setting off, I sit on the sculpture by the harbour, and read the sagas through again. It strikes me that neither is very focused on Erik. He is almost taken for granted – given a few matter-or-fact pages and left. Erik's Saga devotes far more space to Christianity – Leif's adoption of it and conversion of the Greenlanders, the rising of ghosts from graves to demand proper Christian burial, the pilgrimage of Greenland's first nun. The Greenland Saga is about the Vinland adventures – the first sighting and the various discoveries – and the conflicts of Erik's children, rather than Erik himself.

Perversely, this makes me more confident that Erik existed. If these writers were so uninterested in him, why would they have bothered to make him up?

～

The boat shoots off at a great pace, leaving a v-shaped wake and disturbing some sea-birds which fly up all around us. Qaqortoq disappears with rapidity, my last glimpse just a smear of colour on the hillside before it is hidden behind a lump of rocky island. I move, with some difficulty, to the front of the boat. The skipper urges me inside but I am rolled up in too many layers of clothing. My coat blows open in the wind and my hair, getting thick and sticky with salt, prickles my face.

We slow, and turn, lurching over two or three waves. The view has changed. We have gone between islands and emerged in a fjord, a narrower place than around Qaqortoq. It has a population of small icebergs. Mountains surround us on all sides: some may be islands, some fjord. We turn further and go deeper. Ahead is an absurdly-shaped mountain, a blue-grey lump rising from the sea.

Around us, the land is green. Now I can spot Narsaq, a scatter of habitation. That means the fjord to the right of it is Erik's fjord, and on my left now, as we approach it, is Erik's Island. It is steep-sided, green with moss and grass. I try to imagine it in winter, thick with snow and surrounded by ice. There is ice still now, but not winter ice, bergs from the glaciers further up the fjord. We weave a wiggly path around them.

Some of the icebergs are melting. In the harbour, one sits wonky-profiled and full of holes, making a sound like rice crispies crackling as air escapes from the dampening bubbles. The skipper kicks it: it's slushy, and bits fly off in sloppy curves.

I dump my bags, and set off to explore. The town, about a third of the size of Qaqortoq, is spread across two peninsulas, either side of a bay. On top of the narrower peninsula is a mound with a flagpole, perfect for surveying. To sea is Erik's island, and water full of ice. On land, behind the scattered houses, a single green mountain rises from nothing to two square tops. From the saddle, a stream falls steeply into the main bay, where it is bridged and where a few groups of children are messing around.

~~

My first exploration takes me down to the beach. I am stalking icebergs, going where they are close to the shore. Remembering the cowboy hatted geologist and his story of sitting on one, I am hoping at least to touch one. One bobs near the shore, and it leads me to two others, a beached pair sitting on the pebbles.

The first is ring-shaped, the second squat. Both are glassy and shrunken, about the size of my small backpack. I stroke one: it is like textured glass, smooth but dimpled, mottled with hollows. I turn it over, laying it flat on its back on the pebbles.

Peering at the second berg, I realise that one part of it is patterned inside, a mesh of surfaces, crystal faces touching each other. The crystals are hexagonal or square, not always even, the pattern sometimes broken by smooth continuous ice or clouds of bubbles. But the crystalline part is intriguing. I can put a fingernail in the gap between two hexagons, pushing them apart, or gently knock the berg and cleave one off, making a geometrically near-perfect ice cube. One trio of crystals meets at a perfect three-way junction, each a 120° angle.

Looking closely at the cleaved-off ice cubes, I find that the crystal surface is slightly wrinkled, presumably where, in a warmer moment, something has slowly melted and refrozen. It is a very fine texture, barely apparent: otherwise the surface is smooth. As the cube – not a cube at all, but part of a hexagonal prism – melts in my fingers, I pop it into my mouth. It crunches between my teeth, the taste cold and clean.

The berg floating a few metres away is bigger: about my size, which is minimal for an iceberg. All but two small peaks sit below the surface. As I watch, the wake from a motorboat reaches the cove, and the berg shudders. A piece of ice breaks off. The berg hesitates, then turns slowly, rocking a little. It emits a couple of pops, then settles down.

Wondering if I'll find more crystals, I return to the one I turned over. Lifting it, I find the underside covered in grit. It won't brush off: in the last fifteen minutes, each piece has moulded a perfect hollow for itself in the ice. I imagine it must be because of some combination of warmth and pressure: it dawns on me that this easy fitting of itself to the ground is a part of how ice erodes landscapes so powerfully.

Later in the evening I walk further round the coast, through knee-deep grass and bushes, to the ruin of a Norse building. It is no more than an outline of walls in the grass, but the sign tells me that parts of it date to 985 AD: one of the first settlers started farming here. Finds – not necessarily from 985 – include a chess piece, and a runic poem. Here, I think, staring dreamily across the cove, lived one of Erik's neighbours. Erik must have visited. He must have explored this point on his first trip too, a good harbour, right opposite Erik's Island.

I walk on. Beyond a mossy stream and more meadow, the coast gets rocky. I sit on an outcrop, watching another iceberg, hoping it will explode. It does not, but a little fish wriggles around below me. The bergs round here are deeply textured, forked all over, some with swans' heads jutting upward. The sloshing of water echoes hollowly inside them. There are pops and gurgles: one time I hear a crash and turn to see water spurting from ice, but the sun is directly behind it so I am dazzled and turn away, blinking. As the sun gets lower, the icebergs stand out more and more against the dark water, gently glowing. On the beach, they are getting stranded by the tide, white visitors to the grey and brown shore.

~~

'Una?'

I score a Danish pastry with an apricot filling. The lady tells me what I assume is a number and I hand her what I know is an excess of money. I mould my tongue into a U and push it back in my mouth.

'*Qujanaq!*'

The standard response to *Qujanaq* is entirely unpronounceable: something like *ith-lith-lieu*. But she says it, as she hands over my change, and I cheer internally: my first conversation entirely in Greenlandic.

No mocking: three words is three words.

~~

I am looking for a lady called Rie Oldenberg. She is to be found, I know, at the museum, and I hope she'll be able to tell me about Vikings and about plans for tourism in this area. But the museum doesn't open until 1pm. I sit on a stone by the harbour and watch the boats going in and out and a raven flapping across the slope, and I write a letter home.

It is impressive that there is a museum here at all. There are less than two thousand people in Narsaq, just a scatter of coloured houses surrounded by mountains and sea. In the museum, there is a photo of a lady fetching water with a yoke and buckets. One of the yokes is on display, used only forty or fifty years ago. Running water only reached Narsaq in the 1960s.

As it turns out, Rie is not at the museum, but at the community centre, at the eye of a whirlwind of activity. All the children in the village seem to be here, playing on bouncy castles, swings and an old ship, faces painted gaudily. Music plays from a ghettoblaster somewhere in the grass. The best bouncy castle, the one with the longest queue, is an old-fashioned ship. I pursue Rie through the café, where I have just missed her, down the stairs, past a room full of Norse artefacts and reconstructed costumes and a grindstone – where she vanishes. Just as I am reading about local finds, I hear a footstep and, turning, almost walk into a brightly dressed, light haired lady.

She is expecting me. 'But you have come at a busy time!' It is a festival they have every summer for the children. 'And each year we have a theme. This year it is the Vikings. You see, we had this opportunity for an inflatable ship…this boat bouncy castle was specially made. It was going to be a pirate ship, but then we decided it should be Vikings instead. Only it still seems to have some pirate elements. There is a strange dragon on the prow, but the Vikings are a bit piratical.' She pulls a face. 'It is a slightly cross-bred ship!'

They are painting faces and making masks today, weaving tomorrow, writing in runes on Wednesday. I arrange to see Rie in the morning, and she lends me a whole stack of books to read before then. 'Homework!' she says, cheerfully.

Fair enough.

I follow a gravel road gently upwards towards the main fjord – Erik's fjord. Part-way, a bench offers a view back over the settlement. I consider settling down there with my work, but the path onwards is too intriguing: I follow it instead.

Soon, the landscape flattens out. Rounded stone stretches to the water. Long before it, a small lake fills one hollow in the rocks, and there is a scattering of low plants: otherwise, emptiness is all around.

As I walk into nowhere, a taxi bowls out of it, bumping and scraping. It races past me, and the figures in the back wave frantically: then silence returns.

I sit on a knoll and pull out my books. Part of my homework is to read the excavation report from the farm site I explored yesterday evening. I flick through cautiously. It's in the usual format: a summary of the excavation, space by space, then specialist sections on the bones and objects of different materials that were found.

The animal bones expert explains that most of the bones were from seal and domestic animals such as cows and goats, though there were also a few pieces of walrus, whale, caribou and bird bones. Most interestingly there were polar bear phalanges – the finger and toe bones, suggesting that the bear had been killed elsewhere and skinned, these tiny bones transported with the skin.

I go on to read about fabric. Pieces of cloth were found at

this site – unusual, as cloth tends to rot away – and work was done to establish how they were dyed. Indigo was a common colour in the Norse world, and found here, but there were also purples and reds. The purples were from lichens, collected from rocks and trees and treated with stale urine. Apparently lichen dye can be different shades because lichen is an indicator: adding an alkali will make the dye bluer, adding acid will make it redder.

They didn't find just one game piece: there were three, one shaped like a chess pawn, one a large drafts piece and one tall and rounded. And they found pieces of ship, and of Saqqaq or Dorset culture tools, and there was a Thule culture occupation too, later.

The runic poem says: *In the sea sea sea is the place where the ana-gods are on their watch. Bibrau is the name of the virgin who is sitting in the blue sky.*

~

At the far end of the road, the fjord comes into view behind a satellite tower. A few fishing groups are making their way home on foot, chatting. I stand for a while, imagining a longship weaving between the few, scattered icebergs.

Erik's colonisation was a settling of an uninhabited land.

Fourteen boatfuls of tired travellers – and nothing here but grass, trees and a few puzzling objects to show someone had been here before. There was no cultural exchange, unless the Norse learned from the centuries-old arrowheads they came across while digging turf for their walls. Greenland was just a space to stretch out into and fill, carrying on with all the old games, bringing knowledge from home about how to live, how to dye fabric, how to sail and to farm and to marry.

I turn back. As I pace along the track, deep in thought, a jeep rumbles towards me. I scramble off into the grass and it scrunches to a halt. I am used to being waved at and greeted by complete strangers by now, but these aren't strangers: it's the Vikings from Jaeren. One leans out of the window. 'Hello! Have you found Erik yet?' he grins. I sigh and confess that no, I haven't. 'How are the satellite dishes?' I retort more cheerfully. 'Getting better and better!' They laugh and accelerate off.

Mentally, I take away the jeep and put the men on horses, the small, tough, shaggy Icelandic breed. I clothe them in purple and indigo hooded robes, made of rough, woven fabric. They move away, chatting and laughing, and I follow on foot. The hill behind the town – whose Greenlandic name translates as Big Mountain – is green and yellow with buttercups, and so full of birds that it seems itself to be singing.

~~

Rie sits surrounded by bookshelves, rune translation worksheets and ancient artefacts, issuing a press release. She smiles at me as she tells me about the local Norse site.

'I remember giving guided tours, saying 'And down here, ladies and gentlemen, you ought to be able to see...' but all there was actually to see was piles of soil, spoil from digs, and buttercups half a metre high. We got funding from the Destination Viking project to tidy it up, put walls in the right places. It was important because it is so near the town – it's do-it-yourself tourism, tourists can visit independently.'

We talk more about tourism and how it fits in the local economy.

'How do I explain this? Greenland's economy is going to be saved by minerals, tourism and cod.'

'Cod? I thought cod stocks were low?'

'Fish, then. Though the cod is coming back. We had a shrimp factory here, which closed in December, and we hope it will reopen for fish processing.'

I have been reading about the minerals. There are more ruby miners in these fjords, and a mountain containing many rare minerals – including a candy-floss pink stone that is only found in three or four other places on the planet. The same mountain contains uranium, at one time extracted by Niels

Bohr.

'Yes, there is uranium, and there is also gold. And there is some local support for mining, because it means jobs. And if Greenland is ever to say goodbye to Denmark – well, tourism and fish cannot support that. So it is a complex issue!'

The difficulty is that, unknown to Erik, his colony was close to some valuable minerals: close enough that it's sometimes a choice between preserving his landscape and mining it. Rie seems to think there's a happy compromise to be had. Meanwhile, the idea of Erik and his colonists fighting against mining interests for their land, or for their story to be told to tourists, entertains me. I wonder what Erik would choose.

~~

But Greenland's links to the rest of the world aren't limited to supermarkets and tourism. There are tensions too, mostly around the subject of whaling.

'With age comes freedom. I think it's exciting to be old, because you can say what you think.'

Finn Lynge was Greenland's only ever MEP, serving for five years in the 1980s leading up to Greenland's vote to leave the EC. I can't imagine his ever not saying what he thinks: when he is talking about politics, he is so animated that his presence is too big for the room, where I am seated in the corner of a sofa under a view of the ice-cap.

'The reason Greenland didn't like the EC was pretty simple: their waters became EC waters, and German – and British! – fleets of fishermen started plundering the waters.'

He sinks back in his chair. 'People have long memories here. They remember the 1700s, 1800s, when whalers came from Europe and emptied the waters. In the 1880s they had destroyed the stocks. This time, it was Atlantic cod, and halibut.' A nostalgic look crosses his features. 'Great, wonderful fish. Very scarce now. The idea of the EC was 'we help you, you help us' and they helped some – they helped the farmers – but in the mean time they were plundering.'

The independence movement stepped up: Greenland won Home Rule and left the EC as soon as they could.

'Now we have Home Rule,' Finn continues, 'there's been quite a bit of bickering about the details. There's a popular expectation that we'll' – his tone of voice shifts to mock an inverted comma – ' "throw off the shackles of the past, stand on the world stage as the people we are." Language is a part of that, speaking Greenlandic not Danish. Economic sustainability is another. The Brundtland approach.'

I look puzzled.

'The Brundtland report you know of course.'

I shake my head.

'You don't? Gro Brundtland was a Norwegian politician

who chaired a World Commission on environment and development. And in 1987 they published a report for the UN. And what came out of that was the catchphrase everyone has used ever since: responsibility and sustainability. Responsible, sustainable use of resources.' I look this report up later and find out it led to the Rio Earth summit in 1992. It all sounds good. I am nodding along amiably as Finn continues. 'We all subscribe to the Brundtland approach. We don't want to abuse nature – we want to use it. Including –'

He pauses and looks at me, steadily, watching for my reaction,

'Including hunting whales and seals.'

I return his gaze steadily, then nod slowly. It is not the first time a Greenlander has talked to me of whaling, but Finn is different because he has lived between two worlds – that of Greenland and that of Europe. He knows my world as well as knowing his own. He sighs.

'If I had two lives – I sometimes wish I had two lives, and I could start again and deal with this. But pretty soon I am glad I have not got two lives. The problem is this new – this new religion, headed mainly by the British, which has declared the whale a totem animal.'

Finn's voice is getting louder, and partly out of nerves, I giggle. He looks at me and I quell it. But it's not just nerves that are making me laugh: there is something peculiarly apt in what he's saying. Images of totem whales, worshipped by crowds of bowing Britishers, drift past behind my eyes. Silly as they are, they stir memories of the whale that was stranded in London the other year, attracting crowds of locals, traumatised by the creature's eventual death. Deeper in memory, thoughts of Save the whale campaigns of my childhood jostle: folders, pencils, every possible item of stationary covered with swimming whales. I even have two wooden whales that I took into exams as mascots. But I need to pay attention.

'It's not just the British: there's a bit from the Dutch, a bit from the Germans, some Canadians... but add to this: recently we have this new idea, respecting others' cultures.'

He runs his hands through his short grey hair. He is becoming a stadium-sized presence.

'This respect: in Greenland we like the idea of respect. But we ask – how shall we do it? For instance, in India the cow is sacred – they have strong feelings about cows. So are we to stop eating beef? To stop using leather for shoes? Tell us how to do it! Maybe you could show us!'

He bangs his hand down on the table.

'Tell us: what are we supposed to do?!'

I cower in the corner of the sofa. I can't fault his logic. He goes on, telling me of his respect for the International Whaling Commission – 'a highly honourable institution,' and running his hands through his hair again as he tells me about the Japanese whaling efforts: 'why is it 'so-called' scientific? It *is* scientific. The trouble with this campaign is that you're not up against sensible politics, you're up against pure sentiment.'

The thought occurs to me that in the climate of feeling about whales at home, it would be hard for a politician to stand up and support whaling. And, crucially, why would they? At home it is no-one's livelihood, no-one's favourite food. To support saving whales is a no-risk policy. It is like hugging babies. I point this out to Finn and he laughs, first genuinely and then bitterly.

'And yet prospecting for oil in Alaska, with damage to who knows how many species, that is fine.

'The real problem is this assumption of superiority in Western culture. It was there in Europe and exported to America. The English language community is the most culturally suppressive there has ever been.'

This one I can argue. I sit up in my corner of sofa and speak out.

'But you welcome it. It isn't just us, imposing. You don't have to watch English language TV, use all these gadgets, live with running water, electricity...'

He sits back in his chair, setting his arms on its arms, and sighs. 'Yes. Yes. At the same time, there are aspects of the West that we do not wish to be without. But there are others...'

I ask Finn about his ideal world, and his response centres

around tolerance – for him, a Christian value.

'Homo sum, humani nihil a me alienum puto... I'm human, and nothing human is foreign to me. Who said that? Some Latin philosopher[5]. Obviously everything is governed by people's attitudes. That's straightforward. What I dearly miss is informed discussions where people sit down and talk about their attitudes to other people's attitudes. Informed and tolerant discussions. We all have attitudes, but to act as if your attitude is the starting point, is God's attitude – how do you know? Let's discuss it!'

'Another story. Once I arranged a tour to Greenland for a group of MEPs, eight highly informed and respected people from various parties. They were all people who wanted a trip to this country. So I showed them and they were deeply impressed by this great land.

'And one day I took them to a place by the harbour where they were cutting up seals and dead birds. And they were polite people so they stood and watched. One of the hunters came up to me then: 'Hey, Finn!' he said 'I see you have some visitors from Europe. I have something to show them – something extraordinary. I've got this porpoise I just caught, and when I cut it up I found this foetus.' And he showed me the foetus, a tiny thing.' Finn is miming holding it in his hand. 'Isn't it beautiful?' said the hunter. 'Isn't it a wonderful sight?' And it

5 Terence, it turns out.

was, and the visitors were polite, so they looked too.

'This man, he knows all about life and death. He would have lost friends and family at sea, out hunting. To that man, death is a natural thing, traumatic when you see it hit your friends, see them drowning: of course it is traumatic, but life and death? Life feeds on death. The good Lord made it that way. It says so on the first page of the Bible: God saw what he created and he saw that it was good.'

～～

Whaling was once part of Greenlandic subsistence hunting, carried out with great respect to the creature and with much effort, tens of men in sealskin wetsuits with harpoons, women on hand to mend skin boats and sew up wetsuits if they tore. Now, whales are easier to kill but it is also less justified: there are better fuels than blubber, and plastic is used where whalebone's flexibility was valued – although the eco-friendliness of using plastic can be queried. But the argument about whaling isn't just about whales: it's about Greenlanders sticking up for being Greenlandic.

'As the Greenlanders are naturally very stupid and indolent,' Egede began the conclusion to his 1741 book about Greenland, 'so they are likewise very little disposed to comprehend and consider the divine truths...for they can neither comprehend the miserable condition they are in; nor do they rightly understand and value the exceedingly great mercy and loving kindness God has shown towards mankind in his dear Son Christ Jesus...'

He continued by recommending the same methods for teaching Greenlanders as for teaching children: endless repetition and 'simple and obvious comparisons'. He blamed their 'stupidity and indolence' partly on a lack of education, and he suggested that they needed to be settled, cured of their nomadic habits, and taught 'a quiet and more useful way of life than that which they now follow.'

To be fair to Egede, there was much he respected in the Greenlandic way of life – hunting skills not least. But he lived in a colonial era: he thought his own way of life better and he had a vision of change. In 2008, Egede's vision had come true to a disturbing degree. Greenlanders are now settled, they no longer rely on hunting for a living, and their ancient mythology is barely known. And Finn Lynge is arguing that the West has not abandoned this colonial attitude – that still, after all these years, and while noisily repenting our colonial past, we think we're better, and we think that our normality is the only one that's right. Worse, perhaps: we think it's the only one that exists.

~~

I would still hate to see a whale killed. But I do see Finn's point. It's like the cuddly seals next to the sealskins: there can be different ways to connect to and to look after the world. And also – as a traveller, I feel strongly about variety. I don't want everyone to feel, to think, to behave, the same way.

~~

'As you approach Igaliko, you should look to your left... you will see a huge satellite dish...' I have bumped into the installation team again in the community centre cafe, sitting over their meal. One is still wearing his luminous safety jacket. I am not quite sure how it benefits him in Greenland where there is so little traffic. Igaliko is my next stop, a small farming community with plenty of Norse ruins: in later Norse times, it was the Bishop's residence.

'Your handiwork?' I ask, referring to the satellite dish,

'I played a part, yes, last year.'

The satellite installation Vikings have assumed a new significance: they are conveyers of the West, modern day Eriks for good or for ill. Perhaps this guy is too modest to be Erik. But – I pause to admire his height, his long light hair, his beard and tan – apart from the jacket, he looks the part.

FREEDOM

CHAPTER 18

GREEN FIELDS, HOT WINDS

Igaliko: I think I was transferred here in my sleep. It is a tiny bit chilly, too early in the day for the rock I am perched on to be sun-warmed, but the sky is already blue. Sitting waiting for the shop to open, I am slowly coming awake.

I yawn. It was an early start: the journey feels surreal to me now. But there was something about polar bears. 'This was two months ago,' said my captain, switching on his computer. I saw an iceberg, water, heard echoey splashing. Gradually a bear's head came into focus in the sea, moved toward the iceberg. A clenching and a splashing later, a bear shape heaved itself onto the ice. Languidly, powerful legs stretching to grip the surface, it made its way up the side, a white silhouette against the blue world. Then it was in the water again, out of focus again, climbing out again. And again. And again. And again. A looping, endless bear.

The boat wound and wiggled around the icebergs until the water cleared. A lumpy mountain grew up the side of the fjord, and grey cliffs grew beside it. We came to shore below a little cliff, so dry land was a red stretch towards the sky, a ladder the only way to get there. I insisted, sleepily, on carrying my own bag up, its weight pulling me back towards the water, my body swaying.

Then I met a man in a white van, and we argued in pointing-language about which way I should walk until eventually I clambered in beside him. We swapped names. We came down at last to a temperate valley, a green green valley with a lake and a farm by the lake and a track running always through it. The track wavered, turned, turned again. It tumbled down a new slope, into a place where the water reached out to the land and houses grew like mushrooms in the grass. A lady with a basket of washing joined us. The road, and we, circled round the houses. I tumbled out, stumbling over thanks. I stumbled here.

~~

Igaliko is about fifty kilometres from Narsaq, deeper in the fjords and across a narrow strip of land. I am no longer on Erik's fjord, but on his friend Einar's.

There is a faint buzzing of flies, a little wind, otherwise complete quiet broken only occasionally by a ruckus of seabird calls on the far shore. Igaliko is right at the head of Einar's fjord, where the water gets shallower and shallower until there is only beach, and then gently sloping farmland. Across the water is a mountain and more rise behind and to left and to right, surrounding the little settlement protectively.

The sea is gleaming turquoise. The beach is full of patterned pebbles, striped sandstone and conglomerates with great lumps of quartz. In the clear shallows, amongst the pinks and greys and blue mussel shells, a shoal of dark flickers catches my eye. Not fish: tiny shrimp that wriggle under stones as soon as the water is jostled by the least wind.

An aeroplane crosses above the distant, snowy mountains, going to a different world. In mine, sunlight shines on the damp hair of Norse settlers who look up and around, at the fields and at their hands and straight at each other as they realise that their rough voyage has not been a wild, wrong quest; that their leader has not deceived them; that they have found a paradise across the ocean.

'To work!' cries Einar, and the boat is hauled up high on the beach and the sheep set free, the first sheep Greenland has ever seen, wobbling and stumbling towards fresh grass. Cows follow, and children, proud to have survived the stormy voyage. Secretly, in bags and boxes, tangled in clothes and on bodies, comes the life that trails behind Europeans: mice, lice, houseflies, seeds of foreign plants. Somebody brought a cat. Somebody starts a fire.

~~

The ruins at Igaliko are picturesque. They stand deep in vegetation, surrounded by a grass with a fat, wheaty seedhead, and rhubarb and buttercups, dandelions and angelica. Arches, once doorways with broad, heavy lintels, open into the air. They are built of cut sandstone, pink-red-brown, bronzed against the dusky emerald meadow, clashing with the turquoise sea.

To walk through an arch is to pass from ancient to modern, from real to imaginary. I am between worlds.

~~~

In Einar's fjord... 'on the right side, as one sails into the fjord to the cathedral, which is at the end, there is a large forest that belongs to the cathedral, and that provides all of its income, both large and small. The cathedral owns all of Einar's fjord, and also the large island which lies off the fjord and is called Renøe, so-called because in autumn countless reindeer run there; hunting is by common rights but not without the bishop's permission. On this island there is the best soapstone, which in Greenland is of such good quality...'

In Greenland there is much silver ore, many polar bears with red flecks on their heads, while falcons, whale tusks, walrus hides, and all kinds of fish, more than from any other country; also marble of all colours, fireproof soapstone... reindeer...

Ívar Bárðarson, twelfth century church official [6]

6 translated by Derek Mathers

The cathedral is still detectable. One of the arches is the doorway to a storage building, up against its wall. The wall is there too, blocks at varying heights and, centrally placed within it, a cruciform building: a cathedral.

I can see its shape best if I clamber up on the stones at one end and look down from that height. Archaeology, says the voice of Danish archaeologist Jette Arneborg in my guidebook, has discovered a man buried with a finely carved bishop's crozier and ring. Dated to the thirteenth century, the bishop might be one of two: Nikolaus, or Olaf, both somewhat before Ívarr's time. And there was something odd going on: twenty or thirty walrus skulls and four or five narwhal skulls have been found buried in and around the church. It is possible that they were buried before the church was built: even if so, it is puzzling.

Shattered pieces of church bells were found here too, suggesting that their sound once rang out across the pastures.

~~

How much Collingwood would have enjoyed this, I think, passing through another archway and remembering his nineteenth century pilgrimage to Iceland. In his honour, I sit on a stone and sketch the scene. In Collingwood's day, somewhat more was left. It was only in the mid-twentieth century that legislation was passed protecting Greenland's ruins: by then three hundred years of local farmers had made the stones into houses. But Collingwood never came here.

~~

I pay another visit to the shrimp in the shallows, watching them dodge in and out of stones and shells. Trying to catch one, I wave my hand around beneath the water, and predictably, they swirl away. But the water is warm, so I take off my socks and shoes and paddle, unevenly on the pebbles. Rocks distract me, flame patterned, red spotted with white, dark and light striped, but out of the water they fade.

Something is nibbling at my feet. I shake them, hard, an instinctive reaction, a mental *eeeuw, leeches*. But they are not leeches, I find as I pick the last one off. Tiny shrimp, the largest as long as a finger-bone, have been clinging to me. Sitting down on the beach, I put my feet back in the water and watch. Gradually, more and more wriggly grey shadows attach themselves to the bottoms of my feet and to the sides of my toes, curling up tight with their heads against my skin. They do not hurt so much as nuzzle, gently until one very faintly digs: I shake my foot so they all flee and collect a new crop.

The same thing happens when I let my hands lie still in the water. If they weren't so small, this would be a great way to catch dinner.

A man, painting his house, waves at me. I wave back, and walk over. He beams at me, and I beam back. But we don't have a language in common.

'You – Engelsk?'

I nod. 'You – Igaliku?'

He nods, 'My house!' and points.

I point. '*Ajungilaq!*'

He looks puzzled, pauses, then realises, 'Ah, *ajungilaq!*'

My contact with Igaliku's present is as broken as my contact with its past. He seems on the brink of telling me something. He is fumbling for English words in the depths of his memory: I wish now more than ever that I had learnt the language.

'You come – nine!'

It is lucky that I am not doing anything this evening, because I would not know how to refuse. At nine I cautiously knock on the door. We sit on the sofa. Opposite us, the television stands next to a large stuffed eagle. On the wooden wall behind hang four saw blades, floor to ceiling; tucked in the corner is a spinning wheel.

Through pictionary, I learn the words for sheep, horse and dog: *savaq, histeq, qimmoq*. The dog is an accident: my drawing of a horse is not good enough, and my host checks with its sound: '*wow wow?*' I shake my head and put a stick person on its back. Then I draw a dog as well.

From inside the television, an immaculately groomed

blonde newsreader is trying to tell me something. On another wall hang a mighty pair of brown wings, left there by an angel on his way to the modern world.

~~

The tallest mountain has a story: I am told it is a Norse lookout point. I am not going to try to climb it: eighteen hundred metres is too much for one day, even if there were a path. But I will walk towards it.

As I climb, the view of Igaliko bay opens up, a wide bright view, houses barely showing, just the grass, the water and the snow patches on the mountains shining out. I am stepping on sheep-nibbled scrub, approaching a crag that, according to my map, has a plateau on top. Once there is a glimpse past it, into Erik's fjord where icebergs cram each other for space. That patch of icebergs is marked on the map, always there, easier to navigate by than the rocks and hillocks on this part of the mountain. A lake rests between two knolls and for a moment I know exactly where I am.

I strip off my coat and my jumper and walk with them bundled round my waist. The terrain is rougher now. Soft-leaved dwarf willow is more common than grass, and a scratchier, darker-leafed plant, dwarf birch, crunches underfoot and springs back at me, snatching at my trousers.

Giving up on the map, and relying on my sense of direction and the view to guide me, I climb past smooth stones. It is as I get hungry that I realise the undergrowth has swallowed my phone, my only timepiece. Is my shadow short enough to eat lunch? I wait until it gets longer again: by then, on a one-rock plateau, I am high in the sky, the fjord smooth below. I could imagine that nobody had sat here before. Silence and wind and the call of one timid bird echo around me. I add wild thyme to my sandwich and feel like an explorer.

I am not quite at the top of this ridge. To my left is still the line of red cliffs, blocking my view of Erik's fjord. The map suggests a route amongst or across them, but I think I have strayed from the path already. The sheep tracks are running out. Experimentally, I walk towards the cliffs. The ground gets rougher but the rocks are climbable, sort of, except that the higher I go the higher they seem to get. And then I come to a patch of scrubby birch, a few metres of flat vegetation. An easy route: I breathe a sigh of relief. I look down, checking its depth before stepping onto it, and start back. It is deeper than I am tall, a tangle of trees, a perilous thicket after all.

The trees' trunks, thick as my arm, are gnarled up with history, twisted with the battles they have fought. This is how Greenlandic forest grows: slowly, in sheltered spots, away from sheep and wind. I wonder about the age of the birches: they have taken many years to grow these few entangled metres.

Retracing my steps, I am conscious of being alone. This landscape is untamed. Humans have not laid down their history here, building and chopping and burning and cultivating, as they have in the settlements. They have not walked here enough to make a path. Even the sheep have not explored every corner. Only the wind and the ice and the rain have touched this bump on the planet's surface, leaving the rock deeply cracked in places, polished smooth in others. I want to see it all. With an intake of breath, I scramble a little way up a crag. In one direction are the hills on the far side of Erik's fjord, and way up the valley is a blue-white strip that I know to be the inland ice. The largeness of the landscape gives me vertigo: that ice stretches, largely unexplored, about twice the length of the UK.

But the lower parts of the land refuse to reveal themselves, hiding behind mounds and outcrops. There is still no sign of a path. I step down, and walk through the grassy patches, avoiding the low, deep birch and willow. I walk faster and faster. I have a survival blanket in my backpack – but it's not so much making me feel safe as reminding me of danger. This landscape does not care what happens to me.

A lake fills a hollow in a cliff-faced valley. Sand surrounds it, then rock. Another lake sits a little lower, waiting. I know where the path is, now: about half a kilometre away, behind the cliffs. I don't want to go back though. Perhaps Erik's influence is getting too great, but I know he wouldn't have stopped. I continue, face and arms hot in the sun, following the stream that leads from the lake until it dries up. The downward slope shrinks more steeply away. Now I can see round the cliffs, and there is a choice: plunge down the valley, traverse the crags, or return the way I came.

Reminding myself that I can always go back up, and taking it as carefully as possible, I step downward. Each step is a new risk, a new chance to imagine the consequences of a twisted ankle or a broken arm in a place where a helicopter couldn't possibly land. The slope steepens, and loosens. Boulders sit between hollows of birch. Scree that shifts at a footstep lies next to thickets of unguessable depth. And then there is a grassy spot and I stand on it breathing deeply, telling myself I'm past the worst before stepping back into the bushes.

No longer caring, I let scratchy branches reach for my trousers: better that than slide on the malicious, heavy stones that pile up together, ready to crush a careless foot. But then there is no more birch. To my left is a shallow gully. I step down, coming face to face with a ram's skull, horns curling threateningly. I have stopped looking up now, no longer wanting to know how stupid a route I have taken, how hard it would be to reverse. I continue down, hands and feet working together, over rocks and past hollows. A snow bunting shoots across my path, under a bridge of boulders. There is grass once more. The birch comes back.

My instinct is to race, to flee from this place as fast as I can. But even now, as the slope shallows, I am walking calf-deep in willow and birch, on uneven ground. A brown bird, one I don't recognise, skitters up the sheep-path ahead of me, dodging from side to side and looking back at me. It flies off. The path winds. Now I know it is not far to safety, I look up: the slope looks back at me, stark. It is still looking over me, could still launch that scree on top of me.

My feet scrape gravel, a track. A lake, round and blue, surrounded by beach, green slopes, a waterfall tumbling steep metres. Peace, and now safety.

〜〜

As I follow the track to Igaliko, alongside a meandering river, a wind gets up. Gusty, it pushes me uphill. Great plumes of dust rise pink-grey from the land. Strong, but not cold, the wind laces the fjord white and sends mauve ripples through the tall grass. 'You're back safe,' says the girl at the hostel, relieved. And: 'You know it can blow for days, this wind, and the boats can't cross the fjords.'

The Föhn whistles round the building. I sit by the window watching.

〜〜

Time passes. In Igaliko, it seems foolish to rush, foolish to do anything but sit and watch the weather change. Sun gives way to wind, which gives way to cloud. One day I climb up high on the other side of the valley, and explore a green hollow marked on my map as bog. It's not – the year has been too dry – but it is networked with thin streams, deep passages in the brown earth. A waterfall tumbles and trickles down a cliff on the upper side. Sheep wander.

The day comes to depart. I set out for the landing place, and arrive there with a few hours to spare. Dropping my bag in the waiting room – four walls, a door and a roof: the only building – I ramble round the headland a little, watching the changing colour of the water, grey to blue to grey again as the sun comes in and out. Boats arrive and depart: a small white one, a large orange one, a tiny black one, each going deeper into Erik's fjord, as I will later.

I explore the headland, pushing through birches and crowberries, crunching on dry grass and lichen. I sit down for lunch above a weathered cliff, red stone swirled with ochre, pebbles far below. Across the fjord the mountains form a background for a castle-shaped iceberg. I imagine longboats sailing in; or one longboat, in springtime, with a crew of explorers.

A sound, and I look up. A man sits next to me on my rock, about my age, his long blond hair in a ponytail and smile-crinkles round his eyes. I recognise him at once, and offer him some ryvita and edam, what is left of my scanty lunch. He crunches on it for a while, somewhat sceptically. Refusing more, he pulls out a piece of dried fish and settles down to chew it.

We sit in silence. Then he sighs, a fast, satisfied breath, looking up across the water.

'*Þetta er góðr staðr, held ek, grænn staðr*'

I catch 'good' and 'green' in there, and nod.

'*Já. Vit sjáum hvernig vit komumst í gegnum vetrinn. En ek held – ek held at þat sé mǫgulegt...*'

'You can survive here?'

He looks at me directly for the first time, and smiles.

'*Vit munum ekki einungis lifa af. Vit munum gera meira en þat. Mikit, mikit meira.*'

I sit in silence, waiting for him to say more, eyes resting on the mountains, smooth and pointed across the fjord, and the clouds that streak across the sky above.

'It is a good place,' I answer. But when I look around, he is gone. I sit for a moment more, pondering, and then make my way back, a foolish route through a knee high forest of willow, soft grey leaves disguising the toughness of the entangled branches.

CHAPTER 19

STORIES, FISH, AND A MYSTERIOUS ENDING

Two pushchairs, a giant pack of nappies, two babies, two adults, numerous carrier bags and more large suitcases are hauled, heaved and hefted up twelve steps of vertical, rust-coloured ladder to the pier where I am waiting. I feel I am a poor exchange as I replace them in the boat.

Swiftly, wake foaming behind us, we are in a circle of water ringed by mountains. The coast we left is bright green, a low saddle with snow-specked peaks behind. Ahead, the fjord splits in two, distant sets of mountains divided by a sharp brown, lifeless peak. As we approach it we come out of the circle of water: we are at a junction. The waterway on my right is packed with ice, the crush of bergs I glimpsed from my perilous mountaintop. I watch the icebergs and the cliffs until the mountains fold round them, as we take the other branch.

Here, the icebergs are fewer, and on our left, the hills are getting greener. A low saddle holds a cluster of small wooden buildings. The right hand side of the fjord is wooded: later I learn that this is Greenland's only arboretum, an extravaganza of tree-cultivation, testing extreme-climate trees from all over the world. For now it is astonishing to see forest, and I think of twelfth-century church official Ívarr Bardarson again, and his descriptions of forests 'from which the cathedral derives income.'

But I am not thinking much about Ívarr. My thoughts are with Erik and his family, coming to settle this fjord. The next stop will be Qassiarsuk, identified as the site of Brattahlid, Erik's farm, presumably the best place in the fjord system. My eyes are on the left side of the fjord, and even from the sea it looks hopeful. We are coming to a bay, green fields set off by coloured houses. We slow. As the boat approaches, I notice that the colour of the water has changed yet again: it is not the clear turquoise of Igaliko's fjord, but a limpid blue, the milky colour of water thick with sediment.

My feet stump up wooden steps and land on a brick-red road. As I pace along it, my boots gradually accumulate red dust, and by the time I reach the hostel – the Leif Eiriksson hostel – they are covered in it. Circling the yellow building I pass a strong, silent man with dreadlocks, who nods at me. On the terrace, another man lies stretched on a bench, asleep, hands folded on the stripey t-shirt that covers his gently rounded stomach.

The terrace is sunny, the view over glacial water decorated with lumps of ice. I sit outside, a little chilly, pausing to rejoice that I have arrived. For I am at the end of my journey now. This is the place – according to archaeologists and reconstructionists, guide book writers and historians – where Erik settled down.

This is the place from which his son Leif set sail for America. And today, despite the icebergs, it feels Mediterranean.

~

It may be the end of the journey but there is still a lot to do. First I climb up to the statue of Leif, way above the town. His calves, which from this angle are my main view, are like treetrunks – not Greenlandic ones, either. He is made of metal, dark with a tint of green. He stares out to sea. A constant stream of visitors potters up, takes photographs, and potters down. The views of Leif were better taken from the beach, where his whole mighty figure would fit in the frame, but the view from up here is worth the climb, a glimpse back along the fjord towards – with a little imagination – America.

Sitting with my notebook, scribbling, I attract almost as much interest as the statue. People ask me what I'm doing, alone on a hillock in Greenland, and I tell them. In exchange, one man tells me of a town near Disko Island, far north of Nuuk, where in winter there live three thousand people and five thousand dogs. 'They need the dogs, for fishing with a sled through holes in the ice. From November to April there is no ship.' A far cry from these fertile fjords.

~

One passage from Erik's Saga tells about a winter at Brattahlid. Two ships, with eighty men and trading goods from Iceland, arrived in Erik's fjord one autumn. The trade went well, and the traders were invited to stay the winter. One of the group's leaders was a man named Karlsefni. The saga continues:

The traders accepted the invitation. Their goods were brought up to Brattahlid where there were plenty of fine large outhouses to store them.

The traders spent a pleasant winter there with Eirik. But as Christmas drew near, Eirik became much less cheerful than usual. One day Karlsefni spoke to Eirik and said, 'Is there something wrong, Eirik? I feel that you are in rather lower spirits than you have been. You have treated us with great hospitality and it is our duty to return your kindness as best we can. Tell me now, what is the cause of your worry?'

'You have accepted my hospitality with courtesy and good grace,' replied Eirik, 'and it does not occur to me to think that our dealings with one another will bring you any discredit. Rather, it is this: I should not like it to be said that you have had to endure such a meagre Christmas as the one that is approaching.'

'There is no question of that, Eirik,' said Karlsefni. 'We have malt and flour and grain in our cargoes and you are welcome to have as much of them as you wish and prepare as rich a feast as your generosity demands.'

Eirik accepted the offer and a Christmas feast was prepared. It was so lavish that people thought they had scarcely ever seen one so magnificent before.

The Christmas feast became a wedding feast and days went by: they all had a splendid time at Brattahlid that winter; there was much chess-playing and story-telling, and many other entertainments that enrich a household.

And: *there were great discussions that winter about going in search of Vinland.*

~~

Within the Vinland Sagas there are many stories of the voyages to that semi-mythical land. Some succeed, the adventurers bringing back riches; others fail, ending in murder and lost battles. But each of them ends with a return to this fjord and those near.

The only Vinland voyage that Erik took part in was an unmitigated disaster:

They sailed out of Eiriksfjord. They were in high spirits and were pleased with their prospects. But they ran into prolonged difficulties and were unable to reach the seas they wanted. At one time they were within sight of Iceland; at another time they observed birds off Ireland. Their ship was driven back and forth across the ocean.

In the autumn they turned back towards Greenland and reached Eiriksfjord at the beginning of winter, worn out by exposure and toil.

And Erik may not have taken part in the voyage: this extract is from Erik's Saga but the manuscripts disagree. *Skalholtsbók*, which I visited in Iceland, says Erik stayed at home: only *Hauksbók*, the Copenhagen manuscript, claims he set sail at all.

~~

But the idea of Brattahlid as a setting-off point, as a start for adventure, stays with me as I search, using my archaeological plan, for the house where Erik is meant to have lived. Only – I cannot find it. There are some ruins of a house, once identified as Erik's, but it is later: the text declares it to have been a false identification. The remains of the only house from the right period 'cannot be seen above ground.'

I approach them nonetheless, and find a gently sloping field of buttercups, behind the blue wooden church. I try to imagine the valley bustling with Norse visitors, trading food, telling stories of far-off lands.

It is easier at the hostel, where explorers and guides sit and pore over maps, planning kayak expeditions between icebergs in remote fjords. '*Ici*,' says one Spanish guide, pointing at Johann Dahl Land on the map, '*ici, c'est très joli*'. We are talking French as it is the only language we have in common, restrictive to both our vocabularies. Johann Dahl Land is up towards the inland ice, a high, barren, barely-visited plateau. Perhaps not one for a day hike. 'Another year!' I sigh.

A pair of Danish fishermen are exploring the sea, telling tales of giant fish caught and eaten. 'We have had so much salmon that we do not want to eat any more,' says the dark one.

A Japanese mother and son are touring the whole country. Their guidebook is so well-thumbed as to be almost falling apart, and the son can always be found seeking new details in it, asking questions, comparing his country to this, to those in Europe and the world. He is full of statistics, most populous countries, tallest mountains. He is smiley and full of thanks and bows: '*arigato, arigato!*' His mother is quieter, speaking English more cautiously, nonetheless energetic.

Qassiarsuk is a place of coming and going, of international adventure, today as much as it was in Erik's time.

～

And then there is Thjodhild's church: a story and a site. The story is that Thjodhild, Erik's wife, converted to Christianity before he did, and had a church built not too close to the farmstead – far enough away not to annoy her heathen husband. In the 1960s, a small church was found here, identified as such by its graveyard since all that survived of the building was the base of three walls. The skeletons were carbon dated to the eleventh century, and the churchyard was in use for less than fifty years.

If Erik's Saga had not kept the story alive, it would have been just another church, albeit a small, early one. But the story of the little church at Brattahlid had the power to bring these remains to life in the imaginations of historians and archaeologists. It had more power still than that: it has been powerful enough to give the church a second life.

~~

The little church stands a few hundred metres away, along the gravel road and up the hill on the far side of the Qassiarsuk bay. Its turf walls make it hard to spot against the grass. The west side is built of pine, most of it taken up with a person-sized door. A low turf wall encircles the church, with a roofed wooden gateway, and outside it is a lady: an Icelander with wild blonde hair and piercing blue eyes telling a story.

'And Erik had a son – you know him? Leif, Leaf, Leivr, every language says it differently. And as the son of the chief it was very important he go to Europe – and of course, in Norway he visited the king.'

The storyteller's voice is lilting, imbuing her words with

rhythm; her rs are gently rolled.

'Now this king, King Olaf, was a Christian and he was conducting a very very bad conversion campaign. Basically, he was going around with a cross in one hand and a sword in the other... you can be baptised or you can have your head chopped off.'

She looks at us, as if asking what we would choose.

'Leifr was converted, and he came back to Greenland with two priests. And Erik was furious! He'd sent his son travelling for a year – all that expense! – and he came back a Christian! Christianity was no religion for a Viking chief; it was the religion of the slaves. So Erik ranted and raved...'

I imagine Erik, an older Erik bellowing like a bull with fury, chasing his heretic son out of the house. The story rises around us, Leif setting off for America, discovering new land, rescuing shipwrecked sailors, coming home a hero. Erik's continued resistance to Christianity takes on new life:

'And when Leifr came back, Thjodhilde converted to Christianity. And then she said to Erik – 'I am a Christian woman, you are a heathen man. Until you are baptised, I do not wish – I will not eat with you, I will not talk to you and I certainly – I certainly will not sleep with you!' And with that, she slammed the door in his face.'

She lowers her voice. 'Erik slept in the cowshed for three days...'

And after finally giving in, Erik also allowed the construction of the little church. 'We do not know much about the church. We know it was three walls turf and one wall wood, and that there was something circular around the whole. But the rest – the rest is free fantasy.' She pauses. 'And this church – it must be one of the smallest churches in the world but it had the grandest opening, about six bishops came.'

Six bishops came because of how the story is being told today: Thjodhilde's church was the first church in the New World, hundreds of miles west of its nearest neighbour. And it was built – just – before the great schisms in the Church split it into Catholic and Eastern Orthodox and eventually Protestant, so the new church is non-denominational, a church that tries to represent the ancestry of every Christianity.

She opens the door of the little church with a big iron key. Inside, it is pine-clad, simple, with a driftwood cross above a wooden altar. It is a peaceful place, a rest from the whirlwind of stories.

∾

Ingibjörg Gisladottir is a teller of legends, myths and folk tales of the North. She is a storyteller from a family of storytellers: in Iceland, her mother and her grandmother were storytellers before her. Next to Thjodhilde's Church is a reconstructed longhouse, and we sit inside on musk-ox rugs, listening to her words.

There are stories that have been told in Ingibjörg's family forever about the *huldufólk*, the invisible people I heard about in the Westfjords. A family of *huldufólk* has a long connection with hers, the children playing with each other for generations. 'I used to vanish as a child,' she says. And she tells the tale of her sister, refusing to come in to dinner because 'I am playing with my friend. Can't you see her? She is wearing a red dress. I ate dinner with her and her family. Can't you see her?'

'Does your sister remember?'

'No. No, not at all.'

'Are there hidden people in Greenland too?'

'Why yes... there are the small people and the giants, they came with the Inuit, and the *huldufólk*, they came probably with the first ships.'

'Have you seen them?'

'No.' She seems – sad. 'As children we see them. Then we are taught in school that they do not exist, that nothing we cannot see and touch and smell is real... our eyes are closed to them. But I can sense when they are here, when they are up to mischief.'

But Ingibjörg is returning to history.

'Something that not many people know,' she says, smiling, 'is that Erik the Red was a very romantic man. Very romantic.

And the trouble with these musk-ox furs is that the hairs fall out: they get everywhere, even in your mouth. So, for Thjodhilde he wanted to do something special...'

～～

I walk up the fjord for an hour or so, coming eventually to a farm where they grow potatoes and turnips and sheep, and a lady knits mittens and makes felt slippers out of the wool. She shows me how she cleans it, by hand, picking it over before spinning. One sheep's fleece makes two pairs of slippers. She makes things out of musk ox wool too, from the innermost layer of fur, so soft I can't feel it against my fingers. Her children swim in the stream in wetsuits, and can watch TV only when the generator is switched on.

This farm is out of sight of Qassiarsuk, round a rocky bulge in the coast, a blue house standing all alone. As far away again, I can see the shoreline reach a point and turn back on itself, the innermost end of Erik's fjord. Sparing it only a glance, I set out to walk back to town.

～～

Later, as I come back from buying groceries, I spot the two fishermen standing on a stone at the edge of the beach, flicking their lines into the sea. I put down my groceries on a handy stone and join them, watching, hoping they will catch something. Instead, they offer me a rod.

'Are you sure?' I am worried about the degree of trust this implies. 'I might break it.'

The lighter-complexioned, more talkative one is called Vagn: he laughs. 'If you use it in even a faintly normal way, it will not break.'

So I take the rod, and they teach me to hold it, to catch the reeling line under my finger, to flick the line up and out, letting go at just the right moment so the fly lands far out in the sea, then to reel it in slowly so a fish might have a chance of following and catching it. And I throw, and I throw, and I throw, and I throw; there is a rhythm to it, throwing and reeling, stepping back as the tide rises up our rock.

My technique goes up and down, the fly sometimes landing perfectly, far away, sometimes splashing down somewhere entirely unplanned, leaving me looking around in bewilderment and the face of Mogens, the darker, quieter Dane, creased with laughter. I catch a lot of weed. 'There are no fish,' I complain, after a while.

'I would give money to see you catch something,' Vagn laughs, and I don't know why. I take a break for a while and they tell me of fishermen's superstitions. Vagn points at Mogens, spread across the rock with his line flicking the water.

'See how he is lying on the rock? That is how he caught the biggest fish. So he lies that way always now.'

'I don't believe you caught any fish!'

But they did: they have it on video. Though I'm shivering, and should probably fetch a coat, I take the line back with renewed determination. The tide is higher now: it is a better time for fishing. I throw and reel, reel, reel, throw and reel, reel, reel, throw and

'It's wriggling!'

The line is tugging back, resisting my attempts to pull it in.

'Aagh, what is it?'

Vagn looks at the line. 'I think it is a cod.'

I have no idea how he knows but have more important things to focus on.

'What do I do?'

'We will wait till we can see it. There... yes...'

A fish about a foot long is wriggling at the end of the line. Vagn picks it up gently and unhooks it. I'm quite distressed at its distress and feel relieved when he slips it back into the water. 'Not that way!' he admonishes it, as it swims shorewards before turning round and heading back out to sea.

Apparently it was not a big fish, not worth keeping. It was so insignificant that throughout the rest of the evening Vagn continues to claim we have not caught anything, and I have to correct him. But I am pleased with it. I think back to the first fjord I visited, in Norway, the one I fell into, connecting accidentally with water that Erik might have swum in. I prefer this way of making contact with the past. Perhaps this was a descendent of a fish that Erik ate - or, as it were, did not eat.

Which reminds me of my groceries. I clamber around to the stone I left them on, and find no stone but cream cheese, milk and an avocado floating merrily around the jar of apple puree that I bought on a whim. I laugh, and go to the rescue, stretching for them from dry land. It is Mogens who sees the real problem. Our rock is now separated from the shore by a widening, deepening expanse of water: we are marooned.

If it had been just me, I would have had to wade. Luckily the Danes have longer legs, and half help me half haul me across to dry land. This time, only my food has been swimming. And even that, I reflect, could be thought of as a vital Viking experience: it may only be cream cheese and apple puree but, like Erik, I have fished my dinner from the fjord.

~

The next afternoon the Föhn starts to blow again. The sea is roughened and green, waves breaking and foaming on the shore. It is strange to sit in such strong wind and not feel cold. I curl up on the grass by the reconstructions and watch the water and the light in the sky until my lips and my fingers are crinkled with dryness. There is a bright, creamy patch over the mountains to the south, where they vanish snowy and purple behind the green slopes at the end of our bay. The cream cloud glows, a contrast to the white froth and the white icebergs. There is something not quite real about the colour of the sea: it is peppermint green.

When I come inside I am absolutely covered in red dust. I shower, and wash my hair, but still the towel comes away red when I dry it, and I have to scrape dust from under my fingernails.

〜

And finally it begins to rain, patchily at first, on and off, the mist coming in and hiding the mountains before revealing them again. Ingibjörg the Storyteller, in her Norse overdress, shelters beneath the gateway of Thjodhilde's Church. The red dust is washed from the grass, and the water's surface becomes textured like sandpaper, smooth but not allowing reflections.

I watch an iceberg turn over, and see first two then four ravens take off, circling, relishing the damp. 'You must never speak ill of a raven,' I remember Ingibjörg saying, 'they understand everything you say, every word.'

I stand in the back of the boat crossing the fjord, and think back to Stavanger, in Norway, to the wildness of Drangar in the north of Iceland, to the rich seafood of Breiðafjörður. I envy Erik's life in all three places, and in this one, too.

There is something peaceful about the end of a journey, I think to myself, waving at the Japanese man who is on the back of another boat. And now – now what?

~~

My journey is over but: 'You should talk to Ole,' I am told. 'He knows all about the Norse. He has walked all the sites in this area.'

Ole is an archaeologist, presently Director at the Narsarquaq Museum, by the airport opposite Qassiarsuk. Casually, entirely unprepared, I go to find him. Perhaps, I think, he will tell me about how to spot Norse sites, or have a funny story about his adventures. It is my last day, a few hours before my flight home. Ole is a tall man with a beige cardigan, an academic complete with bookshelves and tea. We sit, and drink, and chat, and then he tells me that Qassiarsuk is not Brattahlid.

But he is not as abrupt as that. First he tells me about his survey, searching out Norse sites. 'How do you spot them?' I ask, curious, for I have not found any without the aid of a map or signs.

'Well,' he answers, 'if I'm looking for a site and I'm not quite sure where it is, I look for the nicest, greenest spot.'

'And that works?'

'Yes – they were just like you and me, chose the best spot.' He laughs gently, 'Also there were changes in vegetation around the farm, it became more grassy and flowery, and you can see that today. The places with more rocks are usually wilder – that's not where you find the ruins.'

Then I ask something that has been puzzling me since I got here. In no book or museum have I found an explanation for why Qassiarsuk was identified as Brattahlid. Ole must know.

'Ah.' He pauses. And then he pauses again: ' – but no, I must take you back to the beginning.'

Ole tells me how, a hundred years or more ago, they thought Igaliko was Brattahlid. I can understand that: lush green Igaliko might well have been my own first choice of home. But that idea was refuted in the 1890s, and then in the 1930s, one particular ruin at Qassiarsuk was identified as Erik's house. That information became so well known that it became hard to refute, even when later work on dating showed that the building was from a later period. A different ruin, less visible, on the same site, was identified in its place. I've been to see it – or to look at the grass under which it lies, at any rate.

But what I want to know is why the archaeologists identified that particular part of the fjord – not Igaliko but Qassiarsuk.

Ole unfolds a map. 'Have you heard of Ívarr Bardarson?'

I have: he's the twelfth century church official whose

descriptions of Greenland I have been reading occasionally during my journey. Bardarson's writing is very useful for identifying sites, for the simple reason that he describes the geographical layout of the fjord, including a hot spring – and there is only one.

Ole takes me through the logic. There are three criteria for suggesting a site is Brattahlid: a large farm ruin, good fertile fields, and the presence of a church. And Bardarson says that the church furthest up the fjord is connected to Brattahlid. Given there are several large, fertile sites in Erik's fjord, the challenge is to work out where these churches lie.

Ole gestures at the map with a penknife. 'Dyrnaes, the outermost church, is near Narsaq. There is no controversy about that.

'Then there are three more churches mentioned and we have found two. One at Qassiarsuk, and one is before it as you sail up the fjord. This one.' He points to a site I must have passed in my travels, between Narsaq and Qassiarsuk.

'So you have one church left to find, then,' I say.

'Yes. We need another archaeological church. And I have found one – here.'

He points to the far end of the fjord, to a place called Qingua, an hour or so's walk from the modern farm I visited, where I learnt about spinning and musk-ox fur. At Qingua, the ruins suggest an extremely large farm, and it's a very good location, with two small streams running through the area and fields that are still farmed today. 'So all that is needed is to find a church there.' And Ole is convinced that he has found one. He shows me its plan – a square building, very different from the shapes of the farm buildings. To my inexperienced eye, it looks convincing.

'And if it is a church – then this is the site of Brattahlid.'

~~

I leave Ole's cosy study and walk along the shore. This is annoying: I have come all this way and I may have missed Erik's home by a mere hour's walk. But I am excited too: if this site has not been excavated, it is a time capsule undamaged by well-meaning archaeologists of the past.

Ole has been fair: he has told me that other archaeologists disagree with him. When I return home I contact Jette Arneborg, and she and her colleague Kevin Edwards tell me about their recent excavations at Qingua. They consider that there is no church: that it is not a church. Looking at the building's plan, there are only a few stones to suggest the square shape, and there's no evidence of a cemetery. It also seems that the area was used for woodland cultivation rather than agriculture, making it less likely to have been a chieftain's farm. I am convinced, but then I was as easily swayed the other way.

~

Oddly, having got over the shock, I really don't mind very much which site is Brattahlid. It would be nice to know for sure that I had stood in the right places, but -

But what?

The point of this quest was to rediscover Erik's life as closely as possible. But I've known for ages that Erik probably didn't even exist. So finding exactly where he lived wasn't the point.

Which raises the question: what was?

The first response: it's not just me. Erik's story has been continuously told, retold and rewritten for a thousand years. Its truth has been argued over for centuries. Statues have been raised to Erik's family. Their homes have been reconstructed. The tales have become part of identity-politics: Icelandic national pride, Scandinavian American pride, Greenlandic contention over who arrived first. It's personal, not just political: Gunnar Marel Eggertsson takes pride in his Icelandic ancestors; pioneering Thule Inuit farmers in this fjord named their children Erik and Leif.

The second response: they're right to be obsessed. That guy lasted out three years in an uninhabited land, sailed three times at least over a nearly impassable ocean and persuaded twenty-five boatfuls of Icelanders to come with him.

And I know him pretty well now. He comes and waves his axe at me when I'm irritating him – feeling pathetic about some new challenge, for instance. And he's not waving his axe now. He's gloating about all the people who still think he's important, a thousand years after he died.

Gloat away, Erik. Stories matter, and whether you existed or not, yours is a good story. As for me – I'm going home, a bit braver and a bit rasher for knowing you. Let's hope it lands me adventures and not exile.

I breathe in the colours of Greenland, russets and whites and pea-green water. I look one last time across the fjord to where Erik might have lived, and then I pace out, reluctantly and joyfully, the few hundred metres to the airport.

NOTE ON SPELLING

Modern Icelandic and Greenlandic names, terminology and place-names are given their local (nominative) spelling including any exotic letters.

However, names of characters in the Norse mythology and sagas, including names of gods, are given modern English spellings. Otherwise things get overwhelming. For instance, Erik – Eiríkur – is spelt Erik. Thor – Þor – is spelt Thor.

For reference, both Icelandic letters, ð/Ð and þ/Þ, are pronounced roughly th although there is a subtle difference: ð/Ð is pronounced as in this, the, heather, and þ/Þ is pronounced as in thing, or north.

ACKNOWLEDGEMENTS

Extracts from Erik's Saga and Greenland Saga on p.26 and onwards (approximately 622 words) are from The Vinland Sagas: the Norse Discovery of America, translated by Magnus Magnusson and Hermann Palsson (Penguin Books, 1973). Copyright © Magnus Magnusson and Hermann Palsson. The extract from Hauksbók quoted on p.54 was translated by Sveinbjörn Rafnsson in his chapter The Atlantic Islands in The Oxford Illustrated History of the Vikings by Peter Sawyer (2001). It is reproduced by permission of Oxford University Press. Extracts from The Earliest Description of Greenland, by Ivarr Bardarson, on p.391 and onwards are translated by Derek Mathers and quoted with his permission, © Derek Mathers. The excerpt from Grágas on p.47 was included by Arne Emil Christensen in his chapter, Ships and Seafaring, in Fitzhugh and Ward's Vikings: The North Atlantic Saga (2000). Extracts from the Elder Edda on pp. 114-117 are from The Elder Edda by W.H. Auden and P.B. Taylor (Faber and Faber, 1973) and copyright © W.H. Auden and P.B. Taylor. Extracts are also quoted from works and letters by W.G. Collingwood, Ethel B. Harley, William Morris, Herman Melville, Heinrich Rink and Signe Møller, Hans Egede, Knud Rasmussen and W. Worster, whose work is out of copyright but whose authorship is nonetheless acknowledged. Every effort has been made to trace copyright holders and to obtain their permission for the use of copyright material. The author apologises for any errors or omissions in the above list and would be grateful if notified of any corrections that should be incorporated in future reprints or editions of this book

THANKS

First and foremost thanks to the Winston Churchill Memorial Trust, without which none of this would have been possible. The WCMT funds travel abroad that brings knowledge back to the UK: if you have a project in mind that does that, check out their website at www.wcmt.org.uk.

Many thanks also to Royal Arctic Line, Jens Andersen, Ivalo Egede, Tina Lynge Schmidt and the Captain and crew of the Nuka Arctica who made it possible for me to travel from Iceland to Greenland by sea – and in what style!

Thanks to Cel Phelan, Kathy Jones, James Alexander and Marco Fugazzola at Event for employing me despite my need to follow a Viking, and bearing with me while I vanished for a few months to do so. Thanks to all my colleagues there for support – particularly to Jenny for the card.

I also owe a debt of gratitude to UCL Library and the collection, in particular, of the Viking Society for Northern Research. Thanks to Islington West Library in Thornhill Square for decent internet in the early 2000s and for stocking a children's historical atlas. And long, long ago, thanks are due to All Saints' Primary School, Putney and my Y4 teacher, Mrs Cameron.

The list of personal debts is endless. To that below should be added all the friendly people at hostels and homestays, at tourist offices and in museums and on buses and on boats, and the people who fed me, invited me in, pulled me out of fjords, chatted, showed me how to fish or offered me coffee. Particularly due thanks are those who ended up, perhaps unsuspectingly (in which case anonymously), in the pages of this book.

More specifically, in Iceland: Bjarni F. Einarsson and team, Gunnar Marel Eggertsson, Christopher Abram, Rósa Þorsteinsdóttir, Jón Jónsson, Sigurður Atlason of the Witchcraft Museum, Addi of the Sheep-farming Museum, the Drangar folk, Hafþor Þorhallson, Óttar Óttoson, Tom Metzger, Friederike Hofert, and last but not least Laura, Birgir and Sara at the Stykkishólmur hostel, who helped me when I was ill, including transporting my abandoned luggage across half of Iceland.

In Greenland: Rie Oldenberg, Inge S Rasmussen, Finn Lynge, Jacky Simoud, Ole Guldager, Kenneth Høegh, Ingibjörg Gisladottir, Georg Nyegaard, Gary McLearn.

Over email and back home, patient answerers of many questions: Sjöfn Kristjánsdóttir, Jeanne Willoz-Egnor, Kristine Leander, Atle Skarsten, Hörður Kristinsson, Gudrun Sveinbjarnardóttir, Morten Kielland, Jette Arneborg, Kevin Edwards, Claire Cavaleri, Alexis Marotta, Derek Mathers, Charles West, Bethany Fox. Thanks to Lucy and Robert Trench for introducing me to the letters of W.G. Collingwood, and sparking my curiosity about other past travellers.

It goes without saying that any errors, misunderstandings, misrepresentations or omissions in the final product are my own.

Thanks to those whose encouragement and support helped this project got off the ground: Todd Whitelaw, Jo Pettipher, Nigel Spivey, Kate Keara Pelen, Jackie Denman, Laura Gould. Lizzy Palles-Clark's and Claudia Zwirn's comments on initial drafts were invaluable – thank you. Miranda Landgraf's comments helped add energy to a much later draft. Sophie Smith's insights into the text and my writing have been transformative. And without Sophie's confidence in Erik, and her willingness to take a bit of a risk, this book would still be sitting on a hard drive.

Thanks to the lovely team at Caper for turning my words into a beautiful book.

Thanks to the friends, colleagues and housemates (on the Cally Road, and later in Peckham and in Kentish Town) who have lived with this project since its inception.

And thanks to my family (Kristina, Anthony, and Rachel, and in recent years, also Chris) who have supported and encouraged in the good times and helped me scrape myself off the ground when the going got tough.

And, I guess, thanks to Erik – for just getting on with it all.

FURTHER READING

I read widely for this project. Rather than putting references within the text, which would have been cumbersome in something which makes no claims to be an academic work, I've pulled out some of the books and articles that I found most helpful and most interesting below.

VIKINGS

Vikings: the North Atlantic Saga edited by William W. Fitzhugh and Elisabeth I. Ward, 2000. (This book also contains chapters on most of the topics below.)

The Vikings – a very short introduction, Julian Richards, 2005.

The Viking Way: religion and war in late Iron Age Scandinavia, Neil Price, 2002.

From Asgard to Valhalla, the remarkable history of the Norse myths, Heather O'Donoghue, 2007.

The Oxford Illustrated History of the Vikings, Peter Sawyer, 2001.

SAGAS AND VERY EARLY TEXTS

The Vinland Sagas: the Norse discovery of America Herman Palsson, 1968.

The Complete sagas of Icelanders, including 49 tales, ed. Viðar Hreinsson, 1997.

Particularly:

The Saga of Erik the Red

Greenland Saga

The Saga of the People of Eyri (set around the area from which Erik departed)

The Saga of the People of Laxardal (set around the area from which Erik departed)

The Saga of the People of Flói (Chapters 20-26, a visit to Greenland)

The tale of Audun from the Westfjords (tale of a man who transports a polar bear to Denmark)

The Tale of Einar Sokkasson (or The Greenlanders' Tale: more bear-transport, and a quarrel)

Stuf's Tale (occurs in the same manuscript as Erik)

Bard's Saga (in chapter five a girl floats to Greenland on an iceberg)

Valdimar's Saga (occurs in the same manuscript as Erik)

Islendingabók, Ari Thorgilsson (Ari the Learned) (various translations)

Edda – Snorri Sturluson, trans. Anthony Faulks, 1987 (1995).

The Poetic Edda, ed. Ursula Dronke, 1997.

The Elder Edda by W.H. Auden and P.B. Taylor 1973

A companion to Old Norse-Icelandic literature and culture, ed. Rory McTurk, 2005.

Old Norse-Icelandic Literature – a short introduction, Heather O'Donoghue, 2004.

The voyage of Saint Brendan: representative versions of the legend in English translation, ed. W.R.J. Barron and Glyn S. Burgess. 2002.

The manuscripts of Iceland, ed. Gísli Sigurðsson and Vésteinn Ólason, 2004.

The development of Flateyjarbók: Iceland and the Norwegian dynastic crisis of 1389, Elizabeth Ashman Rowe, 2005.

BOATS AND VOYAGES

Boats of the North : A history of boatbuilding in Norway, Arne Christensen, trans. Elizabeth Seeberg, 1968.

The Skuldelev ships; 1, Topography, archaeology, history, conservation and display, Ole Crumlin Pederson, 2002.

Boathouses in Northern Europe and the North Atlantic, Frans-Arne Stylegar and Oliver Grimm, in the *International Journal of Nautical Archaeology* 2005.

Ships and navigation, A. Christensen, In *Vikings: the North Atlantic Saga*, 2000.

Ships and seamanship, J. Bill, 1997. In *The Oxford Illustrated History of the Vikings*

PREVIOUS TRAVELLERS' TALES

Ruins of the Saga Times: being an account of travels and explorations in Iceland in the summer of 1895. T. Erlingsson, 1899.

A Girl's Ride in Iceland, Ethel B Harley (Mrs Alec Tweedie), 1889.

Icelandic Journals, 1871 &1873 William Morris, (1996)

A pilgrimage to the saga-steads of Iceland. W Gershom Collingwood and Jón Stefansson, 1899

The life and death of Cormac the skald: being the Icelandic

Kormáks-saga / rendered into English by W.G. Collingwood and Jón Stefánsson. 1902

Letters from Iceland and other essays, WG Collingwood, (1996).

Travels in Iceland 1752-1757, Eggert Ólafsson and Bjarni Pálsson, (1975).

Description Of Greenland, by Hans Egede, 1741 (1818 edition).

Eskimo folk-tales, collected by Knud Rasmussen, edited and rendered into English by W. Worster, with illustrations by native Eskimo artists. 1921

The Principal Navigations, Voyages and Traffiques of the English Nation – vol.3. R. Hakluyt, 1600 (1810 edition)

Account of the Sea-Cow and the Use made if it, by Molyneux Shuldham, 1775 (In *Philosophical Transactions of the Royal Society* 65, 249-51)

Land under the Pole Star, Helge Ingstad, 1966. Trans. N. Walford.

Tales and traditions of the Eskimo, Henrik Rink, 1875 (1974).

The settlement of Iceland: a critical approach: Granastaðir and the ecological heritage, Bjarni F. Einarrsson,1994.

Norse settlements of Greenland. A visitor's guidebook. Jette Arneborg, 2002

Traces – 4400 years of man in Greenland. Greenland National Museum, 2004

Contact, continuity, and collapse: the Norse colonization of the North Atlantic, ed. James Barrett, 2003.

The frozen echo: Greenland and the exploration of North America, ca. A.D. 1000-1500, Kirsten Seaver, 1996.

Approaches to Vínland: a conference on the written and archaeological sources for the Norse settlements in the North-Atlantic region and exploration of America, 9-11 August 1999: proceedings, ed. Andrew Wawn and Þórunn Sigurðardóttir, 2001.

The Arctic Frontier of Norse Greenland. Thomas McGovern, in *The archaeology of frontiers and boundaries*, ed. S Green and S Perlman, 1985.

The Farm of Erik the Red. Guðmundur Ólafsson, In *Approaches to Vínland*, ed. Wawn and Sigurðardóttir, 147-193

Medieval Farmsteads in Greenland: The Brattahlid region, 1999-2000. Ole Guldager, Steffen Stumann Hansen and

Simon Gleie, *Meddelelser om Grønland* 2002.

Things and Wonders – the Norsemen in Greenland and America.
Jens Rosing, 1973 (2000)

Brattahlid reconstructed, some thoughts on the social structure of medieval Norse Greenland and the location of Brattahlid. Ole Guldager, *Archaeologica Islandica* 2002.

Approaches to the Greenlanders, Klavs Randsborg, in *Archaeologia Islandica* 2004.

HISTORY OF ICELAND AND GREENLAND

The History of Iceland Gunnar Karlsson, 2000,

A history of Greenland F. Gad, 1970

Food in South Greenland for a thousand years. Rie Oldenberg and Finn Larsen, 2000

Aron Kleist and Cecilie Kleist – two Greenlandic artists and their magic world. Birte Haagen, 2003

Icelanders, Unnur Jokulsdottir and Sigurgeir Sigurjónsson, 2004.

PRACTICALITIES: GUIDEBOOKS AND LANGUAGE

Iceland, Paul Harding, Joe Bindloss. Lonely Planet 2004

Greenland and the Arctic, Etain O'Carroll and Mark Elliott. Lonely Planet 2005.

A course in modern Icelandic Jón Friðjónsson, 1978,

Greenlandic for travellers, Birgitte Herthing, 1995

West Greenlandic, Michael Fortescue, 1984.

ABOUT THE AUTHOR

Alexandra has lived in London almost all her life. Since following Erik to Greenland, she has evaded all conventional career paths and discovered a lot of interesting stories. If you would like to know what she does, and has done, for a living, you can visit her website, alexandrafitzsimmons.me.uk